PRAISE FOR
FROM WHAT IS TO WHAT IF

"A serious book on an important subject. Without imagination, where are we?"
—SIR QUENTIN BLAKE

"Rob Hopkins has long been a leader in imagining how we could remake our societies for the benefit of nature and humankind. His new book is a powerful call to imagine a better world. It should be widely read and appreciated."
—CHRISTIANA FIGUERES, former executive secretary, United Nations Framework Convention on Climate Change; lead negotiator, Paris Climate Agreement

"Few things distinguish human beings from the rest of life on Earth. Among the most important are our unique powers of imagination. Ironically, our use—and abuse—of those powers has now wrought a complex crisis in our relationships with the planet and with each other. As Rob Hopkins eloquently shows in this powerful and passionate book, to survive and thrive we have to become more imaginative, not less, in how we live, work and connect. He demonstrates the transformative power of imagination in all areas of our lives and the dangers of its neglect, especially in the education of our children. *From What Is to What If* takes us on an inspiring and urgent tour of the people and communities around the world that are reimagining the present to create more hopeful and sustainable futures for us all."
—SIR KEN ROBINSON, educator; *New York Times* best-selling author

"Day after day, week after week, the climate is changing and biodiversity is fading away. For a long time we tended to look the other way, but now, being on the edge of the cliff forces us to understand that we must act urgently. And because of this emergency it is our utmost duty to join forces. Not only among states, but among mayors, NGOs, associations, companies, and citizens. Among all those who are determined to act here and now.

"Towns and cities have already begun transition. Together, mayors have chosen to press ahead toward a healthier and safer world. Whether in Paris or in Totnes, initiatives are being launched and are encouraging us to shift from 'why not' to 'how' and from 'how' to 'when.' The movement must gain momentum and expand.

"We must act wherever we are with the resources we have at our disposal to fight global warming. It's no longer about thinking global and acting local; it's about acting local in order to act global in a better way.

"People like Rob Hopkins give us the courage to move forward. By setting an example, he shows us that we are right to place our hopes in a future in which men and women can act as stewards of their environment. The many stories in this book are evidence of the fact that for some people this future has already become a reality."

—ANNE HIDALGO, Mayor of Paris

"If we could set our imaginations free to explore the possibilities of how to make this world a better place, it would be remarkable indeed. And as this brave and powerful book argues, our very survival may depend upon it. We have nothing to lose by following the ideas set out in these pages, and everything to gain."

—SCOTT BARRY KAUFMAN, psychologist, Columbia University; coauthor of *Wired to Create*

"I couldn't stop reading this book, and ideas just wouldn't stop popping into my head. Rob Hopkins puts imagination back at the heart of future-dreaming, offering us an irresistible invitation to dream bigger and then make those dreams a reality. For anyone seeking a renewed sense of possibility, this one's for you."

—KATE RAWORTH, author of *Doughnut Economics*

"What if we are looking for solutions to our myriad challenges in all the wrong places? Hopkins, cofounder of the global Transition movement, reminds us that an essential ingredient to navigating the various unravelings of the coming decades isn't just our community resilience, reskilling, and activism—but our civic imagination."

—CHUCK COLLINS, Institute for Policy Studies; author of *Born on Third Base*

"I love this book. It is an extraordinary, reality-based report on people around the world applying the power of imagination to rebuild relationships and create a fulfilling, creative, and possible human future together. An essential read for all who care."

—DAVID C. KORTEN, author of *Change the Story, Change the Future* and *When Corporations Rule the World*

"When it comes to tackling climate change or the numerous other threats to our global environment, the greatest challenge we face today may be the belief that the damage is beyond the point of repair, that we lack agency in addressing the problem, for that leads us down the same path as outright denial—a path of inaction. In *From What Is to What If*, Rob Hopkins shows us a different path, one of action, hope, and engagement. Read this book and join the battle to preserve our planet."

—MICHAEL MANN, distinguished professor, Pennsylvania State University; coauthor of *The Madhouse Effect*

"Reading this book is like listening to the voice of Rob Hopkins. A voice full of kindness, optimism, brightness, humor, and imagination. And that spirit is precisely what we need to build a better future and to reconnect with each other and the better part of ourselves. With this book, Rob poses a crucial question: How could we create another world, one in which human beings live in harmony with each other and with nature, if we are not able to imagine it first? We can't—and that's why this book is so necessary."

—CYRIL DION, writer, filmmaker, and producer of the film *Tomorrow*

"At last, a design for our dreams. I believe we have a debt of honour to take action. Please read this book and defy the herd. Are we golden or are we debris?"

—MARK STEWART, musician, The Pop Group and Mark Stewart & The Maffia

"*From What Is to What If* is a profound look at imagination's potential to enact progress and a call for us to make space for the things we often overlook. Hopkins confronts the most pressing issues of our times and urges us to look closer, reconnect with our roots, adapt slower modes of production, and work collectively. Imagination is within reach; it can and it will continue to salvage and elevate communities while driving us towards more sustainable and resilient futures."

—THEASTER GATES, artist; founder and director, Rebuild Foundation

"Today our choice is simple: Change quickly or contribute to a catastrophic collapse. It's a daunting challenge, and it will be impossible unless we can imagine what a low-carbon, high-cohesion society looks like—not on paper, but in our towns and neighborhoods day-to-day. Here Rob Hopkins helps us envision a dramatically different, ecologically sustainable social environment, and invites us to build it together. This is a powerful, inspiring book."

—ERIC KLINENBERG, author of *Palaces for the People*

Also by Rob Hopkins

The Transition Handbook:
From Oil Dependency to Local Resilience

The Transition Companion:
Making Your Community More Resilient in Uncertain Times

The Power of Just Doing Stuff:
How Local Action Can Change the World

21 Stories of Transition:
How a Movement of Communities Is Coming Together
to Reimagine and Rebuild Our World

FROM WHAT IS TO WHAT IF

UNLEASHING THE POWER OF IMAGINATION TO CREATE THE FUTURE WE WANT

ROB HOPKINS

Chelsea Green Publishing
White River Junction, Vermont
London, UK

Project Manager: Sarah Kovach
Developmental Editor: Brianne Goodspeed
Copy Editor: Eliani Torres
Proofreader: Katherine R. Kiger
Indexer: Nancy Crompton
Designer: Melissa Jacobson

Printed in the United States of America.
First printing September 2019.
10 9 8 7 6 5 4 3 2 1   19 20 21 22 23

ISBN 978-1-60358-905-5 (hardcover) | ISBN 978-1-60358-906-2 (ebook)
  | ISBN 978-1-60358-907-9 (audiobook)

Library of Congress Cataloging-in-Publication Data is available upon request.

Chelsea Green Publishing
85 North Main Street, Suite 120
White River Junction, VT 05001
(802) 295-6300
www.chelseagreen.com

Dedicated to Emma, Rowan, Finn, Arlo and Cian.
To my parents, for the precious gift of an imaginative childhood.
To the Stansted 15, because our imaginations need heroes.

And to the memory of Max Hamilton.

We all, adults and children, have an obligation to daydream. We have an obligation to imagine. It is easy to pretend that nobody can change anything, that we are in a world in which society is huge and the individual is less than nothing: an atom in a wall, a grain of rice in a rice field. But the truth is, individuals change their world over and over, individuals make the future, and they do it by imagining things can be different.

—NEIL GAIMAN

CONTENTS

What If Things Turned Out OK?

One might say that human societies have two boundaries.
One boundary is drawn by the requirements of the natu-
ral world and the other by the collective imagination.
—SUSAN GRIFFIN, 'To Love the Marigold'

I wake, well rested, in the straw-bale-walled apartment my family and I call home. Built fifteen years ago as part of a sustainable-construction initiative throughout our city, the three-storey-high apartment complex costs virtually nothing to heat, its basement hosts composting units for all the building's toilets, and the solar panels on the roof generate all our electricity needs. I wake my kids, get them dressed and fed and accompany them to school – a walk that takes us through shared gardens with a diversity of food crops, including young ruby chard whose deep red leaves radiate like stained glass caught in the brilliant sun of this late spring morning. The streets are quiet, due to sparse motorised traffic, and they are lined with fruit and nut trees in early blossom. The air smells of spring. Each bus stop we pass is surrounded by a garden on three sides, part of the Edible Bus Stop network that now includes most bus stops across the United Kingdom. Anyone can graze while they wait for the bus.

In our community, the kids seem to have radically different feelings about school than they did ten years ago. The education department's decision to eliminate testing, to give ample space for unstructured play and to provide students with opportunities within the community to acquire meaningful skills that enable them to live happy and healthy lives by their own definition means that most kids here now love going to school. My son, for example, recently upped his cooking skills by spending a week at a local restaurant.

My kids and I approach the school through intensive food gardens, planted and managed by the students, and walk into a building where we are greeted by the smell of baking bread and the sound of happy chatter. After we say our goodbyes, I pick up a public bicycle and head into the city on one of our cycle networks. With more bicycles and fewer cars on the road, air quality has improved, and public health along with it. I call into my favourite bakery to buy bread. Launched fifteen years ago on the premise that 'baking is the new Prozac', the bakery's mission is to provide meaningful work opportunities for people who lack housing and job security, and who struggle with mental health.[1] The bakery prioritises local produce, grows a thriving rooftop garden and uses bicycle-powered delivery around town.[2] With the bakery's support, many of its employees have launched other successful businesses across the city.

I pass what used to be one of the district's supermarkets, most of which closed down about ten years ago. The explosion in community food production and rapid shift of community investment led to a withdrawal of support from supermarkets, which precipitated the collapse of the industrial food model over the space of only a couple of years. The building was repurposed and became home to a variety of local food processors, small-scale manufacturing and a training centre linked to local schools. The place is buzzing. Our former supermarket houses a mill that processes locally grown grains, as well as a sawmill that processes locally harvested timber. What had been extensive car parks are now intensive food gardens – modelled on those that surrounded Paris a hundred years ago – and they provide local food for local markets.

I call by the train station to buy tickets for a trip the following week. Bringing the trains into public ownership twelve years ago eliminated the days when every train station looked the same, with the same cafes, chains and shops. Now every station is a manifestation of the local economy – its innovators, its unique flavours and tastes. Ours now has twice the number of outlets as before, and it reflects the cultural diversity of our community. There is even a brewery on the station; you can have a drink, surrounded by the fermenters, while you wait for your train.[3] Oh, and the trains now run on time. The many people from other places who arrived here during the times of great migration have assimilated, and now it's hard to remember this community without them. While that transition wasn't without its challenges, the culture, the richness, the enterprise they have brought have much enriched us all.

I call into work. I'm working a half day today, as part of my three-day work week. Adopted nationally ten years ago, the three-day work week, together with the introduction of Universal Basic Income, has resulted in measurably lower levels of anxiety and stress across all income classes. People spend free time working on community projects and enjoying their lives. Some of my colleagues are away today. A scheme was recently launched where up to 10 percent of staff from any company, at any given time, are embedded in the local community, offering managerial, marketing, financial planning and project management skills to organisations that are working in various ways to support residents and make our community more resilient.

I pick up my kids from school and we stroll home down streets where many of the houses are painted with eye-catching murals and mosaics. There are lots of kids playing in the street, a phenomenon that occurred naturally once the number of cars on the road diminished, which in turn encouraged residents to periodically close their streets entirely to motorised traffic, so children can play out; all the neighbours look out for the kids, something made possible when adults began spending more time at home, rather than trapped in long commutes to distant workplaces.

After supper, I head out to a Neighbourhood Assembly meeting. A few years ago, a group of residents, not aligned to any political party, were voted in to run our city government. They altered the city's governance model to enable and support the initiatives emerging at the neighbourhood scale, and to remove obstacles. They even created a Civic Imagination Office to better inspire and support the imaginations of local communities, and to enable their ideas to become reality. About seventy people are at this particular meeting, and we discuss our vision for the future of energy in our neighbourhood, and some other pressing local issues. Policymaking has improved hugely. Thanks to the community-owned energy company set up in 2021, the majority of the city's energy is now locally generated, and most citizens have some kind of financial investment in it; it generates a far better return than the banks do.

When I reach home, I visit with several of my neighbours, who are sitting outside chatting. We hear an owl, and notice the bats swooping overhead. The move to designate our city a National Park City slowed the decline of biodiversity to the point of recovery by reunifying previously fractured wildlife corridors, green spaces, and woods, so that I now regularly notice new kinds of insects and louder and more complex birdsong. With so much around me moving, changing and thriving, I settle down to sleep with a feeling that the future is rich with possibility.

––––––––––

It sounds made up, doesn't it? It is. Mostly.[4] The story is my imagining of the near future, a story of How Things Turned Out OK.

Of course, this imaginary life isn't perfect. This imaginary community is not Utopia. It still rains, friends fall out and people have bad days. Some impacts of climate change are still felt. And the vision is likely very different to what your story of How Things Turned Out OK would be. But I start with it because we live in a time bereft of such stories – stories of what life could look like if we were able to find a way over the course of the next twenty years to be bold, brilliant and decisive, to act in proportion to the challenges we are facing and to aim for a future we actually feel good about.

I've come to believe we desperately need stories like this – stories of How Things Turned Out OK – because if there is a consensus about anything in the world at this point, it seems to be that the future is going to be awful. And with good reason. In 2018, the Intergovernmental Panel on Climate Change (IPCC) reported that the world's temperature warmed by 1 degree Celsius over the past century. To avoid exceeding 1.5 degrees, they say, we would need to cut emissions by 45 percent by 2030, and to zero by 2050.[5] And their findings are actually pretty conservative. Others argue that even staying below a 2-degree increase would, in reality, for 'developed' nations such as those in the EU, necessitate cuts of 12 percent a year, starting now, far beyond the EU's current target of 40 percent by 2030.[6]

The longer our inertia persists, the steeper and more demanding that task becomes. As Jim Skea, co-chair of IPCC Working Group III, stated when the report was released, 'Limiting warming to 1.5°C is possible within the laws of chemistry and physics but doing so would require unprecedented changes.'[7]

And of course, we can already see the impacts of climate change (and other ecological destruction) in real time with extreme weather events, the loss of biodiversity and a food system dependent on the use of vast quantities of pesticides and herbicides to coax crops from the earth. More and more people seem to be feeling accumulated pressures in their personal lives as well. There is an epidemic of loneliness, an epidemic of anxiety (estimated to have increased twentyfold over the past thirty years), a mental health crisis of vast proportions among young people, the rise of extremist movements and governments and much more besides.[8] Looks hopeless, right?

Sadly, it seems far easier to imagine almost any dystopian scenario than the possibility that we might actually still have the competence to act, to create something else, to dig ourselves out of the many holes of our own making. The message that 'it can't be done' is strong and pervasive. As Susan Griffin puts it:

> Among those who would seek or want social change, despair is endemic now. A lack of hope that is tied to many kinds of powerlessness. Repeating patterns of suffering. Burgeoning philosophies of fear and hatred. Not to speak of the failure of dreams. Where once there were societies that served as models for a better future, grand plans, utopias, now there is distrust and dissatisfaction with any form of politics, a sense of powerlessness edging into nihilism.[9]

Given the state of the world, the message of despair is pretty convincing. Things look grim. But something about that doesn't sit quite right with me. In fact, there's evidence that things can change, and that cultures can change, rapidly and unexpectedly. And that's not just naïve, pie-in-the-sky thinking. In *How Did We Do That? The Possibility of Rapid Transition*, Andrew Simms and Peter Newell tell the story of Iceland's 2010 Eyjafjallajökull eruption, which sent fine dust into the sky that spread for thousands of miles and grounded most of the world's planes.[10] Then what happened? People adapted. Quickly. Supermarkets replaced air-freighted goods with local alternatives. People discovered other, slower ways to get around, or decided they didn't really need to travel at all. People held business meetings online. The Norwegian prime minister, Jens Stoltenberg, ran the Norwegian government from New York . . . with his iPad. This isn't the only example. We might be focused these days on how we are only nine meals from anarchy, but there are stories from throughout history about how rapid transitions lead to ingenuity, flourishing, imagination and togetherness.[11]

I've seen this with my own eyes, thanks to an experiment a few friends and I initiated more than a decade ago in our hometown of Totnes in Devon, England (population 8,500). Our idea was a simple one: What if, we wondered, the change we need to see in response to the biggest challenges of our time came not from government and business, but from you and me, from communities working together? What if the answers were to be found not in the bleak solitude of survivalism and isolation, in the tweaking of ruthless commercialism, or in the dream that some electable saviour will come riding to our rescue, but rather in reconnection to community? As we put it: 'If we wait for governments, it will be too late. If we act as individuals, it will be too little. But if we act as communities, it might just be enough, and it might just be in time.'

As we began floating this idea with our friends and the wider community, the term 'Transition' arose to describe the intentional act of shifting from high resource use, high carbon dioxide (CO_2) emissions, extractive business practice and fragmented communities to communities with a healthier culture, more resilient and diverse local economies, more connection and less loneliness, more biodiversity and more time, democracy and beauty.[12]

As 'Transition Town Totnes', we began asking these 'what-if' questions, and things started unfolding apace in our town. People planted fruit and nut trees in public spaces, grew food at the train station, and connected neighbours who wanted to grow food with neighbours who had unused garden space. We crowdfunded to buy a mill – the first new mill in Totnes in more than a hundred years – to grind local grains and pulses for a range of flours, and we hosted an annual local food festival celebrating food grown in and very near to Totnes. As I write this, Transition Homes is building twenty-seven houses using local materials for people in need, and Caring Town Totnes has developed a network of caregiving organisations so they can work together more effectively. Through it all, we've held community conversations so people could come together to imagine and discuss the kind of future they'd like to create.

In 2013, we mapped the local economy with our Local Economic Blueprint and argued the financial case for a more localised approach to economic development.[13] Our annual Local Entrepreneur Forum invites the community to support new businesses and has now helped launch more than thirty enterprises.[14] Recently, some friends and I started a community-owned craft brewery, New Lion Brewery, which brews delicious beers using many local ingredients, often in collaboration with other emerging social enterprises.[15] And early on, Transition Town Totnes created the Totnes Pound, a local currency that has inspired many other local currencies around the world. When people asked us, 'Why do you have a £21 note?' we asked, 'Why not?'

Around the same time that we were mapping the local economy, Transition Streets brought together approximately 550 households in groups of six to ten neighbouring households. Each group met up seven times to look at issues such as water, food or energy consumption and to agree on actions they could take before the next meeting to reduce waste, cut costs, and develop community resilience. By the end, each household cut their carbon emissions by an average of 1.3 tonnes, saving around £600 a year.[16]

What was fascinating about Transition Streets was that when organisers asked participants what was most impactful about taking part, nobody mentioned carbon. Or money. They reported that they felt like part of the community, they felt as though they belonged, they knew more people, they felt connected. This has been true across the board. More important than any of the actual projects was the sense of connection, of feeling part of something, of the underlying story starting to shift. A collective reimagining of what the future could be. I began to see that our efforts were starting to become, at least in part, a different story our town told about itself. And in the process, our collective sense of what was possible began to shift. We discovered that if enough people came together, we could create an entirely new kind of story from the collective experiences of so many people trying to make good, and better, things happen in our community.

Part of the beauty of Transition is that it's all an experiment. I don't know how to do it. Neither do you. In Totnes, we were just trying to spark something that might unlock a creative spirit, a renewed sense of possibility, a fresh and hopeful way to think about the future, without any thought that it could spread to other places. But spread it did. As early as 2007, Transition groups started popping up in communities in the United States, Italy, France, Japan, Holland and Brazil. The Transition movement now exists in fifty countries and in thousands of communities. Every group is different, and emerges from the spirit and culture of the place. It's a process that, from the outset, has invited and supported people's creativity and imagination. It has also profoundly affected how I think about our world's biggest problems.

What I saw ignite with the Transition movement taught me that we're often looking in the wrong places for the solutions to our biggest threats. Yes, political action is a vital part of democracy, and can lead to very real change, but in addition to thinking we always need to campaign and lobby harder, design bigger and more disruptive demonstrations and rally more people through more online petitions, perhaps we need sometimes to stop, stare out of the window and imagine a world in which things are better. Maybe it's time to recognise that at the heart of our work is the need for those around us to be able to imagine a better world, to tell stories about it, to long for its realisation. If we can imagine it, desire it, dream about it, it is so much more likely that we will put our energy and determination into making it reality. As my friend and mentor the late David Fleming wrote, 'If the mature market economy is to have a sequel . . . it will be the work, substantially, of imagination.'[17]

To experience the Transition movement in Totnes and see it take off around the world made clear to me how prescient Fleming's remarks were. Bringing about the world we want to live in, the world we want to leave to our children is, substantially, the work of the imagination, or what educational reformer John Dewey describes as 'the ability to look at things as if they could be otherwise'.[18] It seems a lot of people are reaching a similar conclusion. In 2009 Paolo Lugari, founder of the Colombian sustainable living experiment Las Gaviotas, wrote that 'We are not confronting an energy crisis, but one of imagination and enthusiasm.'[19] In 2016 the writer Amitav Ghosh described climate change as 'a crisis of culture, and thus of imagination'.[20] A year later journalist George Monbiot wrote that 'political failure is, in essence, a failure of imagination.'[21] In 2018 David Wallace-Wells wrote of how, in relation to climate change, 'We suffer from an incredible failure of imagination.'[22]

And yet nobody seems able to explain why our imaginations are failing us so spectacularly. Why are we so incapable of coming together to create, sustain and carry out a vision in which we capably address global crises and enjoy our lives more in the process? It seems as though we are becoming *less* imaginative at the very time in history when we need to be at our most imaginative. Our imagination muscle should be taut and well exercised; instead it is flaccid and untoned. I worry that the deeper we get into a crisis such as climate change, the harder it becomes to imagine a way out. Given everything humanity has accomplished, all of it driven by leaps of the imagination, why is envisioning a safer, saner, happier, more peaceful path forward so consistently beyond our reach? Indeed, why does it seem *increasingly* beyond our reach?

This book arose from those questions, and others like them, as I was trying to understand why on the one hand, Transition had taken off beyond everyone's expectations, as we were swept up in positive change we could never have imagined, while on the other hand, so many problems – big and small – seem so intractable, even when we apply our most rigorous thinking to them. As I was thinking about this, I stumbled on a paper by a researcher named Dr Kyung Hee Kim at the College of William and Mary. Analysing more than 250,000 participants between kindergarten and adulthood from the late 1960s to the present, Dr Kim found that while creative thinking and IQ rose concomitantly until 1990, at some point between 1990 and 1998, they parted ways, with creative thinking heading into a 'steady and persistent' decline.[23] Dr Kim attributed the decline to children's having less time to play, more time spent on electronic devices, greater emphasis on standardised testing and a lack of free time for 'reflective abstraction'. Her findings were picked up by *Newsweek*, and suddenly Dr Kim was inundated with invitations to appear on radio and TV.[24]

Dr Kim's comments and her findings prompted me to look more closely at my life and my community, and what I see people grappling with in the world. It seems as though most of us have less and less space to think creatively or imaginatively, if at all. Even among people who work within the 'creative industries', their imagination seems increasingly harnessed to create demand for things nobody really needs, whose production is increasingly pushing our human and ecological systems to the brink of collapse – almost as if imagination has been coopted in the service of our own extinction.

But what if imagination is exactly what we need to prevent it?

There is a body of research to suggest that it is.

Close your eyes, if you will, and imagine that you are holding a lemon in your hand. Feel its cool skin against your palm. See its bright yellow colour. Run your fingertips over its shiny textured surface. Throw it up in the air and catch it again, feeling its weight in your hand as it lands. Then, with your other hand, reach for a knife and cut the lemon in half. Pick up one half and slowly squeeze it into a glass, hearing the drops fall. Smell the aroma of the fresh lemon juice. As you squeeze the lemon, some of it squirts into your eye.

When psychologists conduct this exercise, they often observe that, at this point, people wince, just as they would if they had actually squirted lemon juice in their eye. The human imagination is a powerful thing. It is not only about images and the ability to hold a picture in our mind. It is multisensory, encompassing smell, touch, sound, emotion and taste. It is more able to effect change than you might think. As we know from the field of positive psychology, imagining a certain outcome can increase the likelihood of its coming to pass.

In a 1995 study, Dr Alvaro Pascual-Leone of Harvard Medical School followed two groups of novices learning to play a sequence of notes on the piano. Each group practised for two hours a day for five days, but one group actually played the piano while the other sat at the piano and imagined playing it. After three days, members of each group had the same ability and showed similar changes in their brains, whether they had played it or not. After five days, members of the group that actually played were marginally more advanced, but members of the other group caught up quickly once they were provided with an actual piano to play.[25]

The same phenomenon can be observed with exercise. A 1992 study by Guang Yue and Kelly Cole found that people who exercised a particular finger muscle increased the strength of that muscle by 30 percent after five days, while a group of people who imagined exercising that particular finger muscle increased their strength by 22 percent.[26]

Jackie Andrade and Jon May, who showed me the lemon exercise, described to me the research they're doing at the University of Plymouth, where they've developed an approach called functional imagery training (FIT), which harnesses the power of the imagination to help people change habitual patterns and behaviours.[27] Let's say, for example, that I want to lose weight. I am determined to succeed, but am then faced with the temptation of a chocolate éclair, which overrides my desire to be fit and trim. But what happens if we imagine our life as a fit and trim person, to such a degree that we can actually see what we'd look like as our muscles start to develop tone they didn't have before; feel our exuberance as we run around the yard with our grandchildren; relish the warmth of the sun on our skin while we're out for a jog; experience the post-run endorphins while we shower and then step back into life. If, Andrade and May argue, we could imagine that, *really* imagine that, the next éclair would have far less power over us compared to the tangibility of our longer-term goal.

Their research suggests it works. In a three-year trial, Andrade and May found that, over the course of six months, when test subjects had up to four hours of FIT through a therapist, they lost an average of 4 kg, compared to members of a control group, who lost an average of 1 kg. Over the course of the next six months, members of the test group had no contact with a therapist at all, and yet they kept losing weight. This is almost unheard of; with most approaches, in that second six months, people put on around 50 percent of what they'd lost. What Andrade and May discovered is that once people have internalised the skills to imagine a future in which they have reached their desired weight or pattern of behavior, they no longer need the therapist.[28]

This research shows that harnessing the imagination can help us improve our lives considerably. I couldn't stop wondering: 'What if we could apply this more broadly, to even more complex problems?' As I ventured into this question, one of the first places I visited was an event hosted by London's Institute of Imagination (iOi), which the author and educational reformer Sir Ken Robinson (one of its patrons) calls 'a celebration of children's imagination and creativity, offering all sorts of practical opportunities for its cultivation'. When I arrive, iOi's *Lab Live: Metropolis* is well under way and I find myself surrounded by kids and grown-ups building a city with cardboard boxes. Elsewhere, kids are being filmed against a green screen (à la *Godzilla*), smashing a cardboard Tokyo to bits. I notice that the adults seem to be enjoying it all as much as the kids. In fact, some parents are so engrossed that they're oblivious to the fact that their children have long since had their attention drawn elsewhere.

Later, I join iOi's director of development, Jennifer Coleman, in a quiet side room, where she tells me: 'There is a lack of opportunities for children to apply their imagination in a meaningful way . . . in a world that doesn't value it. We see imagination as much more fundamental. It enables children to understand the world – imagining different scenarios and then testing them out, using imagination to empathise with others.'[29] She goes on to restate what will be a theme of this book, namely that we don't give imagination enough time. It is not given enough time in school and not enough time at home, as we increasingly pack our lives, and our kids' lives, with classes and screens. Imagination, in other words, is being shunted into a siding.

Our conversation leaves me with the familiar feeling that we have a problem with valuation. That is, we don't have a good sense of what really matters, and why. A few weeks earlier I had spoken by Skype with Scott Barry Kaufman, scientific director of Philadelphia's Imagination Institute, a centre for rigorous academic study under the leadership of positive psychology guru Martin Seligman. Although the Imagination Institute is light-years away from iOi's cozy familial feel, Kaufman told me much the same thing: 'We believe that imagination is an essential skill in the world. It is essential . . . to empathy, to perspective taking. It is essential to our own personal sense of well-being, allowing us to realise our personal futures and much more.'[30]

I was particularly struck by the assertion, from both Coleman and Kaufman, that imagination is fundamental to a person's capacity to function in society, or as Kaufman put it, 'an essential skill in the world'. Yet imagination, rather than being seen as an 'essential skill', is commonly perceived as messy, unpredictable, a bit cheeky, potentially uncontrollable and a frivolous and unprofitable use of time. It's considered the domain of children, while a capacity for innovation (and creativity to a degree) is highly prized and richly rewarded. As David Fleming put it, it is 'widely seen as a dissident to be suppressed, removed or re-educated'.[31] And yet Andrade and May's work seemed to offer so much insight as to why, in a very real way, imagination could be central to the changes we need to make over the next twenty years.

What if we could apply these same techniques and invoke that 'essential skill' to imagine that we did every single creative, ambitious, brilliant thing possible to avert the worst impacts of climate change? What if, in response to the IPCC's 2018 report conclusion that we need 'rapid, far-reaching and unprecedented changes in all aspects of society', we were able to imagine those rapid, far-reaching and unprecedented changes?[32] What if we rushed to embrace such an invitation to reimagine and rebuild everything?

And what if we don't?

I often wonder how future generations will perceive this moment in history: When newly discovered sea creatures in trenches eleven kilometres deep were found to have plastic in their stomachs. When society became dangerously polarised and we saw a resurgence of toxic ideas we thought had been consigned to history. When we lurched from financial crisis to financial crisis without changing the fundamental imbalances that make their occurrence almost inevitable. When bees and other insect populations collapsed because we were unable to adjust how we grew our food or rein in pesticide companies. The missed opportunities when climate change could have been averted, if we hadn't dithered and procrastinated.

A recent paper on climate change known popularly as 'Hothouse Earth' stated: 'Incremental linear changes . . . are not enough to stabilise the Earth system. Widespread, rapid and fundamental transformations will likely be required to reduce the risk of crossing the threshold.'[33] As the writer and activist Naomi Klein puts it, 'There are no non-radical options left before us.'[34] I believe imagination is the only thing we have that is – or could be – radical enough to get us through, provided it is accompanied, of course, by bravery, and by action.

This is not a book of despair, however. During the course of writing this book, I interviewed nearly one hundred people. (You can find all those interviews in full at the *Imagination Taking Power* blog that accompanies this book, www.robhopkins.net.) I visited dozens of projects and places, read hundreds of books (not so easy as it used to be, as we'll discuss) and had conversations with people around the world in an attempt to understand how far we can get with these two little words: 'What if . . . ?' That question and the people I met who were asking it led me on a journey, during which I rekindled my own sense of playfulness by learning to improvise, visited the former High Street bank that re-opened as 'an act of citizen money-creation,' took part in the transformation of a depressing bus turning circle into a vibrant 'village green', joined kids and families in Bristol who shut down their street to motorised traffic so they could ride their skateboards and scooters in the street – and so much more.

I came away with the firm conclusion that David Fleming was not only correct in his thinking that the work before us is substantially the work of the imagination, but that this work is under way in communities around the world that have much to teach us. I discovered that there were people the world over asking questions, large and small, about how things could be otherwise in schools, in neighbourhoods, in our relationship to nature, in our approach to health care, in how we spend our time and attention, even using it as the basis for reimagining the economic and democratic realities of their cities and towns.

At every step I fell more and more in love with those two words, 'What if . . . ?' What if we wasted a lot less energy and generated most of what we do use from renewable sources? What if we made refugees feel welcome and supported in their newly adopted homelands? What if we measured the economy with metrics other than how much bigger it is from one year to the next? What if we could think about car-free cities, no prisons, a more equal distribution of wealth without our brains getting completely discombobulated? What if we lived in a world in which the police didn't shoot unarmed young men of colour, and our education system didn't generate a mental health crisis in young people? What if we phased out the aviation industry and embraced a life of slow travel instead? The Israeli historian Yuval Noah Harari argues that humans became the most powerful creatures on the planet because of our imagination, our ability to tell stories and to ask 'what if?'[35]

What if we revived that capability, in great abundance, starting now?

CHAPTER 1

What If We Took Play Seriously?

The drive to play freely is a basic, biological drive. Lack of free play may not kill the physical body, as would lack of food, air, or water, but it kills the spirit and stunts mental growth . . . nothing that we do, no amount of toys we buy or 'quality time' or special training we give our children, can compensate for the freedom we take away. The things that children learn through their own initiatives, in free play, cannot be taught in other ways.

—PETER GRAY, *Free to Learn*

I t's a Wednesday early evening in the St George area of Bristol, and I'm visiting Howard Road, which is part of a national initiative called Playing Out. It's a simple idea. Playing Out supports parents who want to close their street off to motorised traffic for short periods of time so that children are in charge, not cars.[1] The pavements are covered with chalk drawings, and kids fly past me on scooters, skateboards and bicycles. There's skipping going on, two adults turning the rope while a queue of children wait their turn.[2]

While it might seem counter-intuitive to parents to encourage their children to play in the street, Jo Chesterman, Playing Out coordinator for the street I'm visiting, tells me, 'We've stumbled across a really good thing here.' The seeds were sown during the Queen's Diamond Jubilee in 2012, when the neighbourhood held a street party, and everyone was surprised by how many kids were in the street, and at how much fun they had. Jo now serves as a local 'activator', supporting people on other streets who want to do the same.

Howard Road is closed fortnightly between April and October for two hours after school, and during the winter, one Sunday every month. And Playing Out now happens in five hundred streets across the country, most notably in Leeds, Hackney, Worthing and North Tyneside. But Bristol is the epicentre, with sixty streets closing down on a regular basis. Having an organisation in place has made the legalities of closing a street a lot simpler. For starters, thanks to the new Temporary Streets Play Order, added by Bristol City Council to the Town Police Clauses Act of 1847, groups can now apply for a year's worth of dates in one go, rather than having to make a series of separate applications.

This 'really good thing' of letting children play in the street has had so many unexpected benefits: It offers kids a blank canvas (unlike, say, computer games, where you usually move through levels of someone else's devising). It encourages play that is spontaneous and inventive. Street play helps kids build confidence. Being out of the house is the first step towards feeling confident about interacting with others. After an afternoon of playing in the street, a kid might then feel more confident about venturing farther afield, maybe walking to school the next day. Street play is also, to state the blindly obvious, on the family's doorstep, not requiring a walk, or drive, to the park or playground. It brings communities together, enabling residents to meet one another and build relationships. This familiarity increases the neighbourhood's social resilience, making it a safer and more gratifying place to live. And the play can be 'semi-supervised', so adults can get things done, knowing that the kids are being watched.

In fact, it's hard to think of an argument *against* closing down a public street so that children can play in it – other than that it's an inconvenience to drivers. As Jo told me, this approach is 'not anti-car, it's pro-community'. I asked Jo if those advocating for Playing Out in Howard Road had encountered much opposition from neighbours, and she told me that during the process of setting it up, there had been no opposition. That arrived a year into the initiative, with what she calls 'Chalkgate'.

She told me, 'a group of older residents were increasingly upset by the chalk pictures left behind after Playing Out and demanded that we wash the pavement down at the end of each session [the "leave it as you find it" philosophy]. I got caught in the middle – the Playing Out folk were incensed at this request and got pretty upset, and the older residents had had enough.'[3]

Everyone agreed to a trial with a designated chalking area, supervised by one of the older children, which would then be cleared away at the end of the session, and to not always have chalk. Washing off the chalk drawings became part of the games, and enabled a conversation with the kids about how, as a community, it was important to take each other into account. Today, some sessions happen with chalk, some don't and some play with chalk happens outside of Playing Out sessions – so it can't all be blamed on those sessions.

But the time and effort given to listening to older residents' concerns proved important. When the street faced more recent antisocial behaviour from older lads on quad bikes, those conversations and compromises meant that the street was better able to come together to respond. 'We have had regular Playing Out sessions for over four years, and I think our relentless enthusiasm wore down any opposition – plus nothing negative happened, only neighbours hanging out and kids playing – we brought back street play, which is now part of our street throughout the week, month, year, and I am so delighted to have been part of that,' Jo said.[4]

Daniella Radice, national project manager for Playing Out and my guide for the evening I spent on Howard Road, points out that 'streets constitute the vast majority of public space in a city'. Visit some parts of the world, and you'll routinely see streets as places for play, conversation, chess, dominoes, singing and dancing, sleeping. Enrique Peñalosa, a former mayor of Bogotá, believes that children playing in the street are actually an 'indicator species' for the well-being of a city.[5] In fact, the purging of children from the street is primarily a problem particular to the more affluent nations of the global North. Maybe it's time we reimagine the role of public streets in our lives and communities and take them back.

Until relatively recently, street play was the norm in many places, and a fundamental cornerstone of our culture. One writer in the 1920s reflecting on the street lives of children in London wrote, 'The street is the cradle of the new-born babe, and the nursery of the toddler, and the playing field of the elementary school child; and running wild in it is responsible for much of the vitality and the wit and the insatiable curiosity that are found animating every grown-up London crowd.'[6]

A poll by Playday found that 71 percent of adults in 2007 played out in the street when they were children, while the rate for children in 2007 was just 21 percent.[7] Our children are increasingly under what Richard Louv, author of *Last Child in the Woods*, calls 'well-meaning, protective house arrest', rarely out of their parents' sight, and on tablets, whether of the pharmaceutical or digital variety.[8] Children today have far less room to roam – just one-ninth of what previous generations had.[9]

Comic books and archive film from the 1970s show that children played mostly outside, and had a rich culture of games, songs and stories.[10] Children created their own worlds which their parents rarely knew about – dens, bases, treehouse, pathways – in a way we now know was vital for their psychological well-being and mental health.[11] But even by the 1970s, unstructured outdoor play was in decline. Urban historian Howard Chudacoff calls the period of the early-to-mid twentieth century 'the golden age of children's unstructured play', and situates the beginning of the decline around 1955.[12]

One of the reasons unstructured play has disappeared from our streets is due to older people's thinking of children as unruly. In 2004 the chief constable of West Midlands Police, Paul Scott-Lee, told the *Birmingham Mail*: 'The interesting thing to me is that when you ask them what they are worried about, it's not young people committing criminal damage . . . it's actually young people just being there. Young people simply existing is now a major source of concern for people.'[13] But people like Jo have started to see really positive changes in the culture on her street by letting young people simply exist there. Before, the kids rarely played in the street. Now, she says, it is starting to happen outside of Playing Out. 'Natural street play has started to emerge,' she told me.

And there's a change in how the kids approach play itself. Louise Davey, a parent from a neighbouring street who brings her kids over to Howard Road on Playing Out days, told me she sees an 'imaginative leap' during these sessions. The kids don't just draw; they invent games with the chalk on the pavement. And they don't just use the skipping rope for skipping;

it becomes the focal point for all kinds of other games, once they've tired of skipping. As Jo puts it, it gives them the space for imaginative play. It's also, by the way, a huge positive for the adults, who have discovered, as one parent told me, 'that we actually quite like each other'. There are now regular evening socials, outside of Playing Out. As Louise noted, 'It's nice to see everyone come out, talk to each other, and not behind a screen.'

What happens when children are denied this kind of spontaneous free play – denied the space to pretend? The most extreme end of the research – and it is admittedly extreme – can be found in the work of the psychiatrist Stuart Brown. After the 1966 shooting at the University of Texas, where Charles Whitman shot forty-six people from the top of a tower on the campus, Brown interviewed Whitman and twenty-six other convicted murderers in Texas to find out what they had in common.[14] It turned out there were two key things: they were all from abusive families, and as children they were never allowed to play. In subsequent work, Brown looked deeper, interviewing more than six thousand people about their childhoods and confirming his initial findings about how serious a play-deprived childhood is. He has written that 'pathological aggression often characterises a childhood blighted by little or no playfulness' and 'the consequence of a life that is seriously play-deprived is serious stuff'.[15]

Estonian neuroscientist and psychobiologist Jaak Panksepp writes that growing up with insufficient opportunities for what he calls 'real play' can lead to depression and other adversity, including an increased susceptibility to ADHD. As he puts it: 'Our postmodern societies have stolen natural play away from our children, to be replaced, all too often, with regimented activities and medication that reduce the urge to play.'[16] The implications are stark. Today, thirty-five thousand children in England are being prescribed anti-depressants; one in ten has been diagnosed with a mental health disorder.[17]

The scientific literature is clear on this point: play is key to brain development. It is as natural as learning how to walk, breathe or speak. It teaches social skills, cooperation, creativity and conflict resolution. It builds resilience and produces adults who are better at finding solutions. Studies show that children use more sophisticated language when they play with other children than when they interact with adults.[18] Role play helps children develop empathy. Free play also helps children learn to take risks; one study showed that children who injured themselves falling from heights between the ages of five and nine were, by the age of eighteen, less afraid of heights.[19] If we want to nurture young people who are resilient, self-reliant, entrepreneurial and adventurous – and I argue that we *need* to – we have to let them take risks. Risk-aversion is the last quality we need to be building in our children. As Stephen Moss put it in a report on play for the National Trust, 'A potential risk is that children who don't take risks become adults who don't take risks.'[20]

The disappearance of children from the streets of our towns and cities has an impact on adults too. Adults need to hear and be around children playing. A recent Channel 4 series, *Old People's Home for 4 Year Olds*, ran a trial, bringing a group of four-year-olds into an old people's home, medically assessing the impacts it had on the elderly adults. While in the United States over five hundred such intergenerational schemes exist, this was the United Kingdom's first. By the end, the impacts on well-being, psychological and physical health, including mobility, were striking. One seventy-seven-year-old participant, Zina, had been suffering from depression. She said, 'Every time the children are happy, we're happy. This experiment has brought us back into something where there's room for imagination. It's nearly impossible not to be affected by the joy of the children.'[21]

Or, as Jo Chesterman put it, 'Future generations are going to look back and go, "What were they doing?" "What were they thinking?"' The main thing that stayed with me after my visit to Howard Road was that imaginative play, creativity, inventiveness are all still there. There is a deep well of it in communities, in relationships and in the human psyche, no matter how assiduously it has been tamped down. We just need to make space for it, in the right way, and it will grow again, spontaneously. As Jo told me: 'Traffic just needs to be, for just an hour or two, put in its place, and then this happens. And it happens every single time, every street that I've worked with. You shut it off, you create the space, and it happens.'

This is a theme that emerged time and again as I was researching this book: imagination is resilient. If we can put to one side the factors that are suppressing it, it will re-emerge, blinking into the light, because it is our natural state. It's a fundamental part of being human. When the right conditions are present, imagination flourishes. It's the natural order of things, in the same way that land, left to its own devices, will revert to forest, provided it isn't mowed, sprayed or grazed. When the space is made, the cars kept out, the right level of hands-off supervision, when the sense of being part of a larger community is created, imagination can flourish. Children instinctively and naturally want to play; it's what they do. It's never far beneath the surface. We just have to take the pressure off it, give this desire the space to breathe.

In April 2017, in my own town of Totnes in Devon, a group of volunteers are doing just that, putting on a Festival of Street Games in the Rotherfold, a square at the top of town. Not many children know how to play games that were once commonplace, like Queenie, Jimmy Jimmy Knacker, Murder Ball and Eggy Moo. The festival has brought adults and children together to play, and on the day of the festival they are joined by some recently arrived refugees from Pakistan and Syria, who bring street games of their own. Toni Spencer, one of the event's organisers, tells me, 'I grew up in the middle of London, but all the different ages of kids would be on the street and there was a sense that we belonged in that place. . . . One of my favourite things was to lie down in the middle of the road and dare the cars to run me over! Which I realise must be because I must have had that sense that I mattered more than the cars.'[22]

One game, Spijkerpoepen – the word translates as 'nail poops' in Dutch – is especially popular. Here's how to play: Tie a screw or a nail to the middle belt loop on the back of your trousers with a piece of string so it comes to somewhere just above your knees. Alternatively, you could tie the string around your waist so it hangs down the back. Then, by looking backwards between your legs, try to navigate it into the neck of a bottle behind you. Try it at your next staff meeting.

The square pulsed with noise, children dashing around, singing, the odd child crying over a grazed knee, laughter. You don't need much in order to play in the street. A skipping rope perhaps. Or a ball. A cricket bat maybe. A piece of chalk. Certainly nothing that needs any batteries. Nothing that needs a Wi-Fi connection. Just you, your mates and some time. It was fascinating to see how naturally most of the kids in the Rotherfold slipped into the mode of playing together, of learning the rules and then adapting them. There was a moment when the skipping – I had forgotten just what hard work skipping is! – turned into tug of war in the space of a few chaotic seconds. Some kids struggled with being part of a big group working out the rules together, prompting me to wonder if this was a consequence of our culture becoming more individualistic. And then, of course, there were the adults: At first, they stood around thinking they were there to enable their kids to play. Then they realised that they could play too.

———————

Howard Chudacoff, an author and professor of history at Brown University, once wrote, 'It's interesting to me that when we talk about play today, the first thing that comes to mind are toys. . . . Whereas when I think of play in the nineteenth century, I would think of *activity* rather than an object.'[23]

In the twenty-first century, play has become all about toys. The toys on offer leave less and less space for the imagination, often having one particular function, not enabling open-ended play, and increasingly being driven by corporate needs, rather than by your child's needs. As Jay Griffiths, author of *Kith*, told me, commercial toys teach kids

> that there is a scarcity within them, that they are not able to provide their own imagination, to make the world otherwise. If a child is given a twig and a pile of leaves, they can transform them into absolutely anything. That's imaginative power, and it's a really important way for children to learn they don't have a scarcity within them, but they have a fullness of imagination, a sense of imaginative self-sufficiency that is profoundly able to disobey when necessary.[24]

I am especially fascinated, and troubled, by the phenomenon of Hello Barbie, the first Wi-Fi-enabled chatbot version of the plastic princess of capitalism that 'talks' to your child and interacts with their responses. Introduced by Mattel in 2015, 'Hello Barbie doll uses WiFi and speech recognition technology to engage in two-way dialogue.'[25] In effect, she's like Siri, drawing on a 216-page script to talk to your child about his or her daily life:

> I'd love to learn more about you. Oh, I know! Let's make a game of it. The game's called Family Town! We're gonna

pretend all of your family members run different shops in a make-believe town! I'll be a visitor and you'll show me around! So . . . what's the name of your family's town? I think I'm gonna like it here! Okay, so every member of your family gets its own shop. One per person! I'll visit each shop and you'll tell me who runs it! Got it?[26]

Experts have set out a series of concerns around the technology of such dolls, including hacking and data mining. Mattel harvests what are referred to as 'dialogue chunks' – your child's answers to the doll's questions – which can be recorded, analysed and stored. These valuable bits of information can then be sold and resold to create targeted and personalised marketing strategies.[27]

Thankfully, sales of this ghastly device plummeted thanks to Hell No Barbie, an operation launched by the Campaign for a Commercial-Free Childhood (CCFC) shortly after the doll was released. Josh Golin from CCFC told me via Skype from Boston that alongside the many reasons to be horrified by such toys was the impact they would have on the imagination of the children they were given to:

> Imagination is such a crucial piece of childhood. Making up stories, playing imaginary games, having imaginary friends, imagining imaginary scenarios, are just such crucial parts of healthy child development. They allow children to work through problems . . . to imagine different possibilities. When we have children spending so much time with these devices that are telling stories to them, rather than allowing them to imagine their own worlds, we're really limiting their imagination.[28]

In the United Kingdom, the Toy Retailers Association have stated that such dolls 'offer no special risk', but alarm is growing. The Federal Network Agency, Germany's telecom watchdog, has classified a similar toy, My Friend Cayla, as 'illegal espionage apparatus', ruling that retailers who continue to stock it would be fined, as would parents who fail to disable its wireless connection.[29]

But it's not just children's privacy and safety that are at stake here. A toy like Hello Barbie elbows its way directly into your child's psyche, rendering his or her own personal imaginary friends unemployed overnight. Who now needs to imagine conversations and create scenarios when Mattel's Hello Barbie script will do it all for you?

As Shoshana Zuboff writes, raising disquiet over the 'surveillance capitalism' model behind such devices,

> The doll that was once a beloved mirror of a child's unfettered imagination, along with all the other toys in the toy box – and the box, and the room that hosts the box, and the house that hosts the room – are all earmarked for rendition, calculation, connection and profit. No longer mere things, they are reinvented as vehicles for a horde of commercial opportunities fabricated from our dialogue chunks and assorted gold dust.[30]

There is, in fact, a strong case for the imagination being best served by children having *fewer* toys. A 2018 study led by occupational therapist Alexia Metz at the University of Toledo in Ohio looked at the impact that the number of toys children played with had on their imaginations. She studied thirty-six toddlers aged eighteen to thirty months, and invited them to come to play twice at the laboratory playroom at the university. On one visit they were given sixteen toys to play with. On another visit they were given just four. Cameras captured how they played.

The researchers found that when the children played with fewer toys, they spent more time with each toy. But where it got more interesting was when they looked at the *quality* of play, the intensity of imagination that was evoked. When the toddlers played with just four toys, they played better, more creatively, with more focused and sustained attention, made possible by their not being distracted by so many toys. 'An environment that presents fewer distractions may provide toddlers the opportunity to exercise their intrinsic attention capabilities,' the team wrote. The children had to imagine more uses for each toy, which meant their divergent thinking kicked in. The team concluded that the fewer the toys, the greater the quality of the play. Having fewer toys allowed the toddlers to see what they were playing with in new and more creative ways.[31]

It's an observation that has been taken to another level by a nursery school in Munich, which removes all its toys for three months every year, initiated by two public health officers who wondered if addictive patterns might be instilled at a young age, and wanted to see how happily children could play without 'stuff'.[32] On the first day, the children arrived to a large, empty room, hesitant and a bit bored. By the second day, they were building dens using chairs and blankets, and by the end of the week were playing 'wildly imaginative' games. Their drawing and painting became far more expressive and creative.

When was the last time you could say that you played? I don't mean played a video game, or chess, or tennis; I mean played in an unstructured, 'let's pretend' kind of way, where you felt spontaneous, sparking off other people, absorbed? I'm guessing it's probably been a while. As adults, the whole idea can feel pretty ghastly, like those awful team-building exercises at work. What used to feel so natural for a child can feel toe-curling for adults. When we run big public events with Transition Town in my community, introducing any kind of exercise which even raises the possibility of talking to another person in pairs or small groups leads to about 5 percent, usually older people, heading for the exits. But is that inevitable? Are play and adulthood mutually incompatible? As author Leah Stella Stephens puts it, 'Who has the time or space to hear the barely audible whispers from our long-neglected imaginations? Our imaginations are banished during the day, locked in our internal jails, only to fleetingly emerge at night, *if we are lucky*.'[33]

One way adults can reconnect to play without it feeling so forced is by learning improv, so I thought it was about time I learned. In September 2017, I joined seven other people in London for a Level 1A Improvisation training, led by Jeremy Finch of the Spontaneity Shop, in order to investigate what play looks like in adults – and why it matters. I wanted to learn how, as an adult, to play again. As Tom Salinsky and Deborah Frances-White, founders of Spontaneity Shop, write in *The Improv Handbook*, 'Many adults have simply stopped being creative, so those muscles are tired and atrophied. The imagination is like a scared animal – it needs cossetting and encouraging.'[34] And so there we were, a young man who worked in finance, a shy young man between jobs, a colourful older woman and a few others – a mix of ages and life experience, gathered in a room in an arts centre in London, looking slightly nervous, but ready to cosset and encourage our imaginations.[35]

Jeremy began by sharing his improv philosophy: 'I suck, and I love to fail.' We had to repeat it like a mantra. The idea was to give ourselves permission to try things, with no expectations of brilliance, celebrating 'failure' because failure means taking risks, stepping into the unknown, putting our trust in the other people around us. I asked Jeremy what the course intended to teach us. He answered:

> Improv is creative collaboration. It's making stuff up, on the spot, often in front of an audience. It involves generating material in the moment. It involves engaging with your creative partners, listening, being present. It has a Zen-like 'in the moment' aspect. It's also about understanding story structures, how we create compelling story narratives that enchant us or move us, or capture our imaginations. It's about becoming an actor and a writer at the same time.

For two days, we played games. The first game came in three parts. First was 'pointing at things and saying what they are', so for a couple of minutes we did just that, walking around the room. Then 'pointing at things and saying what the last thing you pointed at was', which took a bit more thinking about, having to keep in mind the last name you had used. Then the third one, 'pointing at things and saying what they're not', might sound easy, but it's fascinating how quickly you start to run out of words. The point of the activity, Jeremy explained, is to start rewiring our brains to the idea that there is no right answer, learning to turn off our internal censor which, since school, has been terrified of giving a 'wrong' answer in public.

We also played 'Yes, and', a game that starts in pairs with one person making a suggestion, such as 'Let's go on holiday!' Your partner shuts down the idea, outraged: 'You know I can't go on holiday, I just broke my legs!' Your partner then makes a suggestion, which you shut down in a similar manner, and so on. In the next phase of the game, you make a suggestion, and your partner responds unenthusiastically. 'We could go on holiday, I suppose. But

I'm really feeling too tired, and I'd rather we didn't.' It doesn't go anywhere, it's not blocking as such, just drowning each other's ideas in a lack of enthusiasm. In the final phase, you respond to your partner's suggestion with a 'Yes, and'. You and your partner then develop an impromptu story in which each suggestion is based on what the other enthusiastically offered, creating a coherent narrative in which both partners are listening and collaborating in a positive way. 'Yes, and' is fundamental to improvisation. When I asked Deborah Frances-White why, she told me that in life, saying no allows us to remain safe, whereas learning to say yes means learning to trust other people and to be open to being changed by the other person.

In another game, we created group stories. The group members take it in turn to add bits to a story, with different prompts:

'Once there was . . .'
'And every day . . .'
'Until one day . . .'
'And because of that . . .' (This one could be repeated several times.)
'Until finally . . .'
'And ever since then . . .'

The game gave us permission to feel OK with uncertainty, and to build off one another's contributions in the same way we did when we played 'Yes, and'. As Jeremy told the group after we'd played, '"I have no idea where this is going" is the improv artist's art.'

Jeremy insisted that he wasn't teaching us new skills, rather that we were 'remembering a more open, childlike state . . . which is part of the deep knowledge we have as human beings.' Play is how we learn, he told us. As we get older, we become more rigid, so a course like this is a remembering of a freer state. As Salinsky and Frances-White put it: 'Saying yes to your partner's idea represents a risk. You have to let an alien idea in, and if you have to build on it, you have to let it influence you. You can't plan your response in advance, it depends on what your partner offers.'

When we finished the course, I asked some of my classmates what they thought. Paolo, the young man between jobs, told me, 'As adults living in the city, we're very good at staying in our little boxes and being a bit scared to come out of them. This gives you an opportunity to come out of your box and experience something a bit different.' For Tony, a cook, 'Yes, and' gave him more confidence to accept other people's ideas. He felt that it left him more open to possibility, to connection, to exploring the potential in other people's contributions. For my part, I immediately sensed that a simple playful game like 'Yes, and' could inspire and mobilise new thinking about seemingly intractable problems such as climate change.

If our adult life contains no play, because we feel too uncomfortable or silly, our ability to generate new thoughts and make new connections depletes. How many great ideas are actually generated in meeting rooms, under strip lighting, with a whiteboard and a manager demanding we 'brainstorm'? Very few. It's why so many great ideas end up on the back of envelopes or beer mats, because they arrive when people are relaxed, with others, in a more playful mood, and the ideas just flow when we least expect them.

What if, instead of having to sign up for a class as I did, play were at the heart of the everyday – even for adults? What if we were to see more and more people bringing play and imagination into politics? What if our daily lives included more opportunities and spaces where play was possible? Would it decrease our anxiety? Would it build empathy? Would it establish connections? And would it help us to be more imaginative and positive about the future and its possibilities?

Antanas Mockus came to national attention in 1993 while president of the National University of Colombia. Harangued by disruptive far-left student activists while speaking at a university event, Mockus dropped his trousers and mooned the audience, later explaining that 'innovative behaviour can be useful when you run out of words.'[36] The action led, understandably, to his dismissal as president of the university, but provided him with an unlikely platform to run as mayor of Bogotá a year later.

Wearing a superhero costume, Mockus canvassed the city as 'Supercitizen' during a successful campaign that led to the first of two non-consecutive terms. Once elected, he appeared on live TV taking a shower to try and convince people to cut water usage in the city. He asked residents if they might be happy to pay an extra 10 percent tax, on a voluntary basis, in order to enable the works the city needed, and sixty-three thousand of them did. He established 'A Night Without Men', where men were asked to stay home and look after their family while the women went out into the city for the night, with the city's female police officers in charge of keeping the peace. He held a gun amnesty and invited members of the army and the clergy to participate in ceremonially destroying the guns.

Mockus even took on the city's notoriously corrupt traffic police. At the time, the death rate on the city's roads was one of the highest in Colombia. Traffic police pocketed most of the fines they collected and had little impact on safety or driver behaviour. So Mockus hired a team of 420 mime artists, who stood at the city's intersections showing red cards to bad drivers, stopping the traffic and applauding good drivers. He sacked the entire traffic police department, offering them their jobs back if they retrained as mimes. Four hundred did. His actions reduced traffic fatalities by 50 percent.[37] Reflecting on his time as mayor, Mockus wrote, 'Here's what I learned: people respond to humour and playfulness from politicians. It's the most powerful tool for change we have.'[38]

The actions of Antanas Mockus provide one example of how we can use play to shape what our cities become. One of the fundamental challenges this book has identified is that we need to be able to imagine positive, feasible, delightful versions of the future before we can create them. Not utopias, but futures where things turned out OK. Having the opportunity to 'test-drive' the future, to experience different versions of the future, can help us feel they are possible (or, conversely, that we really don't want to go there). And play is central to that. It can bring the future alive, to the extent where we can see it, feel it, taste it, smell it. If we can harness play in our activism in order to bring the kind of future we dream of to life, that's hugely powerful. Designer and futurist Grace Turtle argues that 'play is a political instrument'.[39] She also says, 'If we're making political decisions around how we want to exist in the world, then we need to think about the impossible. . . . Play opens us up to unknowability.'[40]

Play can also reawaken our ability to think *positively* about the future. Community arts practitioner Ruth Ben-Tovim and others designed an activity called 'Transition Town Anywhere' for the 2012 Transition Network conference.[41] About 380 people were ushered into an empty Great Hall at the Battersea Arts Centre for an event on the final morning of the two-day conference, the nature of which had been kept under wraps. We squeezed into a small strip of the hall, which symbolised the present, separated from the rest of the hall by a red ribbon, before being told:

> Please come in. . . . Thank you for joining us, this morning we are going on a journey together, a journey into the near future, look ahead of you into the empty space, into the future, we are heading for Transition Town Centre Anywhere. . . . All we have to take with us is our experience, each other and our imagination, we have the chance today to build a thriving, connected town centre together. . . . Are we ready to go? . . . Once we cut the ribbon, we will be there.

The ribbon was cut, and we spread out into the hall, into the future. We were each given a blackboard and a stick of chalk. We were invited to find our space, a spot in the hall that called to us. That would be our 'home'. We then introduced ourselves to our closest neighbour, and shared a story, documenting the essence of one another's story on their blackboards as 'I heard a story about . . .' Next, we formed into groups of three or four people, a 'street', and discussed projects we could do together to make our lives better on this imaginary street. We documented these stories on our chalk-boards and then roamed the hall to see what other groups had cooked up.

For the next stage, we were told: 'We are going to build a town centre together. . . . A town needs different things: food, governance, education, innovation, enterprise, celebration. . . . What would you like to see happen in your town under these headings? . . . Write your requests on the walls.'[42]

This we then did, through dialogue with others, and self-organising into groups with others who shared our interest, whether it be food, transport, celebration, finance, whatever. Once each group agreed on a project – some endeavour they would open on High Street of Transition Town Anywhere – each group was given a plot number and members were told to help ourselves to the vast pile of cardboard boxes, bamboo canes, string and sticky tape, and to build our contribution.

Once the High Street had taken shape, a participant was randomly chosen by the organisers as the 'Mayor of Anywhere', given a gold chain (made from cardboard covered in kitchen foil) and invited to cut a ribbon strung across the street and declare it open. Once that had happened, to much cheering and celebration, an organiser announced: 'We are ready to go. Go and visit other ventures, see how you could work together, what could you exchange, and some of you stay at home to host other people to your venture.'

For hours, we were lost in laughter and creativity, working together to imagine the future, and make it real. Our cardboard-and-string shops, banks, doctors' surgeries and bike-repair workshops took on a reality – and that reality assumed a deep significance. People were proud of what they had created. Engaging one another in conversation as if this imagined town were a functioning reality made it more so. By the end, some people were moved to tears by how much what we created together meant to them. Ben-Tovim later told me: 'It was one of those memorable moments where collaboration, imagination, play and creativity took flight.'[43]

What's most remarkable is that quite a few of those participants have, since then, created the things they dreamt about that day. Me, I had gathered with other people to create 'The Yeast Collective', a combined bakery and brewery. As I write this, the brewery has now been up and running for five years, and is shortly to move into a shared space with an amazing sourdough bakery.

Isabela Maria Gomez de Menezes, a Transition activist from Brazil, told me she had had a similar experience. 'It was one of those magical moments that we live in life and never forget. I was in the group that created a cultural and artistic space. It was like a square where everything artistic could happen. I returned to my country, dreaming of being a local producer.' A few years later, she was given a kombucha culture by a neighbour, and started making probiotic drinks for friends and neighbours. Then she started selling it at a local market, which she describes as 'full and vibrant with all the local small producers in our region: honey, beer, bread, sweets, salads, vegetables, fruits, vegetables and many other products', which she says has just the same feel as Transition Town Anywhere's High Street. 'And I can tell you that I've never been happier,' she told me.[44]

Filipa Pimentel, a Portuguese Transition activist, was also moved by the experience: 'When we were all invited to build the High Street, to build what we dreamt, it was absolutely magical.' She told me how she had spent much of the event in tears. When I asked her why, she told me: 'I deeply felt that everything is possible, that from nothing and with very little, by playing, we understood that it is OK to make your dreams into reality. You open the road to what's possible by dreaming.' She remembered walking through it, marvelling at the shops, the relationships, the street carnival, the swimming pool ('I remember it in such detail'). 'I go back to that event very often,' she concluded, 'whenever I think "it's not possible", it gives me a real feeling of possibility.'[45]

Whatever work we do to engage people in making change can be deepened and expanded if it has play at its heart. We need to play at living in the kind of world we want to create. We need tools like Transition Town Anywhere to, as futurist Franco Berardi puts it, uncover 'the future . . . inscribed in the present'.[46] If we refuse our children their right to play freely, creatively, if we make adults feel play is silly, if our campaigning and activism are so serious that there is no space for play or for taking risk, if we assume our children's childhoods exist to start planning their careers, compiling their CV from the age of four, we risk shutting down the very creativity and imagination upon which our future depends.

In an article in *Time* magazine, Walter Kirn and Wendy Cole capture what is at risk by quoting Alvin Rosenfeld, co-author of *The Over-Scheduled Child*: 'Today's mania for raising young Einsteins might have destroyed the real Einstein – a notorious dreamer who earned poor grades in school but somewhere in his frolics divined the formula for the relationship between matter and energy'.[47] The relevance is hard to ignore. Or, as Peter and Iona Opie, who wrote extensively about the cultures children developed, put it: 'The more children have their "free time" organised for them, and the more they have equipment provided, the more they lose the traditional art of self-entertainment.'[48] Who's to say that today's dreamy child swinging in a tree isn't divining the solution to climate change – or any of the other existential crises we face? Free, unstructured, cheeky, loud, reflective, spontaneous, crazy, attentive, wild play is vital to the health of our children, and also to our ability to reimagine the world. Without it, we are all the poorer, our streets fall silent and our imagination begins to dessicate.

CHAPTER 2

What If We Considered Imagination Vital to Our Health?

*'Because fear kills everything,' Mo had once told her.
'Your mind, your heart, your imagination.'*
—CORNELIA FUNKE, *Inkheart*

In August 2018, the journalist Will Hutton reported on a new colloquialism being used by doctors in the United States and United Kingdom to describe 'a tangled mix of economic, social and emotional problems', which 'consists of low mood caused by adverse life circumstances'. 'Shit life syndrome' (SLS), as the doctors call it, is when 'finding meaning in life is close to impossible; the struggle to survive commands all intellectual and emotional resources . . . It is not just poverty, but growing relative poverty in an era of rising inequality, with all its psychological side-effects, that is the killer.'[1] Although Hutton was primarily describing SLS as an argument against austerity and growing inequality, it seems to describe how an awful lot of people, rich or poor, are feeling these days.

Nobody should be surprised by this malaise. Anxiety disorders have increased twentyfold in the past thirty years.[2] A 2018 survey found that three-quarters of Britons have experienced levels of anxiety at least once over the past year where they felt overwhelmed or unable to cope, one in three reported having felt suicidal, and one in six have self-harmed. Young people are faring especially badly. In the same survey, 84 percent of eighteen-to-twenty-four-year-old Britons reported having felt unable to cope.[3]

A 2018 survey for the Prince's Trust found that 18 percent of sixteen-to-twenty-five-year-olds disagreed with the statement 'I find life really worth living,' and 27 percent disagreed that 'I find my life has a sense of purpose.'[4] In the United States, the number of teens who felt useless and joyless, a defining symptom of depression, rose by 33 percent between 2010 and 2015.[5] A 2018 report noted that we are witnessing 'an epidemic of self-doubt, anxiety, low self-esteem and correspondingly aggressive behaviour among the young'.[6] Research shows a steady fall in young people's sense that they have control over their own lives.[7] We are also seeing a rise in interest in books and films that tell dystopian stories of the future and are, as Christopher Schmidt – author, poet and professor of English at CUNY – puts it, 'unusually obsessed with ruination and the post-apocalyptic'.[8] There are increased levels of loneliness and isolation.[9] Eighty-three percent of people report that they spend no time whatsoever 'relaxing or thinking'.[10]

What do these troubling statistics and that 'tangled mix of economic, social and emotional problems' have to do with imagination? Absolutely nothing if you look at our current political and cultural priorities. But absolutely everything if you look at how the brain works, how the best conditions for the imagination can be cultivated, if you're interested in what we might learn from initiatives that are actually successful in nurturing it.

To see what I could learn from people who seem to be getting something right, I set off for Dundee, Scotland, to visit a project called Art Angel.[11] Originally named the Arts Advocacy Project and part of the Dundee Rep Theatre Company, Art Angel was founded in 1997 with the goal of helping people with experience of mental health difficulties find their voice through the arts. In 2003 the project's *Life at Liff* exhibition was held at McManus Galleries to tell the history of Royal Dundee Liff Hospital, the city's psychiatric hospital, and, more important, to showcase the art, photography and creative writing of people who had been treated there. An estimated fifteen thousand people attended. A few years later, the project (newly named Art Angel) began to receive funding from the National Health Service, expanded its offerings and moved to its own building at the Dudhope Art Centre. It has since moved again to its current location in the centre of the city.

I visited Art Angel one day in October 2018, arriving at a well-lit first-floor office suite with large south-facing windows, walls adorned with art and photography, and shelves full of paintbrushes and a variety of paints, crayons, pencils and art books. Artistic Manager Rosalie Summerton greeted me and invited me to take part in the day's programs, which I happily did.

Art Angel offers an alternative – and perhaps an antidote – to mainstream psychiatric treatment and hospitals, which many people experience as disempowering, robbing them of the autonomy to make even simple decisions themselves. What meagre support mainstream psychiatry offers often involves a long wait, at a time in someone's life when the need for care, listening and support is at its most urgent, and the support they eventually receive may provide only temporary relief, if any at all. Funding for these services has been cut to the bone in recent years. And yet, in many cases, it's all there is.

Art Angel, on the other hand, offers people the personal warmth and connection that should be part of all psychiatric care, as well as structure, routine, community and the chance to create something tangible and meaningful. The space itself is designed to feel as un-clinical as possible. Participants are not called 'patients' or 'clients' – they are 'artists' – and everyone on the staff team has had personal experience of mental illness within their own lives. At Art Angel, there are biscuits and there is lots of tea.

How does art help people, exactly? I asked Rosalie. She gave me a list:

- Art is another form of communication.
- Art is (or can be) a social activity.
- Art is a challenge.
- Art is educational.
- Art is collaborative. (People spark ideas off each other.)

- The process of art is therapeutic.
- Anyone can do it.
- You can share art with others in your community.
- Art is a meaningful activity which reduces isolation and improves your life.[12]

Significantly, art allows people who have lost the ability to make decisions to make them again. Which pencil, what colour, what kind of paint – these are small but vital decisions. Derek Ramsay is Art Angel's chairperson and has been involved since its inception. He told me that at Liff in the 1990s, when it was time for a cup of tea, everyone was given a mug of tea with milk and two sugars. 'What are the odds', he asked me, 'that all twenty-five people in that room took tea with milk and two sugars?'[13] In 2005, University of Dundee geographer Dr Hester Parr published a research report about Art Angel, in which she quoted one artist as saying: 'When I first started, it was huge to just choose the colour of paint that I was going to use. I felt really naked in that, I was very fragile.'[14]

'The main things we promote here are safety and hope. It's not written down anywhere, but it's our purpose,' Derek told me. 'People's difficulties are usually the result of something,' he continued. 'Stuff happened and they didn't understand it and they got scared. If the people who come here have anything in common, it's that they are all scared of life.'

I chatted to Sandra (not her real name), who has struggled with her mental health since the age of fourteen, and now at thirty-seven suffers from long periods of depression, especially since the recent death of her parents. Last year, she came close to taking her own life. 'Before Art Angel,' she told me, 'I always felt quite numb, in a very dark place. I couldn't think of anything. There was just nothing. With Art Angel, something clicked. It's like someone turned a light on inside and literally my imagination just bloomed. I went from having a blank canvas to having a colourful piece of art.'

I wondered if or how Sandra's experience at Art Angel affected how she thought about the future. 'I see it more positively,' she told me. 'Somewhere down the line, I may decide to go to art college, something that I've never ever had the confidence to do. I never felt I was good enough to be there, but now I think I can do it. I now see so many things with imagination, even my home. Decorating my home, making things. Future plans. Places I would never contemplate going.'[15]

Sandra's remarks affected me and reinforced my impression that Art Angel has stumbled on an approach far more aligned than mainstream psychiatry with what we know about how the brain – and, in particular, one small but mighty part of it – works.

The hippocampus, so named due to its seahorse shape, is actually in two halves in humans, one on each side of the brain and joined at the top, like a wishbone. It is the hub of memory, a sort of time machine which reintegrates the details, turning our short-term memories into long-term memories we can refer back to throughout our lives. The hippocampus is also associated with context processing, pattern separation and spatial awareness, helping us find our way around and remember where we've been.

For fifty years it was believed that the role of the hippocampus was purely to do with memory, but more recently there has been a paradigm shift. It is now generally accepted that the hippocampus is also involved in our ability to think about and imagine the future. One of the leading researchers in this area is Donna Rose Addis, Canada Research Chair in Cognitive Neuroscience of Memory and Aging and a senior scientist at the Rotman Research Institute in Toronto. Her work has redefined the function of episodic memory as being 'primarily future-focused', and she recently discovered that some parts of the hippocampus are more active during imagination, especially of future scenarios, than when remembering.[16]

Initially puzzled, she was later able to make sense of it. She told me: 'When we imagine a future event, we have to integrate details that may never have been integrated before. When you remember something, you are reintegrating details that already had linkages so it's not as demanding for the hippocampus.'[17]

In other words, in the hippocampus, past and future are inextricably linked; we may create scenarios in which we replay past events or imagine future ones, changing what we said, what they said, what happened. The exact mechanism for this is not yet understood. What is the task common to both? It could be our experience of space, or the more sensory experience of different events and scenarios. Research is ongoing to answer these questions. When the hippocampus is damaged or deteriorates, a person may lose the ability to recall the past, but also the ability to imagine the future.

While the hippocampus represents the vibrant epicentre of our imagination, it is also uniquely fragile. It is packed with glucocorticoid receptors, which render it especially vulnerable to cortisol, the 'stress hormone' that for many people today seems a near-constant companion.[18] In small doses, cortisol is useful. It helps you to break apart stored energy so you can outrun danger, play dead or stand and fight. High levels of cortisol, however, can damage or destroy hippocampal cells, reducing the hippocampus's overall size and volume. When a woman experiences chronic stress during pregnancy, for example, its impact can be passed down a generation, affecting her child's brain development, including impairment and decreased volume of the hippocampus. Researchers can actually observe the hippocampus contracting during states of high anxiety and fear.[19]

Trauma, to varying degrees, runs through society. One in four Americans grew up with alcoholic relatives; one in four was beaten by a parent to the point of marks being left on their body; one in five was molested as a child; and one in three couples engages in physical violence.[20] Professor Gordon Turnbull, a psychiatrist, specialist in PTSD and the author of *Trauma: From Lockerbie to 7/7*, described to me how trauma can affect our ability to imagine a different future. I asked him to estimate, from his clinical experience, the percentage of the population suffering from trauma in some form. He tells me the commonly quoted 10 percent is wide of the mark; the real figure is closer to 50 percent.[21]

Once the hippocampus has been damaged, we may begin to experience everyday events as more stressful, negative potential future events may come to mind more easily and we may seek out information that confirms an increasingly pessimistic world view. This vicious cycle results in the release of more cortisol and more damage to the hippocampus. As Daniel Schacter, a professor of psychology at Harvard University who often collaborates with Donna Rose Addis, told me: 'Anxiety has an important relationship to imagination, because it can lead us into a position where we're focusing on imagining negative future outcomes that may further cause us to become even more anxious.'[22]

Addis's remarks are striking in the context of what Sandra, who attends the photography classes, went on to tell me at Art Angel, which offered a taste of what it might look and feel like when that negative spiral is reversed:

> I used to walk past the most beautiful things, unaware that they were there, and now when I walk down the street, I'm always looking for different unique pieces. Art Angel opens your mind up to a realm of possibilities. Nothing is impossible. It used to be that a lot of the time when I went out, I could only see all the negatives. Because there are a lot. Especially living in the city, there are so many negatives.
>
> You see homelessness, you see drug addicts, you see litter lying about, but then if you look deeper, yes, you still see the homeless people, but you see them as a person, and you see that even though they're going through what they're going through, they've still got some positivity, they'll say hello to you and smile at you. Drug addicts . . . I look at them and I think they're someone's son or daughter, or they're a father or a mother. I don't think there's anything that I now see as a negative. Not anymore. I always see the positive side of things.[23]

The fact that Sandra's experience at Art Angel empowered her to start thinking about her future with a greater sense of possibility, as well as to experience even stressful everyday events in a more positive light is, to put it bluntly, huge. It's as though Sandra was able to apply the brakes to that vicious cycle, stop it and then begin to run it in reverse. It was like seeing a wasted muscle starting to exercise again, or a desert starting to bloom after rain.

I talked to many of the artists at Art Angel that day and heard echoes of Sandra's comments, as though some combination of the safe and welcoming physical space, the egalitarianism, the sense of community, the honouring of personal stories and the learning once again to use their hands and experience their imagination allowed people to start telling themselves different stories about their lives and see their experiences through new eyes.

It brought to mind the work of Sarah Corbett and the Craftivist Collective. Corbett's approach, of 'gentle activism', focuses on 'anything that links craft with activism'. It is, as she told me, 'about curiosity and about questioning'. She uses craft in a way that creates safe spaces for nervous or introverted activists, finding that the lack of contact while people are looking down and knitting or stitching, while still able to have conversations, is ideal for introverts. 'As soon as people do something, and pick a colour, and do a few stitches,' she told me, 'that confidence suddenly makes people think, "I can do this. Well, what else could I do?" Or, "I've actually made something."'[24]

At the end of Art Angel's photography class, I sat next to Mark (not his real name) in front of a large computer screen as he reviewed photos he had taken on that morning's walk around the city. They showed details he had spotted, such as water droplets on a phone box that clustered together like a jigsaw puzzle, a pile of autumn leaves which included one golden toffee wrapper nestled in like one of the leaves, an overflowing dustbin in front of a house, a wasp on a window, part of a bus reflected in the puddle it was passing through. It was as though he were learning to see again, to notice, to pay attention to the world around him, to see his world in more detail, more colour, more focus. It was coming alive to him.

Whether artists were silk-scarf painting, wire weaving, or painting on canvas, I began to see that one of the most important things happening at Art Angel was that people were in the process of reimagining themselves, who they saw themselves to be in the world. While chatting to Terry (not his real name), a former council worker who had been off work for some time due to depression and low self-esteem, and whose paintings were inspired by Indian art he found in a children's book, I asked him: 'So, do you think of yourself as an artist?' He paused, as though rolling the possibility around in his mind, trying it on for size. 'Aye,' he said, 'why not?'

Rosalie echoed this. 'It's a place you come and you're not bipolar, you're not depressive, you're not this or that,' she said.

> You're an artist . . . working on your piece of art. You're learning things, you're thinking about what you're going to be doing next, learning about other artists, going to an exhibition and building up your interest and passion for art . . . Recovery isn't about regaining what you had before. The reason you got ill, quite often, was because you were doing things that made you ill. To go back to that just seems pointless. It's about developing a new life, and new things that are going to help you get well, stay well, have an enhanced life . . . be part of something, part of a community.[25]

Rosalie's remarks are significant, I think, because it's not just individuals making individual choices that make them ill. Socially and politically, we're promoting policies, regulations and lifestyles that are making people ill to such a degree that stress, trauma and anxiety are being woven through and through the social fabric. Indeed there is a strong case to say that stress, anxiety and depression are, in fact, the entirely appropriate response to a world in which people are increasingly disconnected from one another and from nature. 'How different would it be', the clinical psychologist Dr Lucy Johnstone told Johann Hari in his book *Lost Connections*, 'if when you went to your doctor, she "diagnosed" us with "disconnection"? What would happen then?'[26]

'Depression', writes Ruth Cain, a senior lecturer in law at the University of Kent, 'may appear almost self-protective: an opt-out from an unwinnable set of continual competitions'.[27] Although stigmatised in many ways, it is the healthy response to a mad, uncaring world.

We know that people are becoming increasingly fearful, with 77 percent of Americans believing the world has become a more frightening place in the last ten years.[28] Meanwhile a 2016 study found 'a quickly widening generational gap in political apathy', with the percentage of young Americans professing an interest in politics declining, and a steady rise over the past thirty years in the number of

US citizens thinking it would be 'good' or 'very good' for the army to rule the country.[29]

Austerity hasn't helped. The politically imposed austerity many countries have experienced since the 2008 economic crisis is as much a problem of inequality as it is of poverty. Since 2008 in the United Kingdom, austerity has led to funding cuts of 49 percent for local authorities, a £950m fall in spending on legal aid, a doubling of the use of food banks, the closure of 478 libraries and the cutting of more than 230,000 library opening hours, a 5.8 percent cut in adult social care, the closure of over six hundred youth centres, and much more.[30] During roughly the same period, the richest one thousand people in the United Kingdom have seen their wealth increase by £83bn – enough, the Equality Trust calculated, to pay the grocery bills of every family currently using food banks for fifty-six years.[31] Research by Richard Wilkinson and Kate Pickett found that in every country where inequality widened, there was an associated rise in the number of people reporting hallucinations, delusions of thought control, delusional moods and the overall quantity of these symptoms. 'The reality', they write, 'is that inequality causes real suffering, regardless of how we choose to label such distress. Greater inequality heightens social threat and status anxiety, evoking feelings of shame which feed into our instincts for withdrawal, submission and subordination: when the social pyramid gets higher and steeper and status insecurity increases, there are widespread psychological costs.'[32]

The Royal College of Psychiatrists has described inequality as a major determinant of mental illness, noting that higher rates of inequality correlate with worse mental health outcomes: 'Mental illness . . . is consistently associated with deprivation, low income, unemployment, poor education, poorer physical health and increased health-risk behaviour.'[33]

Rosalie told me that over the past eight years, she has observed the growing impacts of austerity on the people Art Angel work with. 'There's a greater number of people presenting with mental health issues of all kinds. Anxieties, depression. All sorts of things. Obviously there's an increase in young people . . . and there's a lot of suicide amongst young men'. Austerity cuts to mental health services and to benefits mean that more and more people with mental health issues are not getting the support they need. Rosalie told me of the struggles that recent changes to the benefits system have had, meaning people are having to make very real decisions between, for example, food and heating their homes: 'Most people that come here initially can hardly look you in the eye. . . . They're broken. They feel quite often as if it's their fault, that they've done something wrong, they've ruined their family, lost their friends, there's a lot of loss involved. They don't think anything of themselves at that point'.[34]

Jamie Hanson is an assistant professor at the University of Pittsburgh's Department of Psychology. His research has shown that growing up in poverty can result in a reduction in attentional processes and working memory, and a measurably smaller hippocampus.[35] While it is not the case, he told me, that everyone experiencing poverty will experience these challenges, many do. He identifies two key areas where the impacts are most severe. One has to do with surroundings. In the 1970s, researchers put mice in 'enriched environments' for forty-five days, with everything mice love – a 'Mouse Palace' full of favorite stimuli, if you like. Other mice were put in environments in which they had nothing they loved and nothing to do, and they were left to their own devices. At the end of the experiment, the hippocampi of the mice in enriched environments were 15 percent larger.

And then there is the impact of the stress resulting from poverty and injustice on the hippocampus. People living in poverty tend towards states of hyper-vigilance. Psychoanalyst Joy Schaverien points out that 'a child who is perpetually vigilant has little space for symbolic play . . . there is little time for reverie, and the life of the imagination may therefore suffer.'[36] Might it be that the more deeply we are immersed in crisis and the more dystopian the future appears, the less able we are to imagine a way out? I put this idea to Gordon Turnbull, who told me that in his opinion, when populations are dejected and depressed, they exhibit the same symptoms that individuals do in terms of a diminished hippocampus. 'They lose their creative thinking ability', he stated. As an example, he mentioned the National Health Service, an organization under great pressure. 'You can imagine', he told me, 'people who work within that community are actually going to have hippocampi which are not working at their optimum. They'll be suboptimally functioning as a result. . . . They'll be losing their ability to think of new things imaginatively which would create solutions to problems. You do see in these organisations the same mistakes, or similar mistakes, being made time after time after time. A repetitive pattern.'[37]

In addition to requiring a measure of safety, security, stability and comfort, the hippocampus also needs us to get adequate nutrition and enough sleep, neither of which is doable when you're having to choose between heating your home and eating. Even for people with relatively stable living situations, getting adequate nutrition and enough sleep is an increasing challenge. The World Health Organization (WHO) has declared sleep loss an epidemic throughout the industrialised world, in the United States, United Kingdom, Japan and South Korea, in particular.[38] As many as 30 percent of adults in the United States report at least one symptom of insomnia, visits to hospital caused by poor sleep have tripled in the last ten years, and between 2000 and 2010, diagnosis of sleeping disorders rose by 266 percent and prescriptions of sleeping medication rose by 293 percent.

Not getting enough sleep – we need at least six hours, ideally around eight – is as damaging to our health as not getting proper nutrition or enough exercise. It triggers chronic inflammation, a risk factor for diabetes, cancer, depression, cardiovascular diseases and neurodegenerative disorders.[39] It can impair our attention, our divergent thinking, our decision-making and our memory, all vital to the imagination.[40] It is the single strongest factor in predicting clinical depression.[41] The loss of an hour's sleep a night can result in a reduction in academic performance by up to two school years, and some researchers believe that sleep problems during a child's formative years can result in permanent changes to brain structure.[42]

Lack of sleep robs the brain of REM, deep sleep, which is when the brain makes associative networks of information, novel links between seemingly unrelated pieces of information, which enables us to wake with solutions to problems. During deep REM sleep, the hippocampus acts like the staff in a library, sorting through the books that have come in that day and returning them to the correct shelves. That is, it sorts through your experiences and decides which ones to file away as long-term memories, and which ones to clear out of your short-term memory in order to make room for the day to come.[43] The hippocampus, it's worth noting, is also vital to our ability to dream.

The hippocampus needs a healthy diet. The developing brain – both in the womb and up to about the first three years of life – has a particularly high demand for iron and zinc. Estimates suggest that in the United Kingdom and the United States, 50 to 70 percent of the population of pregnant women are not meeting dietary recommendations, with resultant impacts on neurocognitive development in infants, including impacts on the development of the hippocampus.[44]

Troubling research by Irakli Loladze has looked at the impact of rising levels of atmospheric CO_2 on food crops. Climate sceptics sometimes argue that the more CO_2 there is in the atmosphere, the higher the crop yields will be, but Loladze's work shows that with higher levels of CO_2, plants pack on more carbohydrates like glucose, and take up less potassium, calcium, zinc, iron, protein.[45] His work, which gathers thirty years of research and looks at 130 varieties of plants, suggests that on average, the rises of CO_2 forecast for the end of the century will result in an 8 percent decline in nutrients. The decline of nutrients means we need to eat more bulk in order to extract sufficient nutrition, one of the drivers of obesity in wealthier nations. A 2005 study by William Jagust and colleagues found that the larger an individual's waist-to-hip ratio (that is, their belly girth), the smaller their hippocampus.[46]

What nurtures the hippocampus, in addition to adequate sleep and nutrition, and manageable levels of stress? Well, among other things, meditation. Meditation has been shown to reduce stress, lower cortisol levels and increase well-being. It can lead to more grey matter in the hippocampus, and result in hippocampi that are up to 15 percent larger than in non-meditators. And exercise. Regular aerobic exercise in both adults and older women can also increase hippocampal volume.[47] Of course, not everyone has equal access to these things. As the nature writer Robert Macfarlane told me, 'In some ways imagination is a function of privilege. . . . I don't for a moment want to suggest that only those who are well off can be imaginative, but I think it's important to note the kind of protected space, the 'what if' space, that you need to think in this way'.[48]

Looked at in this way, government-imposed austerity, especially following the 2008 financial crash, represents an act of violence against the most vulnerable in society, whether through fuel poverty, cuts to the welfare state, increased homelessness or lack of support for the mentally or physically unwell.[49] But maybe we should also think of it as an attack on the imagination. As the columnist Aditya Chakrabortty puts it, 'One of the great casualties of austerity is likely to be imagination, the sense that alternatives to this broken regime not only exist, but can be built by us.'[50] Henry Giroux, a scholar and cultural critic, writes: 'State and corporate sponsored ignorance produced primarily through the disimagination machines of the mainstream media and public relations industries in diverse forms now function largely to erase selected elements of history, disdain critical thought, reduce dissent to a species of fake news, and undermine the social imagination.'[51]

'Disimagination machine': the phrase leapt out at me, and for so many reasons.[52] If there is a disimagination machine, it certainly seems to be working. Attention spans are in decline. We have an increasingly superficial approach to facts and knowledge. Curiosity in the classroom is falling.[53] Thirty-four percent of children living in London agree with the statement 'I don't have enough time to use my imagination,' as opposed to a 21 percent national average. A third of adults (33 percent) and a quarter of children (26 percent) feel as though they do not need to use their imagination for their work, study or schoolwork. Only 51 percent of retired people, and 47 percent of those not working, say they used their imaginations 'regularly'. A recent survey showed that only 40 percent of respondents feel they use their imagination when online.[54] A survey of people working in the creative industries found that 48 percent of them believe levels of creativity have stagnated in the last decade.[55]

There is a strong argument that neoliberal economics and growth-based capitalism are, at their core, disimagination machines. As the scholar Richard Sennett puts it, 'Modern capitalism works by colonising people's imagination of what is possible.'[56] Thomas Piketty has shown how the creation of inequality is fundamental to capitalism's model, built into its DNA.[57] It is a model that thrives by imagining us as isolated consumers, cultivating desire for things we don't actually need and a sense of inadequacy if we fail to attain them, promulgating the myth that the route to happiness is through the accumulation of 'stuff'. All of which has led to some terming capitalism as 'a mental illness generating system'.[58]

But that sense of our being frogs in the boiling pan of imaginative decline goes deeper. As I write, global CO_2 concentrations are around 410 parts per million (ppm); they were 321 when I was born in 1968. By mid-century they look set to hit 550 ppm, and to reach 1,000 ppm by the year 2100. Researchers estimate that concentrations of 1,000 ppm would reduce human cognitive ability by 21 percent.[59] Even the 660 ppm by 2100 set forth in the Paris Agreement on climate change would still result in a 15 percent decline in our cognitive abilities. If we are to avoid the worst forecasts, and to respond in a vigorously creative way, reimagining many of the ways the world works at the moment, such as Paul Hawken sets out in his book *Drawdown*, it will be because we successfully rallied our imagination.[60] And if we can't, if our task now is to navigate an inevitable lurch into climate breakdown, we will need our imaginations more than ever to adapt as best we can to a rapidly changing world.[61] And, just for the record, there is no third 'green growth', business as usual, 'just pop solar panels on, and it'll be OK' option. It's too late for that now.

Another contribution to the 'boiling frog' analogy comes from research that looked at billions of Twitter posts between March 2014 and November 2016 and how people were discussing weather extremes.[62] Apart from extreme weather events, climate change is mostly a gradual shift, a shifting baseline of what we think of as 'normal'. The study found that people comment more about weather that is different from normal, but that they do so far less when such weather persists for several years. They estimate that it takes around five years for such extremes to become completely unremarkable, a 'new normal'. 'It may be easy', wrote Nick Obradovich and Frances C. Moore, the study's authors, 'to normalise a climate that is, at least on geological time-scales, rapidly and dramatically changing.'[63]

The thought that keeps me awake at night is that the further we get into the big challenges of Now – economic inequality, climate change, the very real risk of the collapse of many of the key aspects of the economy we depend on, mass migration and so on – the less able we are to imagine a way out of them. That might be because of the very real anxiety and distress felt by those experiencing fires, flooding, displacement or destitution due to climate impacts, or the subconscious anxiety caused by the amount of mental energy it takes to look away from these issues and pretend they aren't happening.[64] It could be because, as recent research shows, the more CO_2 there is in the atmosphere, the slower our minds get, the cloudier our thinking becomes, the more difficult it is to generate new ideas, the harder it is to formulate complex thought and take in new information.[65]

Where does this leave us? If stress, trauma and anxiety are eroding our imaginations precisely at the time when we need to be at our most vitally imaginative, then where do we find the clues for how to reverse this process? I don't think we'll find them from politicians or think tanks. I think we're far more likely to find them at places like Art Angel, which seems to have understood the optimal conditions in which the imagination can be rekindled and can flourish. Remember Sandra? She has something to teach us about how to apply the brakes to that vicious cycle, stop it and to then begin to run it in reverse. When the future disappears from our imagining, when we get stuck in the present or in the past, we're in trouble. Rather than it being some kind of academic concept to suggest that creating spaces of safety and hope is fundamental to our being able to start rebuilding our imaginations, in Sandra's story we can see how it functions in reality.

Indeed, at Art Angel I started to get a taste of what the rebuilding of the collective imagination might look like. Those spaces of safety and hope need not necessarily be art based. They could just as well be gardening, or welding, or building, or cooking, or baking, or working in the woods, or making music, or dancing, or meditating, or space to sit and talk with other people, or working with animals. It could be school, if school were different to how it is today.

We need to start to see differently, too, like 'Mark', to connect with the world around us again, rather than whizzing through it, distracted, eyes on our screens, doing our utmost to avoid contact with others. Everyone I met at Art Angel was learning to see again, learning to see with new eyes, in new ways, through new filters. One of the biggest challenges Art Angel faces – and which, in turn, the imagination faces – is how to thrive in a world that wants to quantitatively assess and evaluate everything, what the author Rebecca Solnit calls 'systems of accounting that can't count what matters'.[66]

'Why are testimonials not good enough?' Rosalie asks.[67] Everyone I spoke to at Art Angel told me how it had transformed their life, and how vital it was to their well-being and recovery. 'I found my way back to life here,' one artist told me.

What if we created the optimal conditions – where we live, where we work, where we study, where we pray, where you walk every day – for the imagination to flourish? What would you do? What would you change?

All of which brings us back to the question of how we might measure imagination. The whole question of how to put a quantitative 'score' onto the imagination is fraught with challenges. But perhaps we're asking the wrong question. Perhaps we should instead be asking what the world would look like if a healthy imagination were, in our everyday, considered indispensable to a healthy life? I have come across two suggestions for how this might look. The first is from an exercise at an event organised by the Institute for the Future, shared with me by Gabriella Gómez-Mont. It says, 'We will measure ideas generated, ideas translated, shared and exchanged, and ideas enacted. We will . . . measure our success by minds changed, coalitions formed, common ground forged and new dreams adopted.'[68]

Eric Liu and Scott Noppe-Brandon, in *Imagination First*, develop this idea further: 'The true utility of imagination is measured not by some ratio of innovations-per-ideation. It is best measured by whether the ecosystem as a whole is richer in possibility, and whether the society we feed with our imagination enables all participants in the market or the community to participate to their fullest potential.'[69]

In other words, we will know the world is becoming more imaginative because our daily life will feel as though it is becoming more rich with possibility, more full of imaginative ideas, more open, less fearful, less anxious, more open to ideas. When I asked Lucy Neal, an artist and Transition activist, for her thoughts on how we would recognise that the world was becoming more imaginative, she told me: 'You could get out of bed and think, "I have no idea what's going to happen today, but I think it might be something quite nice. I'll go round the corner and have a look". . . . There would be joy in the air, and joy is very radical. Joy is a radical force, because it connects us all to life, and life is enthusiastic for life.'[70]

While it is clear that, in the present, very few places in the world actually feel like that, the story of Art Angel offers us a tantalising taste of how we might start to move it more in that direction.

CHAPTER 3

What If We Followed Nature's Lead?

To the eyes of a man of Imagination, Nature is Imagination itself.

—WILLIAM BLAKE, to Rev. John Trusler

When was the last time you heard the dawn chorus?
I don't mean when was the last time you happened to be awake after leaving a window open. I mean when was the last time you deliberately woke up before dawn sometime between February and early June and went outside just before sunrise, simply to listen. I'm racking my brains to try to think of the last time I did something like this. I tend to think of dawn as a time for deep sleep, not sitting in misty early morning fields.

Still, one May morning in 2018, I had to pry myself out of bed at 4am – as the writer Henry Porter once wrote, this is 'easily achieved by drinking a lot of water the night before' – to take part in Dawn Chorus Day at the Dartington Hall estate near Totnes.[1] Dawn Chorus Day is an annual event held on the first Sunday of May, and has its roots sometime in the 1980s, when the broadcaster and environmentalist Chris Baines hosted his birthday party at 4am so his guests could enjoy the morning song. The art collective SoundCamp now coordinates a global twenty-four-hour live recording of the dawn chorus and uploads this 'Reveille', so anyone can listen as the music of morning spreads around the world. The collective also organises a network of 'soundcamps' where people can participate in real life. My local camp is run by the community radio station SoundArt Radio. Now in its third year, the camp brings together sound recordists, artists and the simply curious for a weekend that includes workshops on field recording, yoga, bodywork and a wildlife disco to make 'good use of all the vinyl wildlife recordings we have between us . . . [including] screaming rabbits, whining squirrels and whistling otters.'[2] Plus, of course, there was that early morning outdoor wakeup call.

It's still dark when our seven-person group gathers in a small car park near where we've been camping. It's quiet, apart from a few robins tricked by streetlights into an early start. It's cool but not cold. All seven of us are focused, purposeful, intent. We set off together on a ten-minute walk. As we walk, we hear some other early risers: the first blackbirds and, as we head down a hill through open farmland, the song of a skylark high above. Our destination is a bend in the River Dart with woodlands on the other side stretching as far as the eye can see. By the time we reach it, the chorus has begun in earnest. The invitation, and challenge, from Tony Whitehead, the ornithologist and sound recordist leading the walk, is to just listen. To be still and enjoy the remarkable concert. I make myself as comfortable as I can, leaning against an oak tree and sitting on my raincoat. A thin layer of mist sits above the surface of the river.

Soon we hear robins, then blackbirds and song thrushes. They are joined by wrens, wood pigeons and crows. Then there's a mandarin duck, with its distinctive squelchy-sounding call. There are mallard ducks, long-tailed tits, chiffchaffs, and chaffinches. Plus the occasional pheasant. Soon, the song of the blackbird arrives in two halves. The first half is roughly the same each time, its signature if you like. In the second, they improvise, something different each time. I am reminded of Charlie Parker (whose nickname, ironically, was Bird), who said, 'You've got to learn your instrument. Then, you practice, practice, practice. And then, when you finally get up there on the bandstand, forget all that and just wail.' This morning, I'm hearing nature's improvisation: jazz birds. The dawn chorus plays in pulses of intensity, something I'm vaguely aware of as I listen, but which is unmistakable when I look at the peak and trough sound profile of the recording afterwards. Apart from the occasional plane going over, or a distant motorbike, we are treated to an intense, spectacular recital.

The dawn chorus, Tony explained to us the previous evening, happens between February and June, reaching its height in May. What we're hearing is almost entirely male birds. In order to attract the female of their species, they are letting the world know 'I'm here, and this is my territory,' and 'I'm so able to feed myself, and am so strong and so great, that I can be awake and make this fine, powerful song.' It's the woodland community communicating with itself. (When a woman points out similarities with social media, Tony agrees, saying the wood was 'literally tweeting'.) As we listen to the chorus, I recall how Tony explained that when birds notice dangers or threats, they have a different call. An experienced birdwatcher can follow the passage of people or animals through a forest just by listening to the calls.

After fifty minutes, the chorus drops from its peak to background noise as the birds become peckish and ready for breakfast. We featherless ones gather to reflect upon the experience. My companions are clearly affected by what they've heard. Tony notes that although he's heard many dawn choruses, he never tires of it and urges us all to make the effort whenever possible. 'You only get so many Mays in your life,' he observes. Later he tells me: 'The richness of the experience is just remarkable. I've had people say that it's been on the edge of life-changing. . . . For some it can be genuinely a very, very deep experience.'[3]

Indeed, for months afterwards, I find myself much more aware of birdsong. It's as though my time by the river tuned me in. I now notice it everywhere I go. That early morning walk gave me a deep reconnection to the natural world and its diversity. The alertness it engendered, the opportunity for undistracted attention was reward enough, but it also boosted my imagination in a palpable way. In the days and weeks that followed, I noticed that my writing flowed easier. I was, in general, less distracted. The magic of that morning carried over to my life. Even many months later, as I write this, I find myself affected by the richness of it in my day-to-day life. I might not be able to identify a given bird, but I notice them in a way I didn't before, and I also feel a bit more present, a bit more in the world.

This kind of experience can have profound impact, both personally and societally. It reminds me of the story of how President Theodore Roosevelt sought out the naturalist and environmental philosopher John Muir after having been moved by reading his books. In 1903, the two of them, accompanied only by two park rangers and an army packer named Jackie Alder, spent three days visiting key sites in the wilderness of Yosemite, including Mariposa Grove, Sentinel Dome, Glacier Point and Yosemite Valley. It has been referred to as 'the most important camping trip in US history'.[4] 'Of all the best people in the world, he [Muir] was the one with whom it was best worth while to see Yosemite,' Roosevelt later wrote.[5] The president, it was noted, slept on, and under, a pile of forty woollen blankets. There is no mention of what Muir slept on.

Muir had a purpose: to change the president's thinking on the need to conserve wilderness areas. 'I might be able to do some forest good in freely talking around the campfire,' he had previously written in a letter to a friend.[6] The two stayed up late around the campfire, discussing the importance of wilderness, and the experience – and those conversations – had a profound impact on Roosevelt. Three years later Roosevelt passed the Yosemite Recession Bill, which put many of the places they had visited under federal protection. During his time as president, Roosevelt created five new national parks, fifty-five national bird sanctuaries and wildlife refuges, and added 147 million acres to the country's forest reserves, creating 150 new national forests.[7] In his autobiography, published ten years later, Roosevelt wrote, 'I shall always be glad that I was in the Yosemite with John Muir.'[8]

What if all our elected officials went out into the wilderness and returned so moved? What if even one or two of them did? What if they participated in a dawn chorus walk, every once in a while – just stopped, and listened, and thought about what they really want to leave behind?

The dawn chorus walk also made me grieve, however, for the precipitous decline in the diversity I listened to that day, despite how abundant it felt to my ear. Since 1970, the number of birds, fish, reptiles and mammals we share the planet with has dropped by 60 percent.[9] There has been a 91 percent decline in nightingales since the late 1960s, a 51 percent fall in song thrush populations over the last forty years and a 75 percent decline in populations of flying insects since 1989.[10] According to the United Nations, we lose between 150 and 200 species every day.[11] Forever. Gone. Environmental journalist Michael McCarthy calls this 'the Great Thinning', a wholesale unravelling of the diversity our grandparents took for granted – and scraped off their windscreens.[12] McCarthy notes:

> Our imaginations are rooted in the natural world. They formed in the natural world. They took their metaphors and similes from the natural world. It's from the natural world that we thought that something might be 'strong as an oak tree' or 'fragile as a reed'. I don't think that human creations on the whole supply us with figures of speech. It is the natural world which does. . . . Our imagination itself takes its root in the natural world, and increasingly the natural world is being distanced from us, and that can only impoverish our own imaginations.[13]

As Robert Macfarlane told me, 'It's a thinning in its most important form of a material basis of life, of a biodiversity, but it's also a thinning of language, and a thinning of possibility.' Simply recalling the names of extinct species gives me a terrible sense of vanished colour, experience and richness. These names fire our deep ancestral imagination, but are now no longer a reality. Ilin Island cloudrunner. Dusky flying fox. Quagga. Tasmanian tiger. Great auk. Caucasian moose. Pyrenean ibex. Red-bellied gracile opossum. Chadwick Beach cotton mouse. Auroch. Bluebuck. Desert bandicoot. Passenger pigeon.[14] According to the American Museum of Natural History, 'Passenger Pigeons once migrated through Canada, the United States and the Gulf of Mexico in numbers so huge that they darkened the sky. One flock was described as "a column, eight or ten miles in length . . . resembling the windings of a vast and majestic river"', before they were killed in the millions as a cheap source of food.[15]

What is the impact on our imaginations of this free-falling biodiversity and abundance? (And, the corollary, is our diminished imagination to blame for our tolerance of such an abject tragedy?) The environmentalist and microbiologist René Dubos said that if we lived on the moon, our imagination would be as barren as the moon.[16] Our imagination needs diversity. It expands or contracts – or plummets, as the case may be – in response to it. Even if we somehow manage to convince ourselves that we are unaffected by the devastation, as Madeline Bunting notes, 'Ignoring something . . . requires a form of attention. It costs us attention to ignore something.'[17] And that takes a toll.

In tandem with the loss of biodiversity, we are losing, as Robert Macfarlane notes, the language that accompanied it. He has documented a dizzying array. 'Feetlings', for example, is an old Suffolk term for the footprints of animals as they appear in the snow. 'Appledrain' is a beautiful old Devon word for a wasp, and 'Dumbledore', a word popularised by the Harry Potter books, is a regional English term for 'bumblebee'.[18] When an animal or an experience disappears, so does the need for language that describes it. Macfarlane talks about 'a deep ancient coding' that connects us to the past, to our ancestors, and to everything we share the planet with.[19] What does it portend that by 2100, over half the world's six thousand languages will be gone? Not coincidentally, we are also losing food crops that sustained people for millennia. The world has also seen a startling decline in the diversity of plants we rely on for our sustenance. Over an eighty-year period, *National Geographic* reports, the United States lost 93 percent of the varieties of its food seeds, such as an 80 percent decline in tomato diversity.[20] In 1903 there were almost 500 varieties of lettuce, and by 1983 just 36. Similarly, the number of cucumber varieties fell from 285 to just 16. Cabbage varieties fell from 544 to 28, and radishes from 463 varieties to 27. Over a similar period, the United States lost 85 percent of its apple cultivars.[21] As the Indian activist Manish Jain told me, 'Imagination is connected to a sense of abundance.'[22]

Imagination – that 'ability to look at things as if they could be otherwise' – needs diversity to feed it. Are we more likely to be imaginative if all our food comes from one vast supermarket, or from a variety of small producers in a vibrant market? If most High Streets across the United Kingdom look identical, with the same massive chains, how does that impact our imagination compared with living somewhere that is home to an abundance of businesses unique to that particular place? And if we replace diverse local economies with enormous Amazon 'fulfilment centres' – one of the most egregious abuses of the English language I've ever encountered – which inflict untold psychological damage on those working there? In *The Creative Spark: How Imagination Made Humans Exceptional*, biological anthropologist Agustín Fuentes argues, 'The big-box store and strip-mallification of the United States are killing our imagination. . . . Over the past thirty to forty years this has created a homogeneity that suppresses the American imagination. If everything is the same no matter where you are as you grow up, your mind will be shaped by that sameness.'[23]

When our agricultural system drives out diversity and sees a huge rise in monocultures, it is accompanied by a decline in the diversity that so underpins our culture and our connection to the world. In the Eastern United States, populations of monarch butterflies have declined by 90 percent because of a decline in habitats, but also due to more land being used to grow genetically modified (GM) soya and corn, and a resultant increase in the use of Roundup herbicide, which has all but wiped out the 'weed' milkweed, vital to monarch butterflies. As Tierra Curry, a senior scientist at the Center for Biological Diversity, told *Newsweek*, 'We're at risk of losing a symbolic backyard beauty that has been part of the childhood of every generation of Americans.'[24]

The imagination draws from the palette of options and possibilities that we carry in our memories. It reassembles, cuts and pastes, and makes unique combinations of experiences and ideas we have seen before. The greater the diversity in the natural world around us, and the greater our capacity to notice it, the more we can draw on it as our muse for how to exist in the world.

We also know the opposite is true: the Great Thinning shuts us down. Psychoanalyst Lise Van Susteren coined the term 'pre-traumatic stress disorder' to describe a condition similar to post-traumatic stress disorder, except that its symptoms are felt in advance of trauma. It has been observed in soldiers who, before being deployed to Afghanistan, experience many of the symptoms they would also experience afterwards: sadness, grief, inability to sleep, nightmares, constant vivid worry. It can be thought of as a kind of anticipatory anxiety, or, as Van Susteren puts it, 'a before-the-fact version of PTSD'.[25]

Van Susteren uses the term to describe the impact observed in climate scientists and activists who spend all day focused on the probabilities of disastrous future scenarios. But I think it's affecting us all. When we're inundated on a daily basis with stories as we scroll through our various news and social media feeds or just follow the news on TV or in newspapers, stories that fill us with dread and hopelessness about the future, pre-traumatic stress disorder is an appropriate response. Indeed, as Van Susteren notes, the term 'disorder' is a misnomer.[26] It's a disorder only in the way feeling concern for a family picnicking on a railway track with an approaching train would be a disorder. In fact, it's the healthy human response to dangerous or dysfunctional circumstances. Attempting to live in a way that ignores these inconvenient truths is actually the disorder. Pre-traumatic stress *condition* is probably a better term. It is another constant state of anxiety quietly taking its toll on our hippocampi. It's what Mark Cocker, in his book *Our Place*, describes as 'a persistent low-level heartache, a background melancholia'.[27]

Reconnecting to the natural world, especially from a young age, can be one strategy for managing Pre-TSD. Spending even twenty-five minutes outside has been shown to relax the brain and increase cognitive functioning, not unlike meditation.[28] In 2012, three researchers set out to understand the cognitive impact a four-day hike with no electronic devices would have on a group of people who had never backpacked before. They found that the backpackers were 50 percent more creative following their four-day immersion than before they set off. 'Our results demonstrate that there is a cognitive advantage to be realized if we spend time immersed in a natural setting,' the researchers noted.[29] The prefrontal cortex, that part of our brain that gets overloaded when we multitask, has only a limited capacity. It is estimated that our brain has a processing capacity of 120 bits per second; it takes 60 bits just to pay attention to and understand one person talking to us.[30] Being outside in nature gives the brain the opportunity to rest, for the default mode network to kick in, putting us in a state neuroscientists call 'soft fascination', in which our mind is at ease, we feel immersed in our surroundings and we have the cognitive freedom to daydream.[31]

A large body of research shows the health benefits of contact with nature. These include reduced stress, better sleep, improved mental health – including reduced depression and anxiety – greater happiness, well-being, life satisfaction, reduced aggression, improved child development, lower blood pressure, better eyesight and improved immune function.[32] In another study conducted at Stanford University, researchers divided a group of sixty participants, sending thirty on a walk through the woods, and the other thirty for a walk along a four-lane road. Participants were given a series of psychological tests before and after. The researchers found that those who walked in the woods were less anxious, had better memory, and felt more positive.[33] Some doctors are now prescribing people time in nature as part of their treatment. In Shetland, in Scotland, every GP surgery is now part of the Nature Prescriptions project, a partnership with RSPB Scotland.[34] They are given a leaflet which offers a number of seasonal activities, such as 'Go look for seabeans after westerly gales' (January), 'Bury your face in the grass' (May) and 'Follow a bumble bee' (July).[35]

We also know that time in nature helps us focus.[36] At a primary school in Liverpool, researchers found that playing a soundscape of birdsong helped children concentrate during the early afternoon 'post-meal slump'.[37] Unfortunately, the average American spends 93 percent of their time either indoors or in vehicles, and three-quarters of children in the United Kingdom spend less time outdoors than inmates of the US prison system.[38]

But we must also recognise that there is a social inequality aspect to this. On a visit to give a talk at a university in Cornwall in late 2018, I was told by researchers that in the most impoverished communities there, many children have never visited the sea, even though it is only a few miles away. This mismatch, where the people who could most benefit from spending time in nature are often those least likely to do so, can be put down to a number of causes. It has been linked to poor proximity, to lack of transport options, to poor access for those with limited mobility, to concerns about safety and a perceived 'lack of time'.[39] Any national approach to rebuilding the imagination must take access to nature seriously, and must also recognise the power of bringing more nature to where people live, to a 'rewilding' of our towns, cities and neighbourhoods.

How can we do better? In September 2017, I took a trip to Germany's Ruhr Valley, which included a visit to Grundschule Pantrings Hof, a primary school in Herne. Twenty years ago students, parents and staff created a nature garden on a paddock next to the school, which evolved into a woodland garden, with trees and shrubs as well as open areas, and a bark mulch path running through. During my visit, a group of kids gave us a tour. Each had a special spot in the garden and had prepared a short presentation about it. We were introduced to the pond and its wildlife, and a stone wall habitat for reptiles, including sticks painted to look like snakes adorning the wall. One girl showed us the courgette patch, bemoaning the fact that the slugs ate their harvest. Other kids showed us their 'bee hotel', built to attract rare bees and other insects. The kids were clearly proud. Their teacher explained that the garden was the main reason he applied to work at the school.

After the tour, we chatted with the school's head teacher. 'If, in maths', she told us,

> we want to teach them to calculate circumference, we send them out to calculate the circumference of a tree. In German lessons, they write essays about the garden. If some students feel they need quiet and focus in order to be able to write, they can come and sit in the garden and work. During their art classes they spend a lot of time here in the garden drawing. Every subject they study makes as much use of the garden as it can.[40]

I wonder, do these children who study in the wildlife garden have lower levels of cortisol in their systems than children in schools without such a garden? And what is the impact on their imaginations? If trauma and poverty can raise the level of cortisol, as we saw in chapter 2, what if we use nature as part of the remedy?

Not far from where I revelled in the dawn chorus is a project called LandWorks, a charity set up in 2013 to provide 'a supported route back into employment and community for those in prison or at risk of going to prison'.[41] Situated in a two-acre former quarry on the Dartington Hall estate, LandWorks is rooted in a natural setting that maximises opportunities for people to immerse themselves in it. LandWorks is clearly onto something. In the United Kingdom, the recidivism rate is 48 percent (higher for youth offenders), at a cost of £13bn a year. For those leaving LandWorks, it is under 6 percent. Ninety-two percent of LandWorks participants find employment afterwards.[42] 'We use market gardening, wood working, pottery, charcoal production, compost production . . . [and] weave [in] softer skills, social skills', founder and director Chris Parsons tells me. Clients and staff dress alike to break down hierarchies, and everyone cooks and eats lunch together every day. Much of the focus of the work is about building trust. 'Once you've got that, then change can happen,' Chris adds.

I am also, of course, especially interested in the impact on participants' imaginations, and their sense of what the future holds. 'Just going through prison causes tremendous shock,' Chris says. 'People's imaginations have been squashed'. So LandWorks works with individuals to heal from this kind of trauma. 'We very much encourage people to form a non-criminal identity here, and to have imagination to do that. . . . The very basic point that there may even be a future for you, is something.'

Chris and I walk through abundant vegetable beds, call in at a workshop where participants are crafting wooden garden furniture, bird boxes and other things to sell at their roadside shop, and visit a cob wall, built using subsoil from the site. Everyone adds a tile with their name on it to the wall, creating an evolving timeline that tells the project's history and all the people who have been a part of it. We are surrounded by big trees, the birds are singing, nature is abundant. LandWorks is a clear and powerful demonstration that alternative ways of managing justice and incarceration are possible.

Chris describes LandWorks as 'a safe place to be vulnerable.' We discuss how replicable and scalable their approach is, given that at the moment the number of places offering similar programmes is very small. 'Many people could come here,' Chris says. For him, LandWorks is entirely replicable, there is nothing magical about what they do. It is about bringing people into natural settings, in a trusting and supportive way, and enabling them to use their hands, learn new skills and connect to other people. 'If imagination could start fundamentally to allow people to look at situations in a different way, I think that would be a great benefit to us all,' he told me.[43]

How can we bring this kind of thinking – namely that a key way to rebuild imagination and well-being is to put nature connection at the centre – to a whole city? Having a big, infectious, inspirational dream helps. Geography teacher Daniel Raven-Ellison set out to visit all fifteen national parks in the UK with his son, and returned home wondering why none of them were in cities. London, after all, is home to nine million people. What if nine million people had a national park . . . in their backyard? Even though London is plagued by the environmental woes that so many cities contend with – air, land and water pollution; traffic congestion; fractured wildlife corridors; overdevelopment; and a hell of a lot of concrete and pavement – it's also home to nearly fifteen thousand species of wildlife, 3.8 million gardens and three thousand parks. Forty-seven percent of London is green space already. Another 2.5 percent is 'blue' space; that is, lakes, ponds and rivers. So it would take only 0.5 percent more – around 1 m² of land for every person in London – to transform the majority of the city into a natural landscape.

Why not build on that? Why not change the story, deepen the identity, and give people tools to develop a different kind of relationship with the Smoke? So Daniel began a campaign to turn London into the world's first National Park City. The idea was to celebrate, enjoy and improve life in the city by building community, stewarding land and playing more Frisbee. Daniel – a self-styled 'guerrilla geographer' – emphasised the health benefits, both physical and mental; resilience to climate change and weather events; economic benefits; and, maybe most important, the casting of a different narrative about the City of London and how its residents and visitors relate to it, and to themselves. He collaborated with designer Charlie Peel to create a map of London showing the city's

> 3,000 parks plus woodlands, playing fields, nature reserves, city farms, rivers, canals and all the spaces that contribute to London's landscape . . . [including] some of the most iconic walks through and around London . . . such as the London

Outer Orbital Path (LOOP) and Capital Ring, along with symbols marking places to swim outdoors, climb hills, pitch a tent or go kayaking. It even shows front and back gardens, but not any buildings![44]

Like the Transition movement, the National Park City initiative is much more bottom up than top down. While there has been political buy-in – notably from London's mayor Sadiq Khan – the project is not a bureaucratic one. It's an invitation. 'It's about providing a loose enough vision that it is welcoming and inviting,' Daniel told me, 'and not so technocratic that it becomes alienating to people, and about making it clear how people can contribute.' It's a story which, for Daniel, is about what we have in common. We all like to walk alongside a clean canal. Everyone wants to be healthier, to live in a city with cleaner air. Pretty much everyone enjoys seeing butterflies. The story of London as a National Park City uses different tools to awaken people's imaginations. They utilize a diversity of media: maps, photography, drawings, and have a firm commitment to involving artists, poets and the city's culture makers from the outset.

Daniel's advice on how to make something like this happen? 'Get it out of the environmental movement as quickly as possible'. He argues that often the people who are trying to drive environmental change are not necessarily the culture makers who will inspire a broad audience. And that 'it is culture and people that will drive change'.[45] For Daniel, the problem isn't that people don't understand what the problems are, rather that the problems are so big that people feel overwhelmed and this in turn shuts down the imagination. London was formally declared a National Park City in July 2019 with hundreds of launches across the city and a charter produced to support other cities to do the same. As their website states: 'We want more bird song, ultimate frisbee, hill-rolling, tree climbing, cycling, hedgehogs, volunteering, sharing, outdoor play, kayaking, clean air, otters, greener streets, outdoor learning, ball games, outdoor art and hilltop dancing in the city. Why not?'[46]

Why not, indeed? And what if? What if your school were a national park? What if you turned your paved front yard into a wildflower meadow? What if we reconnected fragmented landscapes to nurture wildlife habitats? What if, in fact, we acknowledged that wildlife is good for public health? London National Park City is a stunning example of a good what-if question, something we'll be exploring in more detail later. The campaign cultivates so many opportunities for people to get involved, have a voice, or become citizen scientists. Diverse organisations and individuals can identify a role and make contributions in a rich, organic and enlivening way. It's a powerful example of how to rekindle the collective imagination, give people a taste of changemaking, and draft a powerful new story for a community to tell about itself. And it's spreading: in collaboration with people around the world, Daniel and his team are working on a 'Universal Charter for National Park Cities', which people in other cities will be able to use to understand if and how their city can become a National Park City too.

This is precisely what I see in the Transition movement: an opening up of the collective imagination, with nature as the model and the inspiration, so that communities can begin to reimagine themselves. I see it happening in communities and organisations all over the world, whether they are running reforesting projects, creating new community-supported agriculture (CSA) farms, gleaning food, establishing woodland cooperatives, developing urban agriculture projects or simply neighbours helping neighbours grow a little bit of food on their balconies. I've seen it more times than I can count: rebuilding the everyday connection to nature brings innumerable benefits.

You'll find it, for example, in Richmond, California, a town in the San Francisco Bay Area struggling with poverty, guns, gangs, drugs and violence, and where there is one grocery store for one hundred thousand people.[47] As Richmond resident Doria Robinson explained, 'People are used to opening up a package, putting it in the microwave and calling it dinner.'[48] Doria is the executive director of Urban Tilth, an organisation whose goal is to grow 5 percent of the food consumed in Richmond within Richmond. Urban Tilth has created thirteen new food gardens, and now manages seven of them, having handed the other six back to the church, school and community groups they created them with. Urban Tilth also manages a CSA farm that feeds 160 families every week. And yet, Urban Tilth's gardens and small farms are only a small (but crucial) part of what they do. As Urban Tilth's website puts it: 'We farm, feed, forage, teach, train, build community, employ and give back.' At root, they are reimagining Richmond's economy, culture and story.[49]

Doria told me that when people first join Urban Tilth's training programme, many are pretty disconnected from nature, just focused on getting by day-to-day, and don't have much mental energy for their long-term future, let alone issues like climate change. After getting involved, however, many people develop a different perspective, realizing, as Doria puts it, that 'we actually are dependent on interdependence'.[50]

And how does the space that feeling more connected to nature brings into people's lives change their sense of what's possible and how positive they feel about the future? 'A lot of the people who grew up in my generation, we were just trying to get out', she told me. 'Now I hear a lot more people saying, 'I want to live here. I want to be able to afford to buy a house here and make my life here.' And they're dreaming out all kinds of other new things and feeling like it's totally within the realm of possibility.'

As at Art Angel and at LandWorks, I could see the path back to the imagination shining through Doria's words. When we create safe spaces, time away from screens, 'Yes, and' spaces, working with other people over tasks that facilitate connection and craft a narrative that offers a hopeful take on the future, the world can start to come back into focus. Being immersed in a diversity of living organisms – even if it's just digging your bare hands into the soil of a community garden bed – creates conditions in which the imagination can flicker back to life. As residents are experiencing in Richmond, and across the globe, the living world points the way towards imagining new economic models, developing climate resilience, fostering social inclusion and so much more.

CHAPTER 4

What If We Fought Back to Reclaim Our Attention?

If consumer capitalism can only go on by continuing to accelerate the 'intensification of nervous stimulation', there would seem to be a fundamental antagonism between this form of economic life and the individual who inhabits it.

—Matthew B. Crawford,
The World Beyond Your Head

We are experiencing in our times a loss of depth – a loss, that is, of the very paradigm of depth.

—Sven Birkerts, *The Gutenberg Elegies*

I magine, if you will, Vincent van Gogh in Arles, France, in August 1888. It is a late summer's day with the mistral winds blowing through the street outside. He has just got back to his small studio in what he calls the Yellow House which he dreams will one day be home to a community of artists. He is carrying with him a bunch of sunflowers, a gift from his friend, the gardener Patience Escalier, whose portrait he completed a few days earlier.[1] He arranges them loosely in a glazed earthenware pot on the plain wooden table.

And instead of what history tells us happens next, imagine he were to sit down, get out his smartphone and check his Instagram feed for updates. Soon he is also checking his Facebook timeline and his Twitter account and, before he knows it, an hour has passed and he finds himself on YouTube watching videos of skateboarders falling down stairs. Thus distracted, his attention is taken firmly away from the possibility of *really* seeing those sunflowers, of immersing himself in their shapes, forms and colours, the way the light plays on them, and how he emotionally relates to them. Forever lost to future generations would be the resultant paintings, which have so moved, fascinated and entranced generations ever since.

What if, for that matter, Albert Einstein had stayed inside posting Instagram photos of his breakfast rather than taking his long, dreamy bike rides? Or if William Wordsworth and his sister Dorothy had been checking their social media accounts while they walked straight past that famous 'host of golden daffodils' at Glencoyne Bay at Ullswater in the Lake District in 1802? If Mikhail Bulgakov had been a YouTube star instead of writing *The Master and Margarita*? What would we have lost? More to the point, what works of inspired genius might we be losing right now, at a moment when we're in dire need of as much inspired genius as we can summon? As Sherry Turkle, Abby Rockefeller Mauzé Professor of the Social Studies of Science and Technology at the Massachusetts Institute of Technology, puts it, 'we are forever elsewhere.'[2]

Of course the technology we benefit or suffer from, depending on how you look at it, wasn't a factor for Van Gogh, Einstein, the Wordsworth siblings or Bulgakov. They didn't have to make a choice countless times throughout the day about whether or not to look at their phone. They didn't have to summon willpower or figure out creative hacks to make it less distracting. They didn't have to decide whether to bring it with them, shut it off, or put it on vibrate just in case someone they love or work for urgently needed to reach them. They could sit, uninterrupted, for hours, giving their entire undivided attention to a problem, to filling a blank page, or to pondering the bunch of sunflowers on that kitchen table in Arles. The ability to have such focus meant Van Gogh was able to reflect 'when nature is so beautiful, I am not conscious of myself any more, and the picture comes to me as if in a dream.'[3]

Who knows what their relationship to technology would have been? They were lucky not to have to figure that out. They never experienced the technological tyranny most of us now live with, and that's part of what gave them the freedom to dream and imagine and notice the world around them in ways that had huge implications for themselves and for humankind.

So what's to be done, for those of us living now, here, today? We are relentlessly bombarded with information, all vying for our attention, to the extent that many people fight a daily battle with distraction. Author Hugh McGuire describes 'the unavoidable siren call of the digital hit of new information' and explains how digital technologies have changed the way he works. 'Work on something important, brain itch, check email, *dopamine*, refresh, *dopamine*, check Twitter, *dopamine*, back to work. Over and over, and each time the habit becomes more ingrained in the actual structures of our brains. How can books compete?'[4] Sound familiar? It did to me. Having spent the last few years working in a way that involved a lot of time online, posting things here, tweeting them there, emailing, Facebooking and so on, I was shocked at how shot to bits my attention span was when I started the research for this book. I could barely read for five minutes before the itch McGuire describes would start up. And for what? What do I gain or accomplish by scratching that itch? For the most part, I'm not totally sure.

In 2018, the average 'total media consumption' for US adults (and that's just electronic media: TV, radio, time online, gaming and smartphones) was 11 hours and 6 minutes per day, up from 9 hours 32 minutes per day in 2014.[5] In 2013, researchers at Cal State Dominguez Hills observed 263 students from middle school through college while they studied and found that they focused on a task for an average of six seconds before switching to something else.[6] Many people are aware of and uncomfortable about feeling so distracted, and yet, with so many things pulling us in so many different directions, especially online, it can feel impossible to keep our attention where we want it to be. The question is: What do we do so that everyone stands a better chance of noticing the daffodils, enjoying life on our own terms and engaging in the kind of imaginative thinking that may be our best hope for survival?

The first thing we need to do is understand that our distraction is not a personal failing. Nor is it an accident. Our attention is being hijacked by vast tech companies, and exploited by many more companies, in ways we are evolutionarily unequipped to resist. These companies (which have names and addresses and shareholders, by the way) use aggressive strategies and have clear objectives for how you spend your time – objectives that are probably massively at odds with your own, including the goals you have for what you want to accomplish in life. As Tristan Harris, a former design ethicist at Google and, according *The Atlantic*, 'the closest thing Silicon Valley has to a conscience' says, 'A handful of people working at a handful of technology companies . . . will steer what a billion people are thinking today'.[7] There is, in other words, a huge amount of competition for your gaze. The author Matthew B. Crawford calls this the 'battle of attentional technologies'. Common Sense Media founder Jim Steyer refers to it as 'an arms race for your attention'. And the author James Williams argues that the Information Age would be better renamed 'The Age of Attention'.[8]

These technologies, which are part of what is known as 'persuasive tech', have been so successful at making life without them feel unimaginable a 2016 study found that half of all Americans reported that they 'couldn't live without' their smartphones.[9] A 2016 survey by Common Sense Media found that one-third of American children aged twelve to eighteen felt 'addicted to their mobile devices'.[10] Nomophobia, short for 'no-mobile phobia', or separation from one's phone, has been linked to anxiety, increased heart rate and higher blood pressure.[11] And just what qualifies as internet addiction now, anyway? As Tony Dokoupil wrote in an issue of *Newsweek* that ran with the cover title 'iCrazy: Panic. Depression. Psychosis. How Connection Addiction is Rewiring Our Brains,': 'Don't kid yourself: the gap between an "Internet addict" and John Q. Public is thin to nonexistent. One of the early flags for addiction was spending more than thirty-eight hours a week online. By that definition, we are all addicts now, many of us by Wednesday afternoon, Tuesday if it's a busy week.'[12]

In 2018 the WHO classified 'gaming disorder' as a mental health condition. Central and North West London NHS Foundation Trust (CNWL) has become the first NHS Trust to set up a clinic to support people suffering from internet addictions.[13] Dr Ryan Kemp, director of therapies at the trust, acknowledges that there is more anecdotal evidence than hard data at this point and that teasing it all apart can be complicated, but that the trust operates, busily, on the belief that there is a very real problem, supporting people with conditions ranging from depression, anxiety and panic attacks to relationship strain directly or indirectly connected to their media use.[14] In what might be the most damning example of all on the danger of our daily tech habits, some Silicon Valley executives don't allow their own children to use the very technologies they help develop. As Chamath Palihapitiya, a former vice president of user growth at Facebook, put it, 'I can't control Facebook. I can control my decision, which is that I don't use that shit. I can control my kids' decisions, which is that they're not allowed to use that shit.'[15]

What, besides *how* to direct our gaze, do these companies understand that most of the rest of us don't? They understand how valuable attention is. If not, there wouldn't be such a battle over it. If we're going to stand a chance of reclaiming our own attention, we have to really understand that our attention *does* have great value, to *us*, to our lives, to our well-being, to our collective future; it *matters* what we give our attention to. For these huge tech companies, capturing our attention translates to huge profits. The question is: What does it translate to for us as individuals, for society as a whole, for our collective future? What is it worth to us? What if we considered it worth fighting back for?

These questions got me thinking about the moments when I feel least distracted, most focused, my attention truly summoned. It is when I draw. I head off, with paper, pens and paint, and find a quiet spot. For the next couple of hours, my attention is totally focused on what's in front of me: the forms, the angles and proportions, the colours, the light and the shade, the textures, the relationships between things. In these moments, I am really looking, far deeper than I usually do. The light changes, the shade moves, I notice details I hadn't noticed at the outset. I feel as if I am connecting to the place, really seeing it, in a way I wouldn't have, couldn't have, otherwise. And when I look back at drawings I did ten, twenty, thirty years ago, I can still feel what that place looked like, sounded like, smelt like at the time I drew it, even what I was feeling at the time. It is meditation. It is multisensory. As essayist and literary critic Sven Birkerts writes, 'Art is the summoning of attention,' and that attention has given me things, both tangible and intangible, that have real and lasting value.[16]

Part of valuing our attention is developing a better understanding of how it works, so we can develop more resistance to the many distractions vying for it. Our brains summon attention in different ways, and via different networks, depending on the task in hand. The executive control network (ECN) is active when we bring our attention to focus outwardly on completing a task, the default mode network (DMN) is active when we are focused inward reflectively and the salience network monitors and modulates the two. (The hippocampus, by the way, sits at the heart of these three networks.) Imagine, for example, that you're intensely writing a screenplay to a deadline. Your ECN is outwardly focused on completing it, while your DMN – or 'Imagination Network', as Scott Barry Kaufman of the Imagination Institute calls it – is inwardly focused on conjuring the creative work.[17]

Some people also refer to the DMN as the 'daydreaming network', since that's how we often experience it. The DMN creates a space in our mental life to think divergently, expansively, and to integrate different ideas, possibilities and scenarios, often without our even realising it. The result? New associations form and unexpected solutions to complex problems emerge – often effortlessly, it seems. In other words, the DMN is where attention and imagination meet.

Have you ever struggled hard to figure something out, only to find that once you stopped thinking about it, the solution became clear? People who understand this, even subconsciously, will often go for a walk or sleep on a problem rather than continue to chew on it unproductively. The mathematician Andrew Wiles talks about his '3B Mantra': his best ideas come when he gives his subconscious time and space to wander, ideally on the bus, in bed or in the bath.[18] Whenever I found myself stuck writing this book, I headed out for a short bicycle ride, under some trees, up a hill, and by the time I returned home, the right idea would have arrived.

The DMN likes tasks that require a little of our attention but also leave enough freedom for the mind to wander. Things such as knitting, podding peas, weeding – things we do much less of than we used to.

Jonathan Schooler, a professor at the Department of Psychology and Brain Science at the University of California, Santa Barbara, and one of the world's authorities on daydreaming and the DMN, told me there are things that seem to engage the DMN: being at rest with nothing very demanding to do; thinking about the self, or self-related ideas, or social situations; and creative problem solving. It's the network that 'the mind naturally gravitates to when not given any other demands.'[19]

Research by Schooler and colleagues asked subjects to do the Torrance Tests of Creative Thinking, and then broke them into three groups for a twenty-minute break. One group did nothing at all during the break. The second was given a demanding task which offered no opportunity for mind wandering, and the third had a non-demanding task that offered the opportunity for mind wandering. When they returned to the creativity tests, those who had had the non-demanding task with the best conditions for mind wandering came up with the most creative answers to the test.[20] As Schooler told me, this may be one of the reasons why people often report having creative ideas in the shower. It's an activity that 'requires doing things but it's not a very demanding activity.'[21] Sherry Turkle puts it this way: 'Our brains are most productive when there is no demand that they be reactive'.[22]

As we fill more and more of our mind-wandering time with screens, social media and random busyness, we need to ask: What is the impact on our ability to think imaginatively? The writer and physicist Leonard Mlodinow explains in his book *Elastic* that 'as our DMNs are sidelined more and more, we have less unfocused time for our extended internal dialogue to proceed. As a result, we have diminished opportunities to string together those random associations that lead to new ideas and realisations.'[23]

I asked Dr Larry Rosen, a professor emeritus of psychology at California State University, whose work focuses on the psychological impacts of new technologies, how he sees the overlap between imagination and attention. He told me that abstract thinking, vital to our ability to be imaginative, is 'taking ideas from various other places in your brain – things you've heard, things you've done, things you've thought – and putting them together in unique but valuable ways. We don't have the attention span to do that anymore, and it's not just young people. It's everybody.' I asked him why he thought that might be, that we are seeing this precipitous collapse of attention, and he told me, 'I would say that our imagination . . . is probably on the decline exactly in the opposite trend of our time spent on smartphones.'[24] As he and Adam Gazzaley noted in *The Distracted Mind*, 'We appear to have lost the ability to simply be alone with our thoughts.'[25] In a troubling corollary, addiction specialist Bruce K. Alexander told me that in his experience, people with addictions are 'totally out of imagination'.[26]

As with so many aspects of imagination, the individual experience also plays out in communities and on a large societal scale. 'The way we live is eroding our capacity for deep, sustained, perceptive attention – the building block of intimacy, wisdom and cultural progress,' Maggie Jackson writes in *Distracted: The Erosion of Attention and the Coming Dark Age*.[27] Our depleted attention spans can mean that the world around us simply seems too complex, too bewildering for us to know how to influence it, so we can be increasingly drawn to simplified versions of why we are experiencing the problems we are experiencing. Our imagination shuts down as a decreasing number of stories we encounter add to our sense that another future, one worth fighting for, is both imaginable and possible. As Jackson tells it,

> We really didn't yet fully know the effects of the vast social experiment that we were undertaking on ourselves and our children. We didn't understand the costs of distraction and the downsides to inhabiting digital worlds, dismantling cultures built on face-to-face human connections, and abandoning the kinds of reverie, musing, and what-if questions that are foundations of imagination and hence building blocks of envisioning and creating a better world.[28]

Our attention and imagination are inextricably linked. One does not exist without the other. Together they are, quite possibly, the most valuable tools we have to envision a positive future and fight for it. But life online puts us into a state of being 'always-on', always chasing to catch up with the present, to get to the bottom of our bottomless Facebook feeds, catch up on all our emails, but we never do. Media theorist Douglas Rushkoff notes: 'The present used to be actually where your body was, where your mind was. Now we think of the now as what's happening on our devices.'[29]

It used to be, Rushkoff argues, that the only people expected to be always-on, managing a steady stream of incoming information requiring instant response, were air traffic controllers and 999 (or 911) dispatchers, and they only worked three-hour shifts.[30] Now always-on is a daily reality for most of us. The risk is that a digital world leads to our getting stuck in the present and we start to lose sight of looking towards the future with hope, optimism and imagination. The future starts to fade away.

What if we begin to value our attention as the blessing and the birthright (and responsibility) it is − what should we do? I think we decide, in ways large and small, to fight like hell to get it back. As the design ethicist James Williams writes in *Stand Out of Our Light*, 'The liberation of human attention may be the defining moral and political struggle of our time. Its success is prerequisite for the success of virtually all other struggles.'[31] We need what the author Tim Wu calls a 'human reclamation project'. 'Over the coming century,' he writes, 'the most vital human resource in need of conservation and protection is likely to be our own consciousness and mental space'.[32] What are the stakes here? American cultural critic Jonathan Beller, in his essay 'Paying Attention', writes about a future where our attention spans have collapsed entirely, a world where 'humanity has become its own ghost'.[33]

What does that fightback look like in real life? Well, for starters, there are the small things: We can remove the social media apps from our phones and change the colour display to black and white, which lessens the allure of many of the more addictive features; notification alerts that keep us reaching for the phone are often red. We can have digital-free days, or weekends, or holidays, such as the Tincan Project's Slow Sunday, 'a weekly day of rest, away from screens and all things digital.'[34] There are apps, such as Mute, Space and Hold that track our phone use, which most people considerably underestimate, and nudge us towards cutting down. We can impose a curfew on ourselves and our kids, making sure our screens are turned off at a certain point in the evening. We can buy an alarm clock and get the smartphones out of the bedroom. The smartphone packs many different functions into one device, which is part of its appeal, but if we start to break that back down by wearing a watch, carrying a separate camera, a notebook, and finding other ways of listening to music, we can start to break its hold over us. We can embrace a more comprehensive approach, termed 'digital minimalism', where we review each of the tools we use, and rather than being at their mercy, we embark on a thirty-day 'digital declutter' and then reintroduce only those tools that serve a specific purpose to our lives.[35]

And there are reasons to hope that a fightback for attention is under way. Some schools are now banning smartphone use during school hours; some workplaces are redesigning their layouts to maximise social interaction among staff members and managers are requesting that everyone put their phones in a basket in the middle of the table before meetings begin.[36] The writer and photographer Craig Mod turns his Wi-Fi off before bed and then doesn't turn it on again until lunchtime, making mornings his most productive time. 'Disconnection helped me remember what the mind felt like before I had lost my attention.'[37]

Recent years have also seen a revival in things such as vinyl records, paper notebooks, and board games. As David Sax, author of *The Revenge of Analog*, told me, 'It's not that analogue is superior to digital. It's just different. In some cases that will work better, and in some cases it won't. . . . Technology should serve your imagination. Your imagination should not serve technology.'[38] And of course, we can make more time in our lives to do the sorts of things that the DMN loves: meditate, study mindfulness, read books, take walks, exercise, cook, practice yoga, knit, dance, canoe – whatever, so long as it peels us away from our screens.

What kinds of experience do people have when they do manage to peel away? To find out, I headed up to the Barn Retreat, near where I live, to speak to its manager, Tasha Bassingthwaighte. The Barn offers Buddhist-based meditation, time outdoors, and week-long retreats in community living. As I sat with Tasha in the Barn's library, she explained that the Barn has no Wi-Fi and little mobile phone signal. Retreatants are invited to leave their phone in the car or in the office. Many of those visiting are from London, and for many of them, this is their first experience of spending meaningful time away from their phones.

For the first couple of days, retreatants report that when they are bored or experiencing nomophobia, they find their hands reaching for the 'phantom' phone in their pockets. 'People talk about how they notice that they reach for their phone every time they feel slightly uncomfortable or bored or unsure what to do next,' she told me. Why does this happen? Tasha suggested that it could be due to a mixture of things, to boredom, to insecurity, to unprocessed grief that they've been suppressing.

'We often hear people say', she continued, 'that they've been living in a dream state of lack of awareness for the past year or decade or many decades. They want to connect enough with themselves so that their lives don't just pass them by'. She told me how, by the end of the week's retreat, she observes 'this very obvious glow that people have', of which a reconnection to attention is a significant contributor.

Unfortunately, not everyone has the resources to head to the Barn for a week. There is a fascinating and troubling degree to which privilege runs through this issue of digital disconnection. When music mogul Simon Cowell gave up his smartphone for an older-style phone because of the impact he felt it was having on his mental health, *Guardian* columnist Arwa Mahdawi wrote, 'Just a few years ago, smartphones were a status symbol; today they are the status quo. . . . Ever heard an Uber driver talk about giving up their phone? Or a Deliveroo rider? No, because without their phones they would not be able to do their jobs.'[39]

While high-end digital detox retreats such as California's Camp Grounded lets participants 'trade in your computer, cell phone, email, digital cameras, clocks, schedules, work-jargon, networking events and conferences for four days of pure, unadulterated off-the-grid camp fun', a deeper problem goes unaddressed: many people, in order to keep a roof over their head and food on the table, are expected to be always-on, always connected, and to answer emails at any hour of day or night.[40] With expectations like this, how can anyone *not* get addicted? We must recognise and fight for everyone's right to disconnect. Might work that erodes our attention and builds anxiety come to be seen in the same way as the impact of passive smoking or asbestos exposure in the workplace?

Rather than just sighing and saying this is somehow inevitable, might we recognise that workers, and the rest of us, need some protection?

Dr Ryan Kemp makes the same point about acknowledging the potential for addiction. 'Recognition would be a good first step,' he explained to me. He mentions software that records and reports screen time use; the idea of forming a government panel to establish safer parameters of use, like those that exist for alcohol; the promotion of physical, artistic, and other activities – for everyone; and getting the industry to fund research and treatment.[41] At the time of this writing, CNWL was piloting a gaming addiction clinic using a mixture of face-to-face and online group sessions to better understand gaming addiction and how it might be treated.[42] But it is one pilot programme, and outside the world of digital detoxes for frazzled, well-paid IT professionals, there is little or no support for people, especially parents, concerned about the addictive impact of the phones in our pockets and the games on our screens.

To a large degree, at least for now, we're on our own. In the absence of meaningful leadership from tech companies or government, we need to do the best we can to take matters into our own hands. That often looks like small acts of resistance throughout the day. We need to wean ourselves from the belief that multitasking is an achievable way of working. It isn't. Multitasking just means doing more things more badly. People who multitask by frequently checking their email suffer a reduction in intelligence equivalent to exhaustion or smoking marijuana.[43] When we multitask, we overload the brain, and the processing shifts from the hippocampus, which enables us to remember and imagine, to the striatum, which is responsible for rote tasks.[44] This makes it harder for us to learn a task or, after a period of multitasking, even to remember what we were doing.

One study at the University of Loughborough found that after reading an email, which took two minutes on average, it then took people an average of sixty-eight seconds to return to their work and remember what they were doing.[45] It is estimated that unnecessary interruptions and the time needed to get our brain back on track after being distracted from our original task now consume an average of 28 percent of our working day.[46] This disengagement of the hippocampus, and inability to just focus on doing one thing well, reduces our capacity to be imaginative in a focused way. Research also shows that zipping from task to task rather than just focusing on one thing is more tiring. Focusing on one thing, such as an hour's deep reading, is far less draining and requires less mental energy than attempting to multitask.

We also need to cultivate our tolerance for boredom. Boredom is not always a great thing. Having a boring job can take its toll on our health and relationships and can lead to absenteeism and increased risk of accident.[47] Boring places can impact our mental health, stifling our 'biological need for intrigue'.[48] But boredom also has a purpose. As Sherry Turkle puts it, 'Boredom can be recognized as your imagination calling you.'[49] For her, such moments are 'signs to attend more closely to things, not to turn away'. It is a moment when our minds want some kind of stimulation, but there is none to be had. Boredom offers a catalyst for action, a moment to reflect, to go inwards, to let our imagination fire, to daydream. It's the moment when our brain might start composing a song or a poem, coming up with a really interesting idea for this evening's supper or a new approach to a problem. Boredom can make us more imaginative and more creative. In one study at the University of Central Lancashire, eighty people were given boring things to do, like copying numbers out of a phone book, while a control group wasn't. Both groups were then given divergent-thinking tests, such as thinking of as many uses for a plastic cup as possible. The 'bored' group came up with more answers, and more creative ones, than the control group.[50]

Matthieu Ricard is a French Buddhist monk and, according to neuroscientists who submitted him to a battery of tests, the 'happiest man in the world'. About boredom, he told me, 'Boring is people who have not realised the incredible richness of just resting in the mind. . . . My ideal situation is twenty-four-hour boredom all year round. Sitting on the balcony of my hermitage, watching the Himalaya. If you call that boredom, it's fine enough for me.' At the end of our conversation he paused, and then added: 'I think the Buddha might have got rid of Twitter with his palace.'[51]

The mythologist Martin Shaw refers to the internet as a 'toxic mimic'.[52] What does he mean? Well, as a species, we have evolved over tens of thousands of years to immerse ourselves in stories, to let ourselves be taken on imaginary journeys. A good storyteller can send us to distant realms and settings, warm firesides in imagined castles, imposing beanstalks in dreamt-up fields, the hot breath of dragons, the gentle glow of gold in distant caves. That desire to let ourselves be transported is fundamental to our humanity. Stories and myths fulfil that deep need.

The internet draws us in by appealing to that same desire, that same instinct to be taken on a journey to anywhere we want to go. It feels as though it fills the same space in our lives as daydreaming. But it really doesn't. As the storyteller Tom Hirons told me, 'It's thin and doesn't give us the same nutrition that the actual experience of using the imagination does. It's fantasy, I'd say, rather than imagination.'[53] In other words, the internet is the mental equivalent of junk food. We travel to places in our minds, but little of what we encounter is nourishing. We return from such a journey with little of real value and a nagging sense that we could have used our time more productively.

Despite that intrinsic human yearning for storytelling, recent years have seen a precipitous decline in the time people, especially young people, spend reading books. Research by the National Endowment for the Arts shows that the number of adults reading at least one work of fiction for pleasure in the previous year had dropped from 57 percent in 1982 to 43 percent in 2015.[54] Research shows that reading, fiction in particular, makes us more creative and more empathic. (Should the rise of empathy-free politics really come as a surprise?)[55] The less we read, the less able we are to solve problems, to put ourselves in the shoes of others, and the more easily we're lied to. It's a recipe for the many disasters we're seeing unfolding in the world today.

The writer Charles Chu points out that reclaiming time for books need not be as difficult as you might imagine. He calculates that at the average reading speed of four hundred words per minute, it would take 417 hours in a year to read two hundred books. This might sound like a lot, except that it's far less than the 608 hours the average American spends on social media, or the 1,642 hours watching TV each year.[56] We don't have to read two hundred books this year. Reading even one book is a meaningful act of resistance – and enough to remind us how pleasurable, calming and nourishing it can be. Let us read more books.

Researcher Sherry Turkle has documented how increased smart-phone use also corresponds with a decline in conversation. 'We are being silenced by our technologies – in a way, "cured of talking"', she writes. She argues that a decline in face-to-face conversation, the decline of the very skill of conversation, has real impacts. 'Without conversation,' she continues, 'studies show we are less empathic, less connected, less creative and fulfilled. We are diminished, in retreat.'[57] Research shows that people who visit social media sites every day are 11 percent more likely to feel lonely, with loneliness increasing the risk of premature death by as much as 30 percent.[58] In purely practical terms, we spend 65 percent of our waking hours in front of screens, which leaves less and less time for time for interaction with other people. A recent study by the BBC found that a sense of community has weakened in almost every area of the United Kingdom over the last thirty years.[59]

Our smartphones, our tablets, are so enticing, so dazzling, that they lure us away from the deeper, more ultimately enriching pursuit of actual conversation. Isolation and loneliness lead to anxiety and depression, both of which harm the hippocampus, shutting down the imagination. Sociologist Elise Boulding calls this 'temporal exhaustion', arguing that 'if one is mentally out of breath all the time from dealing with the present, there is no energy left for imagining the future.'[60] Face-to-face conversation, on the other hand, is such a vital spark for the imagination and for the cultivation of empathy. 'My argument is not anti-technology,' Turkle writes. 'It's pro-conversation.'[61] Striking up a conversation with a stranger at a pub, asking an actual human being for directions, or inviting a neighbour over for a cup of tea – these are all small but mighty acts of resistance in reclaiming our attention.

It's easy to forget that the information age is an experiment that has been under way for only the past twenty years. We are just beginning to see the consequences.

Some people say we are entering a 'New Dark Age', in which human attention, connection, democracy and privacy are all eroding, in which the amount of data being extracted about each of us is staggering, and the power of what distant actors can do with that data to affect how we vote, shop, behave and interact is unprecedented.[62] And of course, it is impacting our ability to imagine alternatives. We are seeing the rise of what is called 'surveillance capitalism', a system that harvests massive amounts of data from our daily lives and uses it to build complex algorithms to predict our future decisions and choices, enabling vast amounts of money to be made betting on 'behavioural futures markets'. This terrifying prospect, and its implications for freedom and democracy, are chilling. This, in turn, not only ruins but also co-opts and monetises our imaginations. As Shoshona Zuboff writes, 'Our dependency is at the heart of the commercial surveillance project, in which our felt needs for effective life vie against the inclination to resist its bold incursions. This conflict produces a psychic numbing that inures us to the realities of being tracked, parsed, mined and modified.'[63]

Maybe the digital revolution, which we thought would liberate us and spark a huge expansion in imagination, is having the opposite effect? As Douglas Rushkoff told me, 'we've ended up over the last twenty years disabling the cognitive and collaborative skills that we would have needed to address a collective problem like climate change.'[64] Or, in the words of Sherry Turkle: 'We had a love affair with a technology that seemed magical. But like great magic, it worked by commanding our attention and not letting us see anything but what the magician wanted us to see. Now we are ready to claim our attention – for solitude, for friendship, for society.'[65]

CHAPTER 5

What If School Nurtured Young Imaginations?

If you design a system to do something specific, don't be surprised if it does it. If you run an education system based on standardisation and conformity that suppresses individuality, imagination and creativity, don't be surprised if that's what it does.

—SIR KEN ROBINSON, *Creative Schools*

I magine for a moment – and give yourself some time, because this might require a fair amount of imagining – that you left school around age eighteen, or twenty-two, or whenever, feeling alive, empowered and excited for the future, as you set off with a spring in your step, eager to build your life and rebuild the world. Imagine you felt no fear in your young mind about how you would make your way in the world, find your place, support yourself, and have a good life according to your own definition and values. Imagine that your sense of imagination felt more vibrant and dynamic than it did when you were a child, not relegated to your past at all, but honoured and honed almost to a superpower, so that you were ready to call on it for every decision you needed to make.

Imagine that you loved your education and felt blessed and grateful to have it, something of real value, unique to you, that nobody could ever take away. Imagine that it involved grappling with questions that mattered to you and solving problems that felt relevant, to which no single solution existed? Imagine that you learned the people's history and that it helped you find common ground with others, so that you felt you could go anywhere and do anything and enjoy a convivial meal in friendship and good cheer with anyone. What if it included lying in the grass beneath majestic trees, gazing up into their cathedral canopies, overcome with a sense of awe and connection to all living things? Imagine that going to school was replete with moments that felt as though they were bursting with possibility.

What if you spent time at the feet of storytellers, rappers, musicians, craftspeople and elders, learning from their examples? What if you had time to daydream, to stare out of the window, to dip your fingers into a glittering stream as it drifted past? What if you spent long hours with your hands and face covered in paint, clay, charcoal powder and ink? If you had ample time and space to play, to bring entire worlds into being because you played them into existence? What if your education included laughter? Lots of laughter. And taught you how to be independent, to manage money competently, to budget and live within limits? What if it gave you time with animals, watching them, feeding them, learning their songs? And gave you hands that were skilled, comfortable with tools, so that you could easily think of yourself as a maker, and actually be one?

I don't know about you, but my schooling didn't look much like this. Or anything like it. And in the thirty-odd years since I left school, it has, in most places at least, only accelerated its retreat.

It seems as though, until school begins, children's imaginations are pretty consistently healthy. Marjorie Taylor, a professor of psychology at the University of Oregon, has spent many years researching the development of imagination and creativity, in particular studying the phenomenon of 'imaginary friends'.[1] In her 'Imagination Lab', she particularly focuses on the imaginative abilities of three-to-five-year-olds. 'I haven't seen any decline at all in all the years that I've been interviewing children,' she told me.[2] Her work reveals the dazzlingly inventive imaginative worlds inhabited by young children. But then, it seems, something happens once kids reach school that not only devalues those worlds but actively undermines them.

Case in point: Thomas Deacon Academy in Peterborough opened in 2007 at a cost of £46.4m, the most expensive new state school in the United Kingdom. But it was built with no playground. Nowhere to play. Alan McMurdo, head of this new 'super school', told the BBC that 'youngsters can play in their own time, play in their local communities. What I want from my teachers is maximum teaching and I want maximum learning from the youngsters.'[3]

High school students in Texas currently spend up to 45 days in their 180-day school year taking tests, and those in grades three to eight spend between 19 and 27 days. One school superintendent said, 'When do we put a stick in a wheel and say, that's enough, stop? Because we are going to spend the next 10 years trying to slow that wheel down, and we've got 10 years of kids that are suffering.'[4] Meanwhile, a 2017 report in *The Times* quoted a secondary teacher in the United Kingdom bemoaning the fact that her Year 7 intake, straight from primary school, were unable to tell a story. 'They knew what a fronted adverbial noun was,' she said, 'and how to spot an internal clause, and even what a preposition was – but when I set them a task to write a story, they broke down and cried.'[5] Eleven-year-olds unable to make up stories? Something's not right here. Eric Liu and Scott Noppe-Brandon, in their book *Imagination First*, write: 'It is pretty clear what makes young humans allergic to imagination: school.'[6]

What if we could do better by the next generation? What if school were an enlivening and empowering experience for them? What if they felt no fear that they were about to get the answers to these big questions wrong (because they'd internalised that there's only one right answer, one way to be in the world, one path to follow)? What if young people felt an unshakeable belief that anything were possible and that they could achieve whatever they felt capable of in that moment when they set off into the world? What would be their first move? And the next? What kind of life would they build? What if we all felt this way? What would society look like?

I'm not exactly sure what the outcome would be, but here's what I envision: A lot more people would emerge as storytellers, with voices purposeful, rich and true. More of us would know the place that is our home, its rivers, its secret places, its history. We would love books. We would know our local community, its entrepreneurs, craftspeople, artists, cooks, coders. We might know how to strip an engine down and put it back together again. We could throw a bowl or a vase or a pot. We would have the project-management skills to take our imaginings and make them real. We would be kinder, more empathic, more thoughtful people. I think more of us would have a sense of safety and belonging. We would be able to sit in silence and relish boredom without reaching for a phone. We would know how to grow, cook and enjoy food and the delight of sharing food we have prepared with our friends, family and neighbours.

More of us might also have a keen love for language, its rich treasure trove of words and metaphors, its rhymes and alliterations, for the delight of rolling words around in our mouths like wine. I think more of us would be aware of the impacts of our actions, and way of being in the world, on those around us. Problems would feel solvable; we could turn our hand to anything. We would feel confident discussing problems we see in the world, sharing them, digesting them because a familiarity with visible solutions would have been part of our experience from the beginning. We would be more competent in actually addressing those problems. We would instinctively seek out connections between things rather than isolating them. We would know the major constellations of the stars. I think we would also be happier, a not insignificant factor given the high and growing rates of anxiety, depression and lifestyle-related disease in the world today, and the costs associated with them.

I'm clearly not alone in thinking this way. In 2011, the British artist Patrick Brill, who goes by the pseudonym Bob and Roberta Smith, penned a letter-painting to then secretary of state for education Michael Gove, chastising him for instituting a new national primary curriculum and making changes to the General Certificate of Secondary Education (GCSE), a two-year course of study followed by final exams around age sixteen – that noticeably sidelined the arts. 'Your initiative,' wrote Bob and Roberta Smith, 'rewards conformity and will cause stagnation . . . take art out of schools and belittle art . . . and you will emasculate British culture.'[7]

Undeterred when his letter went unanswered through traditional channels, Bob and Roberta Smith, who says that art education 'taught him how to think, not what to think', convened the inaugural Art Party

Conference at Scarborough Beach in 2013, where artists and art lovers held a demonstration calling on Gove to reinstate the role of the arts in education.[8] According to a BBC report, Lesley Butterworth, general secretary of the National Society for Education in Art and Design, described Gove's policies as 'the most toxic thing to happen to art and design in education in my professional lifetime', and sculptor Cornelia Parker claimed art was 'under attack'.[9]

The artists are right to be concerned. While in the private sector the arts are resourced and flourishing, in the state sector, art, music and drama are increasingly seen as 'non-essential', leading some to suggest that art in schools is 'facing extinction'. According to the UK Department of Education, between 2010 and 2017, in the nation's secondary schools, the number of teaching hours for arts subjects declined by 21 percent, and the number of arts teachers by 20 percent.[10] Nine thousand arts-subject teaching jobs were lost during that time.

The introduction of tuition fees has hit arts education at university level. While there has never really been a golden age where imagination was revered in the way I argue it should be, the art schools of the 1950s and 1960s in the United Kingdom had an enormous impact on the cultural life of the country, a window of time when working-class people could, for the first time, go to art college. Think David Bowie, Grayson Perry, David Hockney, Mary Quant, John Lennon, Vivienne Westwood, Pete Townsend and others. As the historian Dominic Sandbrook puts it, 'All in all, the influence of the art schools on Britain's pop culture can hardly be exaggerated.'[11] But now that door is closing again, thanks to funding cuts and tuition fees, and the arts are again becoming the realm of the privileged.

In the United Kingdom, entries in the Arts for the GCSE have declined by 35 percent between 2010 and 2018.[12] One of the drivers is the growth of the English baccalaureate (EBacc), which offers five key areas: English, maths, sciences, foreign languages and history or geography – but not the arts. The government wants 90 percent of students taking GCSEs to be taking the EBacc by 2025.[13] While universities still recognise both, EBacc has an added cachet, a 'premium' value, which is important for schools in competing for students and in trying to nudge their way up league tables. (UK schools' exam results and other factors are compiled into a league table, ranking the nation's schools from best to worst.) Mention the word 'EBacc' to anyone working in arts education in schools and you'll observe a mix of horror, deep anguish, fury and resignation. Outside of school it's not much better, with austerity leading to closures of hundreds of libraries, as well as arts programmes for young people and music tuition for lower-income families. The role of the arts as the champion for imagination in school can't be underestimated, however. It is not a disposable add-on; it is vital to the mental health of young people. As the author Philip Pullman puts it, 'We shouldn't be wondering whether children need art and music and stories and poetry any more than wondering why plants need water.'[14]

If the emotional well-being of our citizenry isn't reason enough to fund and value the arts, its importance to the well-being of the economy should be enough to convince policymakers that it's counterproductive to cut arts funding. The United Kingdom's creative industries are forecast to represent 20 percent of the entire economy by 2020, generating £84bn a year and creating 2.9 million jobs, more than aerospace, automotive, oil and gas and the life sciences combined. Being involved in art at school can increase cognitive abilities by 17 percent and improve attainment across all subjects. Students from low-income families are three times more likely to get a degree and twice as likely to vote if they do art in school. They are also more employable.[15] As English artist Ryan Gander puts it, 'Art is the source of creative citizenship and art education makes innovative thinkers that filter into every part of our society.'[16]

The decline in the acquisition of hand and craft skills, in particular, is having knock-on impacts across society. The researcher Shirley Brice Heath observed a decline in primary school children's ability to discern visual elements in maps and other graphic design, as well as in creative hand work.[17] If this seems inconsequential, consider the 2018 remarks of Dr Roger Kneebone, a professor of surgical education at Imperial College, London, who reported that the amount of time young people spend in front of screens was showing up as a lack of basic manual dexterity for tasks such as stitching or sewing up patients. 'It is a concern of mine and my scientific colleagues that whereas in the past you could make the assumption that students would leave school able to do certain practical things – cutting things out, making things – that is no longer the case,' Kneebone said.[18]

The policy response to this sort of problem is to double down on instruction, lengthen the school day, lengthen the school year, enforce tighter school uniform codes (Kyung Hee Kim told me of research she is conducting suggesting that wearing a school uniform leads to a decline in imagination), test earlier and more often, impose more standards, shove the kids full of yet more facts and cut anything deemed non-essential to the production of compliant workers who will dutifully serve the world economy.[19]

In a TEDx presentation, Peter Gray – whose book *Free to Learn* is essential reading on the subject of the importance of play – says: 'In the 1950s, when I was a child, we had ample opportunity to play. We had school, but school was not the big deal it is today . . . the school year was five weeks shorter than it is today. The school day was six hours long, but at least in elementary school, two of those were outdoors play . . . homework, for elementary school children, was essentially unheard of.'[20] Today, there's barely time for breaks, even though research shows that kids behave worse when they have fewer breaks.[21] The testing of everything, from an earlier and earlier age, creates a level of stress that damages the hippocampus. Teachers are observing an upsurge in mental ill health, depression and panic attacks in children as young as four.[22]

To get a sense of what the sidelining of imagination in the education system looks like from the inside, I spoke to two friends who work in teaching. One teaches at a school in the North of England. She started by telling me what education looked like from her vantage:

> Stuff kids full of facts, test them at the end. Set targets, measure schools on their ability to meet the targets. Measure teachers on their ability to meet the targets. Force pupils down a narrow academic route. Downplay the role of critical thinking and enquiry-based learning in favour of traditional memorising of facts. Imagination is stifled, job satisfaction plummets. Teachers suffer and so do the pupils. The current

curriculum direction is moving to squeeze out imagination, to devalue its expression and to marginalise enquiry in favour of conformity.[23]

Another friend was midway through her training to become a teacher. After almost a year of training, and placement in a South London school, she told me: 'Basically there is no room for imagination. . . . The students', she went on, 'are not encouraged to use their imaginations, nor even their brains very often.' Following her placement, she wrote to tell me, 'The state of health of the imagination within the comprehensive school system in South London I would say is terminal, currently critical and without hope.'[24]

The UK Department for Education is currently obsessed with replicating the high performance of schools in China and elsewhere in South East Asia, as measured by the Organisation for Economic Co-operation and Development's (OECD) Programme for International Student Assessment (PISA), which every three years tests fifteen-year-olds around the world for their abilities in reading, maths and science. When it was launched in 2000, it attracted little interest, but now they are a source of intense international competition. As Sir Ken Robinson puts it, 'Ministers of education now compare their respective rankings like bodybuilders flexing their biceps.'[25] Andrew Brewerton, principal of Plymouth College of Art in the United Kingdom, a regular visitor to colleges in Shanghai, told me: 'My friends in Shanghai just laugh. They say, "How do you *think* we do it?" But it is no substitute for childhood.' Ironically, the huge interest in China right now is in imagination and creative learning. It will be interesting to see how an encouragement of imagination finds itself able to sit alongside an authoritarian government.

This obsession with measuring everything is, as Brewerton put it to me, hollowing out the motivation of learners. He said: 'If you wanted to design a system to undermine creative learning, you'd be hard-pressed to better what we've done [in the UK].' He told me that this target culture, which generates the metrics upon which league table positions, institutional reputations and leadership careers depend, is 'destroying creative learning'. 'Nobody believes in [it]', he added. 'Nobody.

Everybody resents it. It is driving a lot of the best people to their wits' end and out of the profession . . . The imaginations of young people survive *despite* the system.'[26]

As Amy Seefeldt, director of the Centre for Imagination, puts it, 'That kind of mechanistic approach of measuring everything and standardising everything . . . constrains the imagination immensely.'[27] Indeed, by 2017, ten- and eleven-year-olds sitting SAT tests in UK schools were denied marks because of 'misshapen commas'.[28]

Gillian Judson, director of the Imaginative Education Research Group, campaigns for more imaginative education in schools, and trains teachers to bring it more into their work. 'We so rarely talk about imagination in education,' she has written. 'We have come to see it as associated with the irrational, "fantasy", "make-believe".'[29] After reading her work, I was interested in speaking with her and called her up. 'When you engage imagination, you wake up emotion,' she told me. 'Any educator knows that you need to emotionally engage your students in order for them to have meaningful learning experiences. . . . The things you most remember and understand are those that have affected you.'[30]

Ruth Sapsed, of Cambridge Curiosity and Imagination, tells me that the decline of imagination in schools is linked to the decline of opportunities for collaboration in school life. For her, the collaborative approach has been 'lost as the curriculum is so dried out and so packed and so busy that they are on this road map that doesn't give them the opportunity to do that kind of collaborative working. [This] is where some of these issues around these mental health problems that we're seeing are coming through. They are just not having the struggle and the joy of connecting with each other in enough ways.'[31]

So why is imagination so distrusted in education? Neil Griffiths, director at a charity called Arts Emergency, puts it like this: 'The way decision-makers see it is that the world is not run by people and systems that require imaginative citizens, that require dreamers and thinkers and makers – we're not needed in the economic models planned out for us.' Griffiths established Arts Emergency alongside comedian Josie Long in 2011 after they were looking at a photo one day of members of the Bullingdon Club – the dining club at Oxford that produced David

Cameron, Boris Johnson, and other powerful men – and began thinking about what privileges allow people to gain power, and which of those could be re-created for people who don't have such advantages. Arts Emergency now works with up to two hundred young people a year, aged between sixteen and nineteen, who have an interest in developing a career in the arts, and helps them explore their dreams, where they'd like to go, and how to get there. They also support a constantly growing alumni of over five hundred former protégés. Arts Emergency pairs the students with mentors in the arts, creating 'privilege for people without privilege', who help them fill out their university application forms and find paid work experience in the arts world, and then stay in touch for up to eight years. Their support is, as Griffiths remarked, 'potent, powerful and long-term'.[32]

This nurturing of the whole person calls to mind a Japanese concept called *ikigai*, which means 'reason for being'. Ikigai is whatever it is that gives your life value and meaning. It is the intersection between what you love, what you're good at, what the world needs and what you can be paid for. Those who manage to find this sweet spot are, reputedly at least, among the happiest and most satisfied people on earth. What if we all decided that the goal of education is to guide us towards ikigai, giving us the freedom to uncover and develop it, uniquely for ourselves? Imagine what a force for good each individual could be in the world.

———

So how could we re-envision education so that it's a force *for* the imagination? My aim here is not to set out a detailed pedagogy or critique of different learning models. I am not an educationalist. But I do think we can learn a lot by exploring different educational experiments, whether they are new schools created with a specific focus on imagination, existing schools that have worked to bring imagination into more conventional settings, or people doing away with the idea of school altogether. What I cover here is only a taste of what's out there. Most of these are stories from the margins. They are people committed to offering a learning experience with imagination at its heart, who have taken to the education system's fertile edges and got to work.

One of the most fertile edges is the Reggio Emilia model. After the Second World War, the Italian city of Reggio Emilia and the surrounding region were in ruins. A group of parents sold a tank, three trucks and six horses left behind by the retreating Germans (history doesn't record whom they sold them to) and used the money to build a school – an action that was both a metaphorical and a practical reflection of the hopes they held for the next generation. One of the founders, Loris Malaguzzi, wrote that they set out to create 'a new human culture of childhood . . . a motive that finds its origin in a powerful nostalgia for the future'.[33]

Under what is known as the 'Reggio Emilia approach', children are viewed as having rights, not just needs.[34] They are 'beautiful, powerful, competent, creative, curious and full of potential and ambitious desires'. They are active constructors of knowledge, what Malaguzzi called 'authors of their own learning'.[35] They are researchers, free to question and explore their interests through project-based learning. They are social beings, encouraged to develop a sense of self through their relationships and their connections in the world around them. The schools have no planned curriculum; the students collaborate with the teachers to design what and how they are going to learn. And the physical environment is the 'third teacher'; schools are full of light and plants, with ready access to the outdoors.[36] Every school has at its center an 'atelier', a workshop where someone is ready to help the child make whatever they desire. The City of Reggio Emilia now finances and runs twenty-two schools for children aged three to six, and thirteen infant toddler centres in and around the city based on this philosophy. People travel from around the world to learn from it.

In fact, there are so many schools and models that can lead us to a better path. Françoise Nyssen and Jean-Paul Capitani run the French publishing house Actes Sud in Arles, France. Following the death of their son Antoine, who they felt was let down by the French education system, Francoise and Jean-Paul started École Domaine du Possible (School of the Possible) in 2015.[37] Initially the school ran in a former church next to the publishing company's headquarters until they moved to Volpelière – a 120-hectare farm fifteen kilometres south-west of Arles – an evolving showcase of permaculture, agroforestry, and animal husbandry, with almond trees, olive groves, vineyards and rice fields. The school sits at the centre of the farm, which the students are invited to get involved in. At École Domaine du Possible, there is an emphasis on self-guidance, curiosity and joy in learning, and cultivating a strong relationship with nature. Students spend time in the garden three times each week with 'fingers in the ground, feet in boots, hair in the wind'. The foundation of their everyday experience is the kind of lifestyle that a sustainable, resilient future requires. Food being grown, processed, cooked, eaten in company. Connection, community, conviviality, conversation. Making things by hand, crafting, creating, sculpting, repairing. Understanding that the future we need to create is most likely not going to leap off an iPad, but must be brought forward into the present, into the real, lived now.

École Domaine du Possible is a response to the crisis in French education. It offers a taste of what's possible if a school's primary role is the cultivation of the imagination. Head teacher Jean Rakovitch told me that the school was shortly to undertake its 'first revolution', and move from a subject-based to a project-based model. The school has the support of a wide community of artists who come in to run workshops and masterclasses. 'Students have a lot of freedom to express themselves', he shared, 'through music, dance, craft, as well as through the projects they do.'[38] Future plans include a University of the Possible to be situated nearby, also rooted in the emerging agroecological landscape.

In much the same spirit, Karen MacLean and a friend started Den Grøenne Friskole (The Green Free School) on an industrial estate in Copenhagen. Karen is Danish American, and her two daughters were at a local Waldorf school, until MacLean became passionate about sustainability and Transition, two passions she came to realise weren't shared by the school. She told me: 'I became more and more curious to know what a school would look like that actually prepared children to participate in creating Transition . . . who would not want to see it as a drudgery in the way that many adults do ("Oh, we have to do things differently, that's so awful!"), but would be thrilled and excited and feel themselves as activists, where being part of Transition gave meaning to their lives.'

MacLean and her friend began planning in 2013, and by 2014 it had opened its doors to forty-three kids. It is now home to 150. They expanded from their original buildings, giving some an 'eco' makeover, and building new ones from scratch, as well as building garden beds on top of existing asphalt. 'You don't think when you walk into our school that it's a school necessarily,' she told me. 'There are no tables and chairs in rows. There are no blackboards . . . There are a lot of various kinds of spaces that are homey and comfortable to be in, and it doesn't look like an institution'. The school is part public and part private. Seventy percent of its funding comes from the state, and parents make up the other 30 percent. The school has to be open to inspection to check that students are at a level comparable to that in other schools, but are otherwise left to their own devices and can teach how they like.[39]

So how does Den Grønne Friskole nurture the imagination? School includes lots of time for art and for stories. Rather than offering formal tuition in subjects such as English, Danish and maths, all learning is project based. Projects offer students the opportunity to explore a subject in whatever way they choose; their final piece can be a work of art, craft, text, a presentation, or whatever the student decides. It is made clear that there is no right answer. Students are free to explore a topic as they choose. As MacLean put it, it means that the student's learning process 'isn't closed down by their having to either come up with a correct answer or having to guess what the adults are looking for'. This project-based approach recently became standard in schools across Finland, scrapping 'teaching by subject' in favour of 'teaching by topic'. At Den Grøenne Friskole, MacLean told me, they always start each project with a sensory experience, whether going to see a play, walking into the ocean in bare feet or going into a forest to listen to the birds. I asked MacLean what, for her, are elements that create the conditions in which imagination can flourish. She told me – firstly, spending as much time as possible outdoors in nature is vital. The school has a garden a short walk away, and has weekly field trips. Secondly, self-determination, the power to make your own decisions. Lastly, it's jettisoning 'the fallacy of the correct answer'. 'To inculcate children', she went on, 'in the idea that the entire work of children and henceforth of adults is to find the correct answers to things [does] a great disservice to the faculty of imagination.'[40]

Of course, it's not possible for everyone to create their own school. Amy Seefeldt set up and runs the Centre for Imagination at the Woodstock School, an international boarding school in the foothills of the Indian Himalayas. What's fascinating about the Centre for Imagination is that it isn't a whole new school; it's a program developed within an existing school, rather like a Reggio Emilia atelier. An outpost of the imagination, if you like. In 2014, when the project was born, Seefeldt had been the academic dean at Woodstock for about six years. She was in charge of the curriculum and teaching and learning, and became increasingly frustrated because she felt as though a lot of change was necessary in the way that schools function. 'You take this subject, and then this subject, and then this subject and you go around through the day – that kind of system can only be tweaked so much', she said. They were failing, she felt, to cultivate the imagination.[41]

She noticed that her most valuable interactions with students were happening between the cracks of the school day instead of during classes or other instructional periods. The real questions, on the order of 'What am I going to do with my life?' were happening in little corners in between. She told me: 'I became increasingly convinced that if education doesn't help young people find their place in the world, then really what is it for if they don't know themselves and the world and how those things fit together better?'[42] She took a year sabbatical to study at Schumacher College in the United Kingdom, and her thesis, *Centring the Ecological Imagination*, documents her process of dreaming and planning the Centre for Imagination.[43] When she returned to India, the Woodstock School offered her the oldest building on campus, and she set to work.

Guided by Seefeldt, assisted only by the occasional intern, the centre has developed a number of initiatives. For example, they invite scholars, artists, professionals, and recently retired lawyers or doctors to visit for three to six weeks with a project they're working on, in such a way that students and staff are able to interact with them. There is a lightly programmed agenda, so students, faculty and staff can find out about, and participate in, whatever they are working on. The centre also supports independent projects that students want to work on – for example, a weather- and air-quality-monitoring station, a gravity-powered lamp, the construction of a non-toxic plastic waste incinerator, as well as explorations on such topics as group dynamics and political behaviour. Seefeldt remarked, 'Any idea or initiative that a student has, [we try] to figure out how we can make it happen for them and facilitate that, freeing them up. Freeing their imagination.'[44]

The centre also hosts events, workshops and experiences to help young people understand what's happening in the world. These might take the form of discussions, films or debates and have included, for example, a workshop in restorative justice to deal with an outbreak of bullying, and dormitory-based conversations about how to support mental health, for oneself and others. It hosts a 'Festival of Ideas' every May, where students present the interdisciplinary projects they've been working on, on topics ranging from local water shortages to the effect of ocean noise pollution on whales, and take questions from the audience. They also run a series of summer sessions, in its third year as I write, which offers over twelve programmes covering topics as diverse as music production and songwriting, social entrepreneurship, Indian heritage and culture and Leadership for Change. Future plans include creating a recording studio, videoconferencing, which will open up formal and informal learning opportunities from around the world, an art and dance studio and a maker space. Seefeldt says: 'The filter is basically, will whatever we're doing help them know themselves and help them understand the world better?' The Centre for Imagination is also a resource for teachers at the Woodstock School who want to make their teaching more imaginative, creative and effective.

Although Amy relates that it was initially viewed with suspicion and incomprehension, the Centre for Imagination has become a vital part of school culture. It has impacted the students' sense of what is possible, and what school can offer. She told me, 'One of the really interesting experiences for me in creating this Centre has been when students come with an idea or a question, and I say yes, they're shocked. Like, "Really, I can do that? I can try to build this? Really?" "Sure, why not?"' Seefeldt stressed that a sense of emotional safety is essential. 'We learn early not to say what we really mean, not to ask the real question, to be afraid that whatever idea we have might be judged. For me it's been really important to create, both physically and emotionally, the space where people feel safe to say what they really mean, that nothing bad is going to happen if their idea doesn't work.' She continued:

> The space should feel calm and inviting. . . . Before we opened this, I visited a lot of university centres for imagination and labs and that kind of thing, and a lot of people go for this all-white, sleek futuristic feel. It's all plastic and steel, and I think something really different happens when people are surrounded by natural materials like stone and brick and wood and fabric, natural textures. People start to think differently.[45]

Of course, artistic, imaginative education is within greater reach for wealthier schools, families and communities. But what about for schools, families and communities that have less money, fewer resources? Unfortunately, imagination is often the first thing to be edged out, a luxury nobody can afford when basic needs are going unmet, or when putting food on the table or a roof over one's head is a daily struggle. For this reason, I was fascinated to hear about Project Ancora in São Paulo in Brazil. Founded in 1995 in the disadvantaged district of Cotia, Project Ancora simply offered after-school activities for local kids (under a big top tent!). Inspired by Escola da Ponte (School of the Bridge), an elementary school in Portugal based on the principles of democratic education, the Project Ancora organisers opened a primary school in 2012. Five years later, they integrated a high school. With the circus tent still as its focal point, the school has grown to 12,000 m², and includes laboratories, learning rooms, a sports court, kitchens, a library, a skate park, a dining room, as well as woods, herb gardens, fruit orchards and a vegetable garden. The school community, which sees itself as an actor for social change ('You must fight the forces that make cities unjust'), is now home to 180 students, 60 percent of whom are from local low-income families, and fifteen teachers.

Although Project Ancora is a private school, it is funded through an intriguing feature of the Brazilian tax system. Companies and individuals can choose to pay a proportion of their tax to selected NGOs rather than directly to the government.[46] Projects have to fall within certain categories (such as projects that support children and young people, the national film industry, the care of the elderly, sport, and a few others), and have to be approved by the respective local government departments. (Companies get a 3 percent discount as an incentive.) It's not easy to get, but the social aims of the school make it possible, with the result that all students are able to attend free of charge.

Rather than starting new schools, some people develop programmes that integrate into existing schools. One of my favourites is Cambridge Curiosity and Imagination (CCI), founded in 2002 by the artist Idit Nathan and colleagues, 'to inspire and enrich communities, to support them "to believe in themselves and find their own voice". We design ways for people of all ages to develop their own curiosity and imagination by inviting them into playful environments, both indoors and outdoors, and giving them the permission to explore.'[47]

While the CCI do many different projects with school groups and community organisations, my favourite is their 'Fantastical Cambridge' work. This work is about 'creatively adventuring with young children and their teachers to share discoveries of real, local spaces in extraordinary, enchanting and intriguing ways'.[48] Working with a team of artists, children, their teachers and families explore a particular place, perhaps a woodland adjoining the school, perhaps a garden, perhaps an area of their town, in a variety of ways, dreaming, imagining, noticing, paying attention. Participants might write, create poetry, draw, model with clay, collect things. They might survey the local wildlife in a twenty-four-hour 'Fantastical Beasts and Habitats' event. They might create huge maps on the floor and invite the kids to 'put what you like on the map, anything'.

'We are embodied imaginations', Ruth Sapsed, a co-founder of CCI, told me, 'the maps came out of a desire to make that visible.' It then falls to artist Elena Arévalo Melville to turn the vast amount of data into fantastical maps. The final product is a printed map, created digitally using up to one hundred layers, which presents the place as a dream, as a capturing of how the imagination has interacted with it. 'We love placing the children as experts in the middle,' Sapsed says of their adventures out to interact with the place that is to be the subject of a map. 'We love their capacity to navigate for others a way into a place, because they are play experts and . . . they don't bring that judgement and anxiety that many of us bring.'

Each map starts with asking the kids where they'd like to go and what they'd like to look at, and is then guided by them, seeing through their eyes, seeing them as the leader. The trips are underpinned by a quality Sapsed calls 'slowlyness' ('I've used it so often, I've forgotten it's not a word,' she says). This involves going slowly, and quietly, so as to give you a chance to notice things. Digital devices are left behind, no iPads are involved. The imagination and the materials in the woods are 'more than enough,' she told me.[49]

The resultant maps are stunning, capturing moods and ideas and dreams and locating them on the lived experience captured on the map. To spend time immersing yourself in these maps is to slip into a child's dream world, a multisensory reimagining, a world that runs alongside our own but which, as we get older, we increasingly lose connection with. CCI create spaces where those two vital ingredients for the imagination, space and time, are given the priority they need, CCI seeing its role as being to 'come alongside' kids and their interests.

Imaginative workarounds to class disparity can be seen throughout the world. In fact, over and over again I've been struck by the fact that some of the most ingenious, imaginative approaches to education aren't in wealthy communities; they're in poor communities, where the resources may be few, but people's minds are often less tethered to notions of 'how things must be'. The city of Plymouth, at the intersection of Devon and Cornwall, is England's most significant naval harbour. There is a lot of deprivation and a lot of economic exclusion. There is also a lot of regeneration, restoration, and new thinking. A new school sits at the heart of it.

The Plymouth School of Creative Arts opened initially as a primary school in 2013 and then expanded into a secondary school in 2014, emerging from Plymouth College of Arts (PCA) and two of the strategic aims of its five-year development plan: creative learning and social justice. The college's principal, Andrew Brewerton, told me how. 'It is unusual for art colleges to create mainstream city-centre four-to-sixteen-years all-through schools in areas of significant multiple deprivations. In fact, we are the only one', he said. He had found that he was having many conversations with sixteen-year-old students arriving to study at the college where they would say they were loving being there because it was so different from school. When pressed, he told me, 'They would tell you that at school they just teach you how to pass exams but here we can think for ourselves'.

And so the idea was born for a new school, in the centre of the city, in the art school ethos of learning through making, in all subjects. 'It's everything', Brewerton told me, 'it's language, it's culture, it's history, it's chemistry, biology, maths and physics, it's project management, it's creativity, it's all of those things.' The initial idea was to take over and convert an old department store in the centre of the city. When this site fell through, they were offered another, and began working with a team of architects, keeping the department store in mind as the template for what they wanted to create. Brewerton summed up his brief to the architects: 'This school needs big open floor plates. No corridors. No room that resembles a cell designed for thirty inmates. Specialist performance and studio spaces. We want it totally accessible to an inner-city neighbourhood. . . . If we can't have the department store, build us a department store that we can occupy as a school.'

Known as 'The Red House', the school is a striking large red cube occupying a corner plot on a busy street across the road from the sea. It is home to one thousand students and two hundred staff. The entrance is through the Atrium, a large open space with tables, near the heart of the school: the school's kitchen and a learning kitchen where students learn to cook. The design is inspired by the Reggio Emilia schools, but instead of an atelier at the heart, the school's kitchen and the learning kitchen play that role. There are also a fully equipped theatre, dance studios, additional performance space, a sports hall and science labs. Walls can be moved; spaces can be reconfigured. The designers felt that the relationship between the inside and the outside was important, so there are many large windows facing onto the street, including in the dance studios, offering a threshold between a private space and a performance space, to help shyer students get comfortable with the idea of performing in front of an audience.

Throughout the school – even in the main part of the school where the classes are held – the concept of the studio and the workshop reigns. Unlike a traditional classroom, a studio is a social space, where the social nature of learning is nurtured; at the Red House, they open into a shared space and don't have doors. The school has no uniform, but rather a dress code guiding different year groups in what colour to wear so as to build a sense of community and identity, and maintain affordability. Students in Phase 1 (up to Year 2) wear red tops, from Year 3 to Year 11 they wear black or red, but the clothes are simple, things people would buy anyway, and, yes, you can wear jeans to school. Teachers are called by their first names. The Red House is also a resource for residents of Plymouth. It hosts weekend and evening non-school events such as markets, church meetings, and sports tournaments.

The school encourages, whenever possible, exploration of connection between subjects. One day, the French class, for example, walked a hundred yards up the road, took the overnight ferry to France, and shopped in the harbour town of Roskoff for ingredients they needed to cook a French meal for their schoolmates. They returned to the school kitchen, learned to cook the meal, and spoke only French the entire time – on the ferry, at the market, in the kitchen. For many, it is their first experience outside of Plymouth. 'They come back with a different sense of possibility,' former PCSA Head Teacher Dave Strudwick told me.[50] Students also travel to the nearby Cremyll Boatyard to restore a 1950s Firefly dinghy, which, at the end of the year, they sail back across Plymouth Sound to the school. The school even struck a deal with the Plymouth Raiders basketball team that the team could use their hall for training in exchange for helping the school's youngest kids with literacy. 'It was wonderful', Strudwick told me, 'to see six feet six teaching two feet six.'[51]

Although it is early days for PSCA, it is leading the way in reimagining how education could be. It isn't perfect. It faces many of the daily challenges any inner-city school faces. It has no green space as such, or opportunity for olive and almond groves. Will it solve climate change? No. But I would argue that our only hope of truly tackling the climate crisis, and many others besides, depends on a shift to an education system that puts imagination at its heart, that nurtures young people who know how to imagine, solve problems and work together.

For some, bringing the imagination back into education requires a bigger leap away from the very concept of school. Speaking to me from Udaipur in northern India, unschooling activist Manish Jain told me that from his perspective, the education system is a part of the problem. 'One of the purposes of modern education is to destroy people's imaginations', he told me. He argues that while the Western model of education that has been adopted by India may have helped it to better fit into the global economy, it has been at the expense of many peoples' connection to their culture, their community and their ecosystem. 'Not only is it irrelevant', he told me, 'but it is also actually creating and reproducing the same sicknesses which are killing the planet'.

Jain's work is underpinned by two key concepts: 'unlearning' and 'unschooling'. Unlearning suggests that education needs to play a vital role in looking afresh at fundamental assumptions, recognising that the crisis we face, as he told me, 'runs much deeper than simple management shifts or technology fixes, that there is a deeper question about how we perceive ourselves in the world'. Unschooling is an approach to learning which is about moving beyond the culture of competition and comparison that runs through most schooling and turning instead to self-learning, in which students co-create learning programmes with each other based on their needs, in communities of other people doing the same, what Jain calls 'intergenerational learning spaces'. 'I believe', he told me, 'that you need at least three generations exploring things together to generate the conditions for real wisdom and imagination to emerge.'[52]

For the past fifteen years, Jain has been part of a project called 'Udaipur as a Learning City'. The concept is that, when viewed through an unschooling lens, a city such as Udaipur is a perfect opportunity to learn from the community, rather than from formal teaching. 'We find that once we step out of the boundaries of school,' he told me, 'we're no longer poor, backward, underdeveloped people. We actually have brilliant, abundant resources of learning all around us.' The project helps young people identify mentors and teachers in the community, people with skills and knowledge they would like to acquire, and enables them to work together.

'We are told there is a shortage of teachers everywhere in India', he told me, 'but if you go out on the streets, there's so many people who know how to do things! Who are brilliant, amazing, doing beautiful things. Our spiritual teachers, awesome mechanics who know how to fix everything you bring them, who are fantastic artisans, farmers. But none of these people are regarded as teachers by the existing system'.

––––––––––

At the end of 2018, across Australia, groups of kids began a series of rolling strikes, to say that they would walk out of school regularly until the government took meaningful action on climate change. In response, Prime Minister Scott Morrison told Parliament, 'We do not support our schools being turned into parliaments.'[53] But isn't that, more or less, what we *should* be aiming for? The cultivation of students who care about what's going on in the world and are willing to take a stand for it? Students who understand their own power, their own interest, and their own responsibility in shaping the world? Schools that discuss, debate and act on ideas the students care about? Andrew Brewerton put it best: 'The new kind of student', he told me, 'is that individual who, from their earliest years, has been driven by their intrinsic interests and curiosity and creativity. They never signed that contract in which the child learns that their job is to double-guess what the teacher wants them to say, [so they are always] learning for themselves, they never fall into the trap of learning for someone else.'[54] In a world in which the imagination thrives, all schools should indeed be art schools, and so much more besides.

CHAPTER 6

What If We Became
Better Storytellers?

*We are what we pretend to be, so we must be careful
about what we pretend to be.*

—KURT VONNEGUT, *Mother Night*

In 2012 in a workshop run by the Centre for Artistic Activism, an activist and NYU professor named Stephen Duncombe was working with a group of mothers in Houston, Texas, who were campaigning for better access to their incarcerated children and criminal justice reform in general, but especially for young people. Their children included undocumented immigrants who were caught in both the immigration and the criminal justice systems, including a mentally ill eleven-year-old boy who had been sentenced to three years in the Texas Youth Commission for a minor infraction. Getting access to their kids was very difficult for these mothers, but something they were coming together with determination to achieve.

Duncombe and his colleagues asked the mothers what achieving their goals would look like. The women replied that it would look like the passage of legislation that would allow families more rights and access to their incarcerated children.

'We said: "That's great. Guess what. We're here from the future and you did it. Now what do you want to do?"'

The mothers replied that they wanted the bill to be implemented and respected by law enforcement agencies.

'We say: "Well, guess what? You've done that as well. What's next?"'

Over the course of twenty minutes, the mothers said that what they actually wanted was a world in which their kids don't have to turn to crime or get pulled into crime.

'We say: "OK, that's happened."'

The mothers responded that they wanted a world without crime, without police, and without prisons.

'OK, well that's happened. What happens now?'

'We'd actually just live together, and we'd enjoy each other. We wouldn't worry.'

'We ask them to describe what that would feel like. They get into vivid detail of literally the sound of children laughing. The smell, in this case, of waffles. What the sun feels like on their backs. Then we'd stop them and say, "*This* is where we start. You start with the dream."'

Their point is that nobody cares about that piece of legislation apart from the activists and their opponents. 'But', Duncombe argues, 'if you want to reach the majority of the population, you have to create this greater dream, because they can access it at all sorts of different points and go on there with you.'[1]

We underestimate the power of these kinds of dreams, these kinds of visions, and the stories we can tell that bring them to life. In fact, one of the things all great movements have in common – those that have brought about real change like the Civil Rights movement, the suffragettes and LGBT rights campaigners – is that the participants are able to create and sustain a vision of the world they want, tell stories about it, and bring forward leaders who are able to make that vision a collective one, such that it becomes a powerful narrative – and a powerful counter-narrative to cynicism and despair. Think 'I Have a Dream'. Sadly, today dystopian and 'retrotopian' narratives thrive – that is, stories whose vision is not of a positive future, but a version of the past filtered through nostalgia and imagined ways in which the past was preferable to the present. Think 'Make America Great Again', for example.[2]

Humans, of course, are a storytelling creature. It's part of what *makes* us human. We tell stories that shape our sense of the world. We have strong cultural narratives, like the story that technology will save us. Or that everything is part of God's plan. Or that the end is nigh and we're on the brink of collapse. We also have strong personal narratives – those we tell ourselves about our lives and identity – maybe that we're a failure and our lives have come to naught, or that we're special enough that the limits that apply to others don't apply to us, or that human beings are so fundamentally evil that anyone's bold, imaginative thinking about a positive future is childish and naïve. These narratives are so omnipresent that we often barely notice them, or notice the fact that they're stories – stories that might be inaccurate, or incomplete, or subject to change – even though they can dictate major decisions like whom to vote for, where to live, and what work to do. Stories influence the shape our lives take and the path by which society charts its way forward. The power of story is, in fact, something we underestimate at our peril.

Neuroscience tells us that amazing things happen when we listen to and tell stories. When we listen to a lecture about climate change, for example, with PowerPoint slides, graphs and bullet points, the parts of our brain that show we are listening and the part where words are processed both light up. But when we listen to a story, something very different happens. First of all, the same parts of the storyteller's brain and the listener's brain light up together. And if we are listening to a story in which someone kicks a ball, for example, the part of our brain that coordinates foot motion activates. That is, we *experience* the story, rather than just absorbing information. We understand it more deeply. We retain it for longer. As author Annie Murphy Paul puts it, 'The brain . . . does not make much of a distinction between reading about an experience and encountering it in real life; in each case, the same neurological regions are stimulated.'[3]

This research jibes with my own experience. Shortly after we started the Transition movement in 2006, I began travelling around giving public talks to spread the message. I always started with fifteen minutes of grim graphs heading sharply in the wrong direction, alongside photos of tar sands and floods. After a while I started to notice that members of the audience would lean back in their seats and detach. But later, during the same talk, I would notice something very different happen when I started telling stories of people doing Transition on the ground, their successes, their failures, their triumphs and disasters. The struggle to overcome an obstacle. The transformation of those involved. The discovery of common ground leading to a shared sense of humanity and connectedness. When I would tell stories like this, audience members would laugh. They would relate. They would lean forward. Hopefully they remember and take it home. And when I invite members of the audience to help me *create* a story, or to tell each other a story, they connect even more. And when we get there, anything feels possible.

What does this tell us? Well, lots of things – including that if we want to overcome our world's many problems, facts are not enough. Facts won't persuade people who don't believe in climate change. Facts won't persuade people who think that economic growth, or technology, will solve our problems. Facts won't persuade someone who feels that collapse is inevitable. What unlocks new possibility is story. As the author Annette Simmons puts it, 'People don't need new facts – they need a new story . . . change their story and change their behaviour.'[4]

We need to deepen our storytelling of one specific kind of story, however – namely, the kind of story that can allow us to imagine a future replete with possibility. The kind of story that can elbow its way in front of dystopian visions. When I say we need to become better storytellers, I mean that we need to become willing and skilful tellers of visionary stories of How Things Turn Out OK – like what Stephen Duncombe and the mothers at that workshop did – and work back from there. Many of us are resistant to these kinds of visions – they seem impossible, naive – and yet, who can say for sure that they are any more impossible than the intellectually lazy dystopian visions we are so awash in these days?

It's December 2018 and I'm standing in a room in Brest in France, conducting a training event for forty community energy ambassadors who will later return home to educate people in their community about energy efficiency. I invite everyone to form into a line, shoulder to shoulder, facing me. I dim the lights and ask everyone to close their eyes. I tell the ambassadors to imagine that in front of them is a door, a door to the future. It crackles with static, a powerful portal to a different world.

I tell the ambassadors that when we step through this door, we shall be stepping two decades into the future. It will be a world that has been completely transformed from our current reality because eighteen years ago, there was a global tipping point, a moment when popular demand for governments to take the lead on rapid and effective action on climate change, injustice and inequality led to previously unimaginable change. Principled and determined people were elected. Communities responded with ambitious initiatives in neighbourhoods and cities across the world. A new economy emerged and flourished. Social divisions dissolved.

'When you step through the door,' I tell them, 'you will be stepping into that world, with all your senses.' I invite them to take a step forward.

I let them stand in silence for a few minutes. You can hear a pin drop. I notice some tears. After I break the silence and invite the participants to share what they are seeing or feeling, a woman speaks up.

'There's so much more birdsong,' she says.

The reflections start pouring out from other people too:

> There are no cars.
> Everyone feels so much more relaxed.
> The city is so green, there are plants and trees everywhere.
> There are bicycles, lots of bicycles.
> From my window I can see fields of crops.
> There are food gardens everywhere I walk.
> I am walking among lots of happy children playing.
> The streets are full of people.
> I see many solar panels.
> There are no homeless people.
> There is a lot of activity.
> There are no big shopping centres anymore.
> I hear laughter.

Several minutes pass, and then it's time to return to present day. The participants step back and, now in a different frame of mind, reflect on how that imagined future felt. An older woman noted how blocked we all are from thinking of the future in this way, and how liberating it felt to get beyond that blockage. Another noted that doing this kind of stepping into the future should be a daily thing, almost like a daily meditation practice. And another reflected with surprise that although she had been involved for many years in campaigning for a low-carbon future, this was the very first time she had tried to imagine it, and she was struck by how difficult she found it, and how odd it was to be so committed to the creation of something she couldn't imagine.

Months later, I followed up to see how the activity had affected them over that time. One participant, Claire, told me: 'Since that activity, I have felt less "militant" but more alive.' Another, Elodie, told me: 'It made me feel as if the future were at hand and made me want to dare more, to fight for a desirable future and to work towards its realisation.'[5]

Why are these kinds of stories so hard to sustain, so often subsumed by negative and dystopian visions when the fact is, *nobody* can predict the future. Assuming dystopias has an element of self-fulfilling prophecy, but it's also unlikely things will unfold exactly as *anyone* predicts. I admit that at the moment, the odds for anything other than collapse don't look that great. I meet more people every day who have given up, who are sure it is too late, who have no doubt that the future is going to be awful, worse than now, a slow – or rapid – slide into collapse. These stories can become the wall that separates us from other possible future scenarios and the capacity to envision and enact a positive future, one in which we've actually tackled our problems with competence and courage. As the French say, 'You can't catch a fly with vinegar'.

I don't for a moment say this is easy. As Donella Meadows, co-author of the *Limits to Growth* studies, asks, 'How did we arrive at a culture that constantly, almost automatically, ridicules visionaries? Whose idea of reality forces us to "be realistic"? When were we taught, and by whom, to suppress our visions?'[6] Point taken. This kind of thinking, at this moment in time, represents swimming against the current on an epic scale, given the sheer volume of bewildering, overwhelmingly traumatic information we all encounter every day.

As the writer Umair Haque puts it, 'It's not easy living in a time like this. It sucks the life out of you, drains you, changes you. Just being there. Just watching it all go down. Just going on to fight through another day.' He argues that the times we live in are leaving many people with low-level PTSD. 'You don't have to be the one who is hit by an abuser to be traumatized by abuse,' he goes on. 'You merely have to be in proximity to such a thing, for the experience to ripple out and strike you, too. . . . This, my friends, is a traumatized time, generation, milieu, society, world . . . something like an age of trauma.'[7]

Frankly, at this point, I consider imagining the future in a positive way an act of immense courage, of resistance, of rebellion.

And yet, imagining the future in positive ways is also, in some respects, our natural condition. As Donella Meadows puts it:

> Children, before they are squashed by cynicism, are natural visionaries. They can tell you clearly and firmly what the world should be like. There should be no war, no pollution, no cruelty, no starving children. There should be music, fun, beauty, and lots and lots of nature. People should be trustworthy and grownups should not work so hard. It's fine to have nice things, but it's even more important to have love. As they grow up, children learn that these visions are 'childish' and stop saying them out loud. But inside all of us, if we haven't been too badly bruised by the world, there are glorious visions.[8]

Research by Denise Baden, an associate professor in business ethics at the University of Southampton, backs up the power of glorious visions. Baden gave ninety-one volunteers two stories to read about the negative impacts of climate change. One was set at the end of the world, and in the other, a woman is caught in a flood. The volunteers then read two positive stories. In one, someone created a 'flower bomb', which covered a bare public area with flowers, and in the other, a young boy is inspired by a TV programme to collect plastic to keep it out of the sea. The volunteers were later asked how the different stories had made them feel, and what, if any, actions they inspired. Most people said the negative stories left them feeling passive despair, hopelessness and discouragement. 'It made me angry and I switched off,' said one person. The response to the positive stories was very different. People reported feeling happier and motivated to do something. 'The story made me think about what I can do,' said one. 'I realised from my research', Baden later reflected, 'that we desperately need cultural offerings with positive visions of what a sustainable society might look like, to inspire hope and positive change.'[9]

And, in fact, people are creating those 'cultural offerings', although not always through traditional storytelling, and you may need to look around to find it. One powerful, if counterintuitive, way is through the visual arts. Enter James McKay, an artist and graphic novelist who also happens to have the very long title of 'Science Communicator and Manager at the EPSRC Centre for Doctoral Training in Low Carbon Technologies at the University of Leeds'. In a nutshell, his work involves creating visualisations of different scientists' research as well as doing a lot of public engagement and outreach. He also creates the best images I've ever seen of what a low-carbon future would look like. While a lot of artists try to capture a low-carbon future by depicting something that either looks so futuristic it's impossible to relate to, or something that is so chock-a-block full of hemp handbags and organic carrots that it feels a bit silly, James's work looks like what the future could be like in thirty years if there were sufficient intentional and political will. It looks like somewhere I'd like to live.

'It's very easy to think of the dystopian ideas,' McKay told me. 'It's almost lazy. Thinking of the good future is actually really hard because you have to envision something that is qualitatively different. Everyone knows what dystopia looks like. It's also exciting, in a dramatic way.'[10] In order to visualise what a positive low-carbon future might actually look like, McKay holds public workshops and asks people what their vision is of it, sometimes setting up an easel in the street, asking passers-by for their additions to the picture he is drawing. He told me it takes real effort to wean people off the dystopian visions, but that he does it by getting something, anything, down on paper.

'As soon as you have even just a rough sketch of something that's optimistic', he told me, 'you then have something that people can react to. The visions can be tremendously powerful in terms of motivating people to make some real changes because they can then start to see there are things that are achievable, and it doesn't have to be the dystopian, lazy thinking that most people have in their minds'.

McKay's artwork is not utopian. It does not capture a perfect future (whatever that is). In one graphic novel he worked on,

> sea level rise . . . of a couple of metres means we've got a giant lagoon in the middle of Yorkshire . . . rather than that being a disaster, people have learnt how to live on the water and use aquaculture and various things that mean they are utilising that new geographical feature. I put a lot of work into trying to see where there were problems, issues that some people might say were a disaster, and what an optimistic society would do to adapt to that.[11]

McKay models his drawings on places that already exist, and then projects forward from there. 'It certainly brings people up short when they see a real place that you've done a fantasy vision of', he told me, 'because they can immediately see what would work and what wouldn't.' Think about this the next time you are walking around your neighbourhood. Find a place you pass every day, sit down, and imagine it in the future – a future in which things turn out OK. What would it look like? Smell like? Sound like? Feel like? What would stay the same? What would change?

Visionary artwork doesn't have to be as literal as James McKay's work. It can operate on a deeper emotional level, evoking what that future would *feel* like, not necessarily describing it in precise detail. In 2010, the Centre Hospitalier Universitaire at Angers in the West of France commissioned more than fifty drawings from the artist and illustrator Quentin Blake for its maternity unit. When I first saw them at a presentation Blake gave at the Hay Literary Festival in 2013, they moved me to tears – capturing the moment when a mother and child meet for the first time, reminding me powerfully of the moment my own children were born.[12] Blake's biographer Ghislaine Kenyon describes a moment when Blake had a meeting with the chief economic administrator of the project, who announced: 'There's one very important thing.'

'We held our breath. Had the money run out? Did the hospital top brass not like the drawings? But no, to this hardened administrator the really important thing was the "exchange of looks between the mothers and babies" in the drawings.'[13]

Their power lies in the portrayal of how giving birth could be. As Blake put it, the drawings were 'a celebration of what's going to happen and a reassurance that it is going to happen'.[14] Perhaps it is the ability to create a sense of deep longing, the sense of celebration Blake refers to, that is what will give positive visions the edge over the dystopian ones.

As McKay notes, 'The dystopian stuff is exciting, in the way that natural disasters and accidents do get people's interest, whereas a good future can sometimes be boring. . . . That's the hardest thing, to make it exciting.'[15] The edge Blake describes is, I think, part of what the writer, teacher and mythologist Martin Shaw describes as 'bone memory'. 'As a writer, I've been thinking recently about the difference between what I call skin memory, flesh memory, and bone memory,' he told me one day over tea in his kitchen. 'Skin memory is the kind of stuff you put on your CV. . . . Flesh memory is the breakups, the travails, the high points, the stuff you remember in your life and feel emotional about. But the magical components to stories are the ones that activate what you could call "bone memory".'

Shaw described research in which the researchers pass the shadow of a pigeon over a chick, and it elicits no reaction. The researchers then pass the shadow of a hawk over the chick and the chick shudders even though it has never seen a hawk. 'All I know', Shaw continued, 'is that when I tell deep stories, this peculiar kind of bone memory comes out, where for an hour, or for two hours or for three days, the bones of people say, "Well, I can't tell you how, but I know parts of this story happened to me this morning." Something utterly relevant *right now* happens. What I'm not seeing a lot of at the moment is . . . bone memory.' Part of our challenge is to begin telling deeper stories, that get to what Blake was getting at with his drawings for the maternity ward, and that honour what Shaw is describing when he talks about bone memory.[16]

Maybe we also need to give some attention to how to make positive stories more exciting. Fantasy author Alexandra Rowland coined the term 'hopepunk' in a 2017 Tumblr message to describe 'the opposite of grimdark' and was shocked when the term took off and came to define a genre of emerging fiction. In the genre known as 'grimdark', Rowland explained to me, the assumption is that 'everyone has a core of malice, greed and selfishness' that society is in a terminal decline, and that 'evil will more often triumph over good because evil has fewer qualms about taking action than good does'. Hopepunk, she told me, 'Says that people are petty, cruel and mean, but also people are amazing and our communities are capable of incredible things . . . We also have a huge capacity to do good and to take care of each other and make the world a better place… [It's about] radical kindness.'[17]

In other words, 'It's about how the first step to slaying a dragon is for one person to say, probably drunk in a bar somewhere, "I bet it can be done, though."'[18]

For Rowland, the stories we tell about the future need to make the things we want to see there commonplace and unremarkable. 'The fantasy books I have written all exist in a world where queer people are just accepted because that's the world I want. I want people to be able to live the lives they choose and love the people they choose to love and have adventures slaying dragons while they're doing it. . . . Telling stories is how we get those stories for people in real life.' And she disagreed with James McKay's stance that a positive future is harder to tell stories about because it's duller than a dystopian one. 'What makes stories exciting is stakes', she told me. 'Solar panels break, they can be stolen. . . . If your tools are taken from you, suddenly you are in a position of mortal danger, where your lifestyle is threatened'.[19]

There is a small but growing body of hopepunk literature, stories that embody the spirit of a future rooted in 'radical kindness' – stories of How Things Turned Out OK. Mohsin Hamid's novel *Exit West* tells the story of young lovers Nadia and Saeed who live in a country being overrun by civil war and fundamentalism and are longing to escape. One day, a rumour starts to spread that mysterious black doors are appearing in random places throughout the city. When people walk through a door, they are transported to San Francisco, London, Dubai or Greece – a way out, to a new life, and the reader, of course, is also transported. What if we could simply walk through a door and go anywhere, to any place, or any life, or any possible future? In one passage, Hamid describes what the future felt like once this had happened, and had all settled down: 'The apocalypse appeared to have arrived and yet it was not apocalyptic, which is to say that while the changes were jarring they were not the end, and life went on, and people found things to do and ways to be and people to be with, and plausible desirable futures began to emerge, unimaginable previously, but not unimaginable now, and the result was something not unlike relief.'[20]

I talked to Hamid from his home in Lahore, Pakistan, after reading an article in which he described the need for writers and filmmakers to take a stand against nostalgia and create 'a radical engagement with the future'.[21] 'Engaging with the future . . . imagining that we are willing to author it together as opposed to having it given to us, is important. And "radical"' is to say that we should be ambitious and slightly crazy and idiosyncratic about how we think that future could be,' he told me. 'It shouldn't just be a future imagined by politicians, technologists and people on the violent political fringe. It should be something very different.'[22]

He argues that we have come to fear the future, and that the constant barrage of negative news that surrounds us puts us into a 'hyper-anxious state'. I asked him for his thoughts as to where we should start in telling stories of How Things Turned Out OK. He told me, 'For me as a storyteller, grounding things in the human is very important. . . . What it is like when it's happening to me? Or if it's happening to you?'

Story is increasingly becoming seen as vital to good campaigns and activism. In his book *Dream: Re-imagining Progressive Politics in an Age of Fantasy*, Stephen Duncombe wrote that 'unless progressives acknowledge and accept a politics of imagination, desire and spectacle, and most important, make it ethical and make it our own, we will bring about our "ruin rather than preservation".' Likewise, the Center for Story-Based Strategy in the United States, a 'national movement-building organization dedicated to harnessing the power of narrative for social change'. Shana McDavis-Conway, CSS's co-director, told me their work focuses on frontline communities who are the most impacted by poverty, pollution and racism, and helps them to change the stories they tell, in such a way that it underpins their campaign. I was curious to know why this mattered, why becoming better storytellers matters. She told me that activist groups are often good at organising and campaigning, but tend to lack storytelling skills. 'If you don't [work to] address those underlying narratives and work to . . . shift them . . . but also create alternative narratives that are about liberation, then it's going to be really difficult to do that work.'[23]

McDavis-Conway described to me CSS's work with 'foreshadowing', where 'you want to give people a sense of where the story is going – early on you give the reader [or viewer] a hint of what's going to happen later on' – the proverbial gun hanging over a mantlepiece that isn't mentioned per se but will clearly come back into the story. Some narratives, such as a 'There Is No Alternative' narrative, shut down foreshadowing. Skilful storytelling allows us to foreshadow a positive vision of the future in the stories we tell. McDavis-Conway tells me about a group of organisers frustrated that their mayor was not putting funding towards childcare. So, they took over the mayor's office and turned it into an impromptu day care centre for the day. 'Is that a long-term strategy that's going to work, turning the mayor's office into a day care centre?' she asked. 'No, but it's really effective at giving you a sense of, "Oh, this is what the world could look like."'

Stories are not just things that we tell as individuals. Communities can tell stories too. And it is when communities come together to start telling new stories about what their future could be that I start to get really excited. It is something that many Transition groups around the world do – bring people together to facilitate a collective imagination of what the future could be. The imagination thrives with constraints (think haiku or *The Cat in the Hat*) – which we have in abundance given the challenges we face – an opportunity rather than a barrier. In fact, I sometimes use a game I adapted from Deborah Frances-White, host of *The Guilty Feminist* podcast and pioneer of improvisation.[24] I tell the audience we're going to tell a story of how the place we're in got Transition under way, constrained only by the alphabet. People shout out suggestions. 'There was a woman called . . . *Amanda*, and Amanda was a . . . *Baker*, and she loved . . . *Cats*, but she was also obsessed with . . . *Dairy* products.' And so on. The story gets dafter and dafter as we hear how Amanda started Transition in that place, whom she met, how she put on her first meeting, what she wrote on the posters, who came, what they did, what happened next. The room fills with laughter and silliness, but a story also emerges of how it happened. A story. Most likely not *the* story, but *a* story, one imagined by that group.

In 2014, Transition Fidalgo and Friends on the island of Anacortes in Washington State created *Vision 2030*, a community-generated story of the future. As Evelyn Adams from Transition Fidalgo and Friends put it, 'It's vital that we have a star to steer by, a positive achievable vision to pull us forward.'[25] The community was already starting to see the impacts of climate change, with melting glaciers, droughts and smoke from nearby forest fires drifting in. Their engaging of people in formulating a new story for their community had an effect similar to James McKay's experience that presenting a sketch drawing can be hugely useful to stimulate people's thinking.

Groups were formed to look at different issues, each one drafting a different section of the plan, setting out a vision for the future, a credible basis for their proposals, and suggestions for how to achieve it. Adams continues by saying that 'by putting down on paper what Transition Fildago and Friends felt the future could look like, we were able to convey to ourselves and others in our community the specific goals we were trying to accomplish. It forced us to really think through the coming challenges, what was possible for the future and then outline a plan to accomplish that.'[26] Parts of *Vision 2030* ended up being included in the island authority's ten-year plan. And from there, residents undertook new solar energy projects, developed a gleaning program that in 2018 provided 20,442 pounds of locally grown food to the area's food-poor, created several new urban food gardens and surveyed the community forest lands on the island.[27]

In the final document, the group wrote, 'The vision that emerged was of a forward-looking, resilient community with a strong localized economy, a secure food supply, clean transportation options, energy-efficient buildings, and engaged citizens who measure wealth not by consumption but by contentment.'[28] While the plan has yet to be implemented on the scale the community has laid out, telling a story about the future enabled them to develop plans that can be implemented quickly and efficiently when it is more widely perceived that the time is right. As the economist Milton Friedman once wrote: 'Only a crisis – actual or perceived – produces real change. When that crisis occurs, the actions that are taken depend on the ideas that are lying around. That, I believe, is our basic function: to develop alternatives to existing policies, to keep them alive and available until the politically impossible becomes the politically inevitable.'[29]

We need to become better storytellers in such a way that we can, through a variety of media, give people a visceral sense of what a positive future would sound, taste, feel and look like. We need to create stories where the kind of future we want to see becomes commonplace, everyday. We need to tell stories with an underlying sense that the mere telling of them can create a degree of inevitability about their becoming a reality, and a sense that speaking them out loud is also of great benefit to our own mind, a powerful antidote to despondency and trauma.

When I spoke with James McKay, I asked him how spending the past ten years drawing and giving visual form to a hopeful, positive vision of the future had affected him personally. He told me, 'I came from a place where I was incredibly bleakly pessimistic. I didn't have any hope. I was originally interested in seeing the optimistic side almost as a thought experiment exercise to break out of that thought process. . . . I've had to be optimistic, but I've found that through that, I'm now quite passionately optimistic.'[30]

We need to tell these stories in a wide variety of media: in films, podcasts, drawings, graffiti art, dance, plays, novels, music. These all help to familiarise us with the future they are portraying in different ways. We need also to use stories to bring to life the future that will be inevitable if we don't change how we do things, and to support people in letting go of and grieving for the things we are losing around us right now.

We need to make intentional spaces for people to tell, share, or co-create these stories, spaces that are well facilitated and feel safe and inviting. We need to ground them in people, in characters we recognise, in places we recognise. Our stories need to try to speak to our deep memories, our bone memory, the things that fundamentally move and touch people, that really resonate. They need to make use of foreshadowing. And most important of all, we need to tell them as often as we can.

Every vital and much needed conversation with people about the gravity and scale of the challenges we and the natural world face should also include a taste of how it could be, a story of the future we could yet create. Every demonstration which seeks to raise awareness of or physically put itself in the way of the global challenges or particular manifestations of them should also be a celebration of the world we could yet create. The demonstrations at Standing Rock, for example, which tried to block the Keystone XL pipeline, modelled the grace, inclusivity, truthfulness and dignity that will be a key feature of the world they were striving to create. The Extinction Rebellion demonstrations in London in April 2019 created occupied spaces full of trees, conversation, connection, food and song which had a profound effect on those taking part, those passing through, and on the police officers who policed it. Telling these stories skilfully and making them everyday will make a positive, connected, celebratory future feel inevitable.

CHAPTER 7

What If We Started Asking Better Questions?

It's time for our society to get going on an intentional, dedicated, and systemic effort to up our imagination quotient – the real IQ – at work, at home, in school, at play, and in our community life.

—Eric Liu and Scott Noppe-Brandon,
Imagination First

The bus turning circle off Tooting High Street in South London is an unloved place, home to buses idling their engines next to homes that overlook the constant coming and going, noise and exhaust fumes. Along one side, opposite the houses, is a huge Primark store. The circle is a place that is as unremarkable as it is unloved, a grey space people walk through without noticing, not a place people would ever meet or stop to have a conversation. Tooting itself is a district that lacks a centre, a heart, a village green, being largely strung out along its busy High Street, one of London's main arterial roads. But if there were a centre to Tooting, it would be this circle. It is not a place that inspires much joy, carnival or creativity – and certainly not dancing in the street.

Until, that is, members of Transition Town Tooting (TTT) looked at the bus turning circle with fresh eyes and asked, 'What if this turning circle were, in fact, our village green?'[1]

And so, one Sunday in July 2017, having crowdfunded nearly £2,000, a team of volunteers set about transforming the Tooting circle into a village green for a day. The buses were routed down the road, and volunteers brought out benches, erected a speakers' platform, rolled strips of grass onto the tarmac, and decorated with potted trees, wheelbarrows full of potted plants, handheld windmills, bunting and an arched entryway for people to pass through as they entered from the High Street. A ukulele band and Sikh dhol drummers provided the music, alongside instruments available to anyone who wanted to strike a chord. Complimentary food was provided by a local restaurant as the smell of Ethiopian coffee wafted through.

The local Neighbourhood Plan group showed up (making use of legislation that enables communities to create their own, legally recognised, local development plans), as did a guy named Dr Bike, who fixed people's bicycles for free. The newly elected MP for Tooting, Rosena Allin-Khan, dropped by to give a short speech. Kids made drawings and brought them to life with a pedal-powered zoetrope. Other kids played in the street, in spontaneous games of four square and hopscotch. One girl persuaded people to lie down on the road – a suicidal thing to do on any other day – and traced their bodies with chalk. Led by the drummers, a parade passed through it all, its participants twirling and turning in circles through and around the bus turning circle.

By the end of the day, the long wall of Primark, which anyone would normally pass by without even noticing, had become the focus of many conversations about what to paint on it – how to use it to tell the best stories about ourselves. I took off my shoes and socks on that sunny afternoon and felt the vibrant albeit temporary 'Green Green Grass' of Tooting between my toes, along with a sense of possibility that in a few years I might return to visit the newly inaugurated Tooting Village Green with even bigger, even more colourful, even noisier celebration.

In addition to creating an oasis of colour and creativity, the Tooting Twirl, as it was called, created something very powerful that day. Rather than asking 'What would happen *if* this space were our village green?' it was giving people a taste of what that would be like *when* it was the village green. As Hilary Jennings of TTT told me: 'I don't think it's possible for anyone who's been here today or walked through it, or walked past it, to not see this space a bit differently. Once you've seen it without the buses and you've seen it like this, it's planted in your mind. . . . I don't see how you could go back from that.'[2]

This chapter is about how we can start asking different questions – specifically questions that begin with 'What if . . .' and that help us unlock the imagination in service to the big challenges we face. It's about more than the question per se, however. The question simply begins to open the door, creating a crack through which we might push and rush to the other side. It is an invitation as much as a question. It is a space we create and hold, and the question is the beginning of that, what the authors Eric Liu and Scott Noppe-Brandon call the move 'from *what is* to *what if*.[3] At a time when such spaces seem in short supply, 'What if . . .' becomes the perfect antidote to 'There is no alternative.'

As TTT organiser Lucy Neal told me during the Tooting Twirl, the event created the expectation of change, seeding the idea in peoples' imaginations, so that nobody can say that it isn't possible. 'What we have today is evidence', she said. 'When a proposal is made, no one can say it's not possible. It is *absolutely possible* to move the buses. We've done that. The joy and the delight of this is to step forward a bit, to be a little bit daring and a little bit courageous, saying, "Well, what if? What if we did that?" We have just played with that idea of what could be possible. But let nobody say after today that it's not possible'.[4]

What was so brilliant about asking '*What if* this turning circle were, in fact, our village green?' is that left within it is enough space for other people to ask different questions, new questions, to consider their place, their role in it, and yet at the same time remain safe, held, celebratory – an element of freedom and an element of constraint. All too often that is not the experience of consulting others, where the outcome has already been determined by the organisers or experts, and there's no role for others to step into.

What else makes a good what-if question? Ruth Ben-Tovim of Encounters Arts (who describe themselves as 'a company of artists, producers, facilitators and change agents who are creating the conditions for a creative, caring, connected world in which all can learn to flourish, living together within the Earth's ecological limits') describes three key elements. The first is that the people asking it have to be genuinely curious because 'the people you're asking will have an instinctive understanding if the question is coming from a genuine place of curiosity and openness or not.'[5] The second is that it must be a question that can be answered in many different ways. It ignites a possibility of response from many different angles, and a trust that the responses will be accepted. And thirdly, it should offer a sideways look at something that triggers a moment of pause, 'like lifting a curtain', she told me, 'a glimpse of something you can step into'.[6] Neal, who often collaborates with Ben-Tovim, adds: 'You have to hold your intention quite clearly, which is that it's a genuine offer, that you're not going to sell them a car or something! . . . We're bombarded with such offers all the time.'[7] As Antanas Mockus puts it, 'What people love most is when you write on the blackboard a risky first half of a sentence and then recognise their freedom to write the other half.'[8]

There is also a necessary element of constraint, or limit, in this openness and freedom. Imagination without limits is like typing nothing into a search engine and expecting to get something useful when you press Return. Narrowing the target area is vital for firing the imagination, what the French call 'bricolage' – meaning 'do it yourself' or a construction made of whatever materials are at hand. The storyteller Martin Shaw explains: 'Boundless, endless freedom, oddly, doesn't engender imagination. What engenders imagination for me is a deadline, and some limits.'[9] Poetic forms give writers shapes to work within, enabling them to create depth and beauty that resonate far beyond their apparent constraints, creating worlds that capture and fire the imagination. Paul Valéry wrote: 'A person is a poet if his imagination is stimulated by the difficulties inherent in his art and not if his imagination is dulled by them.'[10]

Fortunately – if we choose to look at it this way – there are many difficulties inherent in the art of solving the world's biggest problems, plenty of constraints, and plenty of limits. One response to the IPCC's 2018 statement that we need 'rapid, far-reaching and unprecedented changes in all aspects of society' is to kick against that, deny it, and say that it's impossible.[11] Another response is to look at it as a historic, once-off invitation to our brilliance. What if we were to massively de-escalate the crisis of anxiety across our culture? What if every university declared a climate and ecological emergency and all of its courses were taught through that lens? What if we created a fossil fuel–free energy system within twenty years? What if every new house built generated more energy than it consumed? What if urban agriculture became utterly commonplace? What if our cities became huge biodiversity reserves? What if single-use plastics were something we only saw in museums?

In what she calls her 'Green Eggs and Ham hypothesis,' the psychologist Catrinel Haught-Tromp argues that constraints can increase creativity, as Dr Seuss found when invited by his publisher to write a book containing just fifty different words: 'Focusing the creative energy on a narrower field of exploration allows for a more in-depth processing of fewer alternatives. Once a frame is in place, the focus can shift to creating something memorable within it.'[12] So perhaps, with imagination, the things that currently look like intractable problems are actually huge opportunities for new thinking. This is another thing Transition Town Tooting did so brilliantly. They looked at a space full of limits and constraints – a bus turning circle, not a blank canvas of pristine untouched land – and still they asked the question.

We see a lot of this kind of imaginative thinking in the context of sometimes self-imposed constraints – and it pushes innovation forward in remarkable ways. The craft beer movement has boomed as small place-based breweries using local ingredients have proved they can make far better beer than vast commercial breweries. 'What if we brewed beer using local wheat, mushrooms, wild herbs, wild yeasts from the air or leftover bread?'[13] The vegan food movement has shown that plant-based food can be colourful, delicious, healthy and satisfying – despite being constrained by no animal products. People and projects around the world have proved that resilient local economies lead to more inventiveness and creativity – and vice versa – than relying on global supply chains to take care of our communities.

This spirit of imagination that arises from bricolage can also be suffocated by policy bureaucracy that sets up false possibilities. For example, in attempts to map the pathway to a low-carbon future, the world's governments have put their faith in negative emission technologies (NETs), magic technologies that don't exist yet but which, if they did, would suck vast amounts of CO_2 back out of the atmosphere. Business-as-usual scenarios, such as those in the Paris Agreement, often assume a large role for NETs. But as Kevin Anderson and John Broderick point out, 'This endemic bias unreasonably lends support for the continued and long-term use of gas and oil whilst effectively closing down more challenging but essential debates over lifestyles, profound social economic change and deeper penetration of genuinely decarbonised energy supply.'[14] This kind of deception about our options creates an illusion of possibility that keeps real imagination at bay. We need to master the art, it seems to me, of asking questions which address the gravity of our situation yet which also create *longing*, which evoke a deep and rich sense of the wonders we can still create, rather than shutting it down or putting it into a deep sleep of complacency.

In our lives today, there are very few real what-if spaces. School and universities rarely offer them. What local and national governments offer as 'consultations' or as 'debates' tend to be very shallow. Spaces in our cities and towns where you can sit down with other people and explore new ideas are virtually non-existent. Ruth Ben-Tovim is skilled at creating such spaces. 'They need to be invitational,' she told me. 'They need to have lots of different ways in, different ways people can respond to the space. The role of the host(s) is really important too.'[15] Encounters Arts use the term 'the Art of Invitation', which Ben-Tovim describes as 'a craft and a practice'. Paying real attention to whom you want to be present and taking your invitation to them in creative and imaginative ways really helps.

London National Park City proposed a good question – 'What if London were a National Park'? – and created a well-held space. Daniel Raven-Ellison and his collaborators started with a question that was simple, but that also opened up possibilities and ideas. They put 'guerrilla signs' shaped like the outline of London in parks and along cycle paths, which read GREATER LONDON NATIONAL PARK* – *OFFICIALLY ONLY A NOTIONAL PARK, with the intention to 'unlock people's imaginations around how an urban area could become a national park'. They put posters in visible parts of the city, asking, WHAT IF WE MADE LONDON A NATIONAL PARK CITY? They crowdfunded to take out ads in the newspapers, and in 2016 held a event at the Southbank Centre called 'Let's Make London a National Park City', after which all the leading candidates for mayor of London announced that they would support the concept if elected.

One of the factors that really helped was the recognition that the declaration of London as a National Park City would need to be from the bottom up, something envisioned and enabled by millions of people. The question of 'What if your street, your ward, your borough, thought of itself as part of a National Park City connected to a much greater landscape?' was powerful and bold. Raven-Ellison told me that framing the campaign around this kind of question 'has been absolutely critical to getting our campaign to where we are now.'[16]

In April 2019, Raven-Ellison and the rest of the National Park City team took to Twitter to ask people to suggest 'What If' questions in relation to the initiative. Here is a selection:

> What if you could swim safely in all London's canals?
> What if all residential streets were play streets?
> What if every street had public art?
> What if birdsong drowned out traffic noise?
> What if there were more trees than people?
> What if a squirrel could get from one side of London to the other without touching the ground, by jumping from tree to tree?
> What if we had a vertical climbable commons?
> What if majestic red kites filled London's skies again?
> What if you could see the Milky Way from every garden?
> What if we rewilded all of London's golf courses?
> What if every park in London were connected to all its neighbouring parks by at least one green quiet way suitable for walking, cycling, and gardening too?

When you start looking, it turns out there are so many other examples of skilfully asked what-if questions – and moving stories of what happened once they'd been asked. Here are five. They are very different, but all arose from people coming together around a good what-if question, rebuilding how we think through the answer, and taking practical steps from there towards a more positive future.

———————

In 1974 the Derby Silk Mill opened as a museum of industrial history located on the site of Lombe's Mill, what may have been the world's first factory, in the Midlands region of England. One of three museums managed by Derby Museums, the Derby Silk Mill was housed in a striking building that still retains many of the original features from the silk mill first built in 1702, such as its central tower. It was home to a collection that reflected the city's industrial past, including large jet engines and historic trains. In 2011 the Derby Silk Mill closed, having rather lost its way. Derby City Council transferred the building into an independent trust, and hired Hannah Fox as the director of projects and programmes. All she had were the keys, a small budget and the invitation to 'have a play'.

That's a pretty limited set of ingredients to cook with, but cook she did, in the spirit of bricolage. What if, Fox asked, we used this as an opportunity to experiment, involve and enrich, co-creating something new with the various communities within our city?

Fox began by opening the doors to the public and putting on a weekend event called 'Shaping the Vision', with live bands, a massive Scalextric track and a huge blackboard with the question: WHAT COULD WE DO HERE? Over the following months, the residents of Derby were invited to imagine what could happen in the building, and then prototype it. Hundreds of community members took part as 'citizen curators and makers', testing ideas through programmes of events and activities. Over time, a collective vision emerged. The Derby Silk Mill's new life would be as a 'Museum of Making' – inspired by the Makers of the Past, made by the Makers of Today, and empowering the Makers of Tomorrow – with 'community participation at its heart'.

'We believe', Fox told me, 'that museums should shift their focus from being didactic educators to "co-creators".'[17] As Fox explained, the criterion for the success of their plans was that 'there isn't anything here that the architect can say 'that bit is my idea', rather they have just synthesised what the people of Derby said they wanted.'[18] Fox and the team built a workshop space on the ground floor of the museum with laser cutters and other equipment, working with volunteers and artists to create a 1,000 m² prototype museum. They brought in a workshop supervisor to prototype the cafe furniture, exhibition cases and displays, even the chairs. By the end of this experiment, they were able to conclude that this approach works, that they wanted to turn the Silk Mill into a Museum of Making, and that it should form the foundation of what filled the whole museum space.

Amazingly, as the community was developing its vision and beginning the work of turning it into reality, the University of Derby was conducting research in which they collected saliva samples and found a fall in levels of the stress hormone cortisol among participants as they took part in the activities.[19]

The community eventually secured the funding to bring its ambitious plans to full fruition – while still maintaining its commitment to co-production. Most conventional big redevelopment projects are just handed over to a big contractor who does everything. At the Derby Silk Mill, the community used a process called Integrated Project Insurance to bring in a team of professionals who were committed to giving the community as much of a role as possible and to working together in new ways.

The aim is that once the basic work has been completed on the building, participants will build a full 'co-production hub', and coordinate the entire fit-out of the building from there, designed and delivered by the community and volunteers, rather than building professionals. The community will design and make key aspects of the building's exhibitions and furnishings in the co-production hub based on some of the prototypes they are currently working on. Of course, all this takes careful planning, especially to ensure the health and safety of non-professionals, but that planning has now become an integral part of the vision.

While the building work is under way, Fox and her team are continuing to find new ways to explore what co-production means in practice. They are creating a Mobile Museum of Making (or the 'Makory' for short).

They host an annual Maker Faire. Anyone who is making anything, and who can demonstrate it in a way that people can get involved, is invited. 'They come from everywhere,' Fox told me.[20] The developing Midlands Maker Challenge will be a programme for young people from the area to design solutions to problems they are passionate about. The community is also involved in the creation of Make Works, a website that maps makers in the region, with a short video about each.[21]

The co-production approach impacted the city's other museums, Pickford's House and Museum and Art Gallery, too. In the museum and art gallery, every new exhibition or gallery now starts with a Project Lab, where the community is invited to help shape the vision. Andrea Hadley-Johnson, the former head of co-production display at Derby Museums, explained that culture shift feels irreversible: 'It would feel selfish and rude to go back,' she said. 'To say, "This is what we think people want," and, "Here go you, people, this is what we've done for you" . . . How can you possibly understand how people might move around a space without moving around that space with them? Everyone brings something different.'[22]

———————

In 2012 members of Transition City Norwich, in East Anglia, asked, 'What if our city could feed itself?'

Transition City Norwich members William Saltmarsh, Nick Hudson and Josiah Meldrum conducted research and concluded that, as Josiah told me, 'Norwich needed to re-create a kind of hinterland of horticultural production – market gardens, effectively, supplying the city's restaurants, shops, homes, cafes. It needed to re-engage with milling and cereal production. . . . It needed to reconnect with the arable land that would surround the horticultural land. And it would need to eat a lot less meat.'[23]

As some group members set about developing a CSA farm with 150 shareholders on the edge of the city, and buying and setting up a new mill in a building in the centre of the city, Josiah, Nick and William embarked on finding soil-building protein sources, which led them to beans, pulses and peas. When they spoke with area farmers, they learned that the peas and beans they had seen growing in local fields and had assumed were being grown for animal feed were in fact exported to Egypt, where they were highly prized, especially for a particular dish prepared for breaking the Ramadan fast, called Ful Medames. A quarter of a million tonnes of beans grown in the United Kingdom, in fact, are exported to North Africa and Middle East every year as food crops.

The three began cooking with these beans and found they were delicious, but that people had lost the habit of eating them, especially as meat became more popular and affordable. And so Hodmedod, whose name comes from the old East Anglian word for 'snail' and 'hedgehog' or anything curled up like a bean, was born. The friends designed a trial – 'the Great British Beans trial', they called it – to distribute the beans to community groups and local shops in order to assess whether there might be a market. 'We began buying half a tonne of split beans', Meldrum told me. 'We put them in little bags and we worked with a local artist to create a postage-paid postcard, with an illustration of beans and a recipe and we asked the people who received them what they thought.'

Hundreds of responses came back, and the response was overwhelmingly positive. How did Hodmedod turn beans no one had heard of into something desirable and appealing? People like talking about the food they're eating, Josiah believes, and to say, 'Look at these beans, and here's the story.' This enables people to share that story and to retell it to their friends, and is a powerful way to propagate an idea. The artwork was important, so was the surge of interest in veganism and sustainable food, not to mention the emerging trend of people taking photos of their dinners and posting them online. 'Our broader vision', Meldrum explained, 'is for a completely new approach to farming in the UK. . . . By demonstrating that there's a demand . . . we encourage farmers to make the shift to growing them.'[24]

The company is now developing UK production of quinoa, trialing beans and pulses in agroforestry systems, and currently sell a wide range of products, from baked beans to curries, made using British beans. In 2017, Hodmedod won a BBC Good Food Award, recognition of how the endeavour changed what people thought was possible and even influenced farmers in what to grow. Hodmedod shows what a good question can unlock, and the energy that it can contain. The friends have built a community (and a company) around their question and invited people to join them on that journey. They have used art and story to ensure the product is beautiful and engaging. And they have used it all to keep asking new questions, and to open up new possibilities.

———————

Housed in a former bank building in Walthamstow, London, the Bank Job is an act of 'citizen money creation' to raise awareness about debt and its corrosive effect on society. The project arose when artist Hilary Powell and filmmaker Dan Edelstyn asked: 'What if a community responded to its debt crisis with art and playfulness?'[25]

They created the Hoe Street Central Bank (HSCB) with the goal of printing and then selling £50,000 worth of their own currency in denominations of 1, 5, 10, 20 and 50. Instead of featuring the queen's face, the currency features local heroes – from the food bank, the homeless kitchen, the youth project and the primary school. That is, people who are supporting the people who are falling through the gaps created by austerity. The project raised the money, donating half of it equally divided among the four organisations whose heroes were featured on the bills. They used the other half to buy £1m of local payday lending debt on the secondary debt market. ('Zombie debt' can be purchased on the secondary debt market for a tiny percentage of the original amount, pennies on the pound.) This debt was symbolically 'detonated' on Hackney Marshes at an event called Big Bang 2 in May 2019. The Walthamstow Bank became a printing shop and a public education space hosting talks and debates about debt and money. Later, they printed 'bonds' in different denominations, which entitled people to attend the 'debtonation' and receive a commemorative coin from fragments of the explosion.

Cancelling debt is a concept gathering speed around the world. The Rolling Jubilee, an outgrowth of Occupy Wall Street, has raised $700,000 in donations, and used it to buy back, and cancel, more than $32m of debt, mostly medical and student loan debt, in what the Rolling Jubilee calls 'a bailout of the people by the people'.[26] John Oliver, host of HBO's *Last Week Tonight*, recently spent $60,000 to buy back $15m of medical debt and cancel it live on air.[27] While buying debt and cancelling it doesn't solve the problem, it is a powerful way of shining a light on the issue and raising awareness of the predatory nature of secondary debt companies, the kind of pressure they can put people under to repay it, and the kind of debt many people are forced to incur simply to meet their day-to-day needs.

When I visited the bank in the spring of 2018, I was taken with the space they created. It looked like a bank, but inside it was full of people wearing banker visors and printing money, whether screenprinting the background colours, block printing the black image and text, cutting out the notes or adding gold foiling. Half-printed notes were hung up around the bank on lines held in place with small clothes pegs, like washing hanging out to dry. Members of the public dropped by to see what was happening, often buying a note or two. The project embraces the analogue. Even though most of our transactions these days are not cash based, there is still something romantic about people printing banknotes. They were making tangible notes, real objects, and people could come in and watch them being made, or even get involved themselves.

Powell explained how important the hands-on element was. People would walk in and say 'this smell takes me back to my Dad's work in the print industry'. There was particular enthusiasm from graphic designers who came to help and lamented that 'they don't get to use their hands anymore'. There was something about the tangible, physical nature of printing actual bank notes that people seemed to love. As Hilary put it, 'people seemed starved of making.'[28] After Edelstyn and Powell invited students from the local primary school to come in and watch notes being printed, many of the children went home, 'locked themselves in their rooms and came out with a whole set of banknotes they'd made for poor people'. Ink, paper, money, dressing up as bankers, all have a far greater invitation to the imagination than a website about how awful debt is and why we should do something about it. Didn't we all play at running our own bank when we were small children? As David Sax puts it in *The Revenge of Analog*: 'Ultimately, analog pursuits connect us to one another in a vastly deeper way than any digital technology can. They allow bonds to form in real time and in physical spaces, which transcend language and our ability to communicate with just words and symbols.'[29]

When I visited in May 2018, I met a woman named Saira, whose family runs a kitchen that provides two meals a day, every day of the year, to people in need. She was helping out at the bank, adding gold foil to the notes featuring her face. 'When they first rang me to tell me I'd been chosen,' she said, 'I thought someone was winding me up and I put the phone down', she told me. 'It was only when my local councillor, who I really respect, rang me to confirm it that I believed it. For us, it's like Christmas.'

––––––––

In 2014 I visited Liège in Belgium to help support Liège en Transition, including a newly launched project called Ceinture Aliment-Terre Liégeoise (Liège Food Belt; CATL) to explore a coordinated relocalisation of the food system. Growing food within Liège, a former industrial city, would be tricky due to soil and water contamination, but the land surrounding the city was much more promising. A cooperative vineyard, Vin de Liège, had just raised €2m in shares, giving CATL the confidence to ask, 'What if, within one generation, the majority of the food grown in this city were to come from the land immediately surrounding it?'

I returned four years later, in March 2018, to find fourteen cooperatives operating under the CATL banner, including Les Petits Producteurs (two shops selling local fresh produce); Fungi up, a coop that grows mushrooms on coffee waste; Rayon 9, which uses bicycles to distribute goods around the city; Cycle en Terre, a seed-saving coop; Les Compagnons de la Terre, a farm; La Brasserie Coopérative Liègeoise, a cooperative brewery; Vin du Pays de Herve, a second vineyard in the model of Vin de Liège; ADM Bio, which processes vegetables from seven local farmers for kitchens collectives; HesbiCoop, a food cooperative; Marguerite Happy Cow, a fair trade milk project; and three distribution coops: Point Ferme, La Coopérative Ardente, and Le Temps des Cerises, which are forming, together with Les Petits Producteurs, a network of local food distribution. Running like a thread through it all is Le Val'Heureux, the region's local currency.

Christian Jonet has been a constant in CATL since the beginning, and now coordinates a network of coops, producers, researchers, institutions and associations. He told me that when Liège en Transition started, there were lots of working groups, but the ones that lasted were the money and the food groups. It became clear that they were not going to Transition the city with volunteers alone, and that they needed to change the scale and, as he put it, 'professionalise the movement'.[30] Belgium has lost a hundred thousand agricultural jobs since 1990. New thinking was clearly needed.

CATL started with an event in November 2013 and invited everyone in the city with an interest in food to consider how they might, within one generation, grow the majority of the city's food on the land immediately surrounding it. People identified elements of what needed to happen: access to land, finance, seeds, know-how, and so forth. What was most important, Jonet observed, was that CATL created a narrative, one that focused on mobilizing citizens to reimagine the food system, as well as on the changes we can make with our consumption choices, and on investing in order to make that happen. They also stressed the importance of people getting involved, volunteering, getting their hands dirty. 'It was a message that really resonated with people', he told me.[31]

It worked. Together with Vin de Liège, which by time of my return visit had raised €3m on its own, the fourteen coops have raised nearly €5m in local investment. 'CATL is based on the narrative of projecting the future and how it could be,' Jonet said, 'and also the fact that Vin de Liège had been a success gave the whole initiative a foundation of confidence.' Each new project inspires more confidence in the next one.

One of those projects is Les Petits Producteurs, a shop in the centre of the city open for just over a year. Its manager, Pascal Hennen, told me, 'Les Petits Producteurs is a cooperative of two hundred cooperators [members of the coop], around fifteen local farmers plus a few further afield, two shops, seven workers and lots of energy.' They had just five weeks to transform the unit into a shop, something achieved by mobilising friends wielding sledgehammers and paintbrushes. It's a very simple concept: a big space, painted white, with food displayed on pallets, and a note about each farmer and his or her story.

Les Petits Producteurs ran a financial forecast with a worst-case, middle and best-case scenario. The shop has already exceeded the best-case scenario; it is a challenge storing stock and managing queues. 'All positive problems', Hennen told me.

Les Petits Producteurs has a principle of not negotiating with the farmer on price, and of keeping costs low: spending the minimum on fitting the shop out, stocking only one kind of jam, one brewer of beer, and so on. The whole shop contains fewer than two hundred products. It is mostly organic, and prices are, on average, 15 percent lower than the Carrefour supermarkets. Being part of CATL helps. CATL builds a relationship among the different coops; they trade with each other and share resources. 'If we have twenty stores,' Hennen said, imagining what the future might hold, 'we will reach the point where the supermarkets will start to say "oh shit". We would love to fragilise [from the French word *fragiliser*, meaning 'to weaken'] them locally.'

Where it is starting to get even more interesting is the impact CATL is having on the city's government. While in Liège, I met with the city's mayor, Willy Demeyer, as well as councillor responsible for agriculture. It is clear something is shifting. Mayor Demeyer expressed how CATL is representative of how the city sees its future. Ten years ago, the city was on the track to become a 'smart city'. 'Now we want to be a Transition City,' he told me.

Jonet is delighted to see the local authorities stepping up. 'They can see what we are doing is good for society, can create jobs, build social links between people, and it is good for health and for the environment', he told me. 'In the future, new projects will be a combination of the forces of the public and citizen-led initiatives.' In the back office at Les Petits Producteurs, Hennen is quietly excited about the increasing involvement of the municipality. 'At the beginning, the municipality laughed, but now they think we are quite interesting. We are doing so well that the municipality will have to follow – I don't think they have a choice actually!'

As I was finishing writing this book, I checked in with Jonet for an update of what had happened in the ten months since my visit. Another seven coops were under development:

- Unis Verts Paysans is a local food shop in the city of Malmedy (Liège Province), based on Les Petits Producteurs' model.

- Invent-Terre and Vent de Terre are vegetable-growing coops.
- Terre d'Herbage is a coop of producers of milk and cheese from the Verviers area (Liège Province), setting up shared warehouse space, shared distribution and other shared facilities, resulting in a more efficient use of resources.
- Vervicoop is a citizen-run local food coop based on Brooklyn's Park Slope Food Coop model.
- Histoire d'un grain is a coop which grows cereals, mills them and bakes bread.
- Novacitis is a coop which invests in buildings it can then let to coop projects. Their first will provide office space as well as dedicated food production spaces.

Les Petits Producteurs has opened a third outlet, and plans to add one new one every year. The Creafarm made land available to Les Petits Producteurs so that two independent vegetable producers could get established and supply them with fresh produce. Les Petits Producteurs will fund the investment to get them started with tools and infrastructure, advise them on what to grow, offer them a fair price for their produce, and offer them work in the shop over the winter to make their livelihood more sustainable.

CATL also organises an annual festival called Nourrir Liège every March. Following a debate at the 2018 event, the municipality voted that food served in schools and kindergartens in the city should be locally sourced as much as possible and totally free from endocrine-disrupting chemicals. CATL now partners with the City of Liège to redesign the city's school lunches, including the proposed purchase of enough agri-cultural land to supply 3,500 meals a day, a new agricultural department within the municipality to train the growers that the model will need, and new processing facilities to wash, cut and prepare the food.

A good what-if question, at best, creates an unstoppable momentum. As Shana McDavis-Conway of the Centre for Story-based Strategy describes it, a good what-if question needs to assume that nothing is unmovable. 'What if we had majority women in Congress?' she asked. 'I would love that, that would be a great question. But it's pretty narrow.

What if women had full equal political power? That's a bigger question. . . . What if we all had equal access to safety and the ability to live the life we want, no matter what our gender was?' For McDavis-Conway, the skill of a good 'what if' question is to move further and further out in terms of ambition, taking people as far into the territory of 'I've never really thought about that' as possible.[32]

Cooperation Jackson (Mississippi) was launched on 1 May 2014 to advance economic democracy in the city by developing 'a solidarity economy' through a network of cooperatives and other worker-owned and democratically self-managed enterprises. The community began with a period of reflection followed by a whole bunch of questions: What if we could make the city fully sovereign by 2025? What if we could reorient the economy to work along cooperative lines? What if we could create a Human Rights Charter for Restorative Justice in the community? What if we had a broad participatory democracy? And then there was the biggest question of all: What if we could create a truly equitable Mississippi?

These questions became the basis of a document called the Jackson-Kush Plan, which lays out the organisation's vision and underpins much of what they do. As Kali Akuno, co-founder and director of Cooperation Jackson, told me, 'it's not like these questions ever stop.' He went on to tell me that for him, the risk of not asking 'what if' questions is you remain stuck in 'a static view of the world', a mindset of, as he put it, 'I'm going to play by the rules as they exist, and I'm going to try to deal with the terms and the alliances that presently are'. This can be very limiting, and prevents us from seeing possibilities and from seeing things differently.[33]

Inspired by the black liberation movement, Cooperation Jackson's aim is to make Jackson 'the most radical city on the planet', creating a solidarity-based, anti-capitalist and pro-feminist local economy. They have started a number of cooperatives, including Freedom Farms Cooperative; the Green Team Landscaping Coop; the Community Production coop, which does 3D printing; and Revolutionary Resonance, an arts and culture coop. Embedded in these projects is a change in Jackson's governance with the creation of People's Assemblies that allow the community to explore and discuss its needs, and Transition Assemblies, which are focused on particular themes and initiatives.

Akuno remarked on how the black liberation movements have managed to keep big what-if questions alive over time. For example, the prison abolitionist movement – with its audacious 'What if there were no prisons, and justice worked in a different way?' question – which has been sustained for decades in the face of an ever-growing prison-industrial complex. Akuno talked about how important it is to be grounded in history, like the prison abolition movement, which sees itself as a long-term project. This means keeping focused on the longer-term goal, rather than being sidetracked by minor reforms and policy changes, what he calls remaining 'consistently orientated towards the North Star'. As he puts it, 'ultimately we're trying to change relationships and hierarchy and exploitation [so] how do we stay focused on that?', adding that keeping that historical perspective means that you can draw inspiration, courage and grounding from people who in far worse conditions kept working towards freedom and change.

Although Cooperation Jackson is a grassroots movement, the election of Chokwe Antar Lumumba as mayor of Jackson, and of his father before him, means that there is a mayor in place supporting the process and helping to drive it forward – or at least trying to in the face of resistance at the state and national level. In a world where many feel there are fewer and fewer possibilities for change, and that the changes we need to make are just not going to happen, Jackson shows that bold questions can open up the fresh thinking, and thereby the new stories and the ambitious solutions, we so urgently need.

We still have a long way to go before anyone can claim to have perfected the art of asking all the right questions. But a lot of people and communities – and those I cover in this chapter are just a smattering – are leading the way and showing how powerful it can be. They show how the right questions can kick past that inner (and outer) critic who says nothing can really ever change, and how they can drive new thinking. The right questions balance imagination and action. As Mariame Kaba, a campaigner in the United States for prison abolition, puts it: 'We have to imagine while we build, always both.'[34]

As my writing of this book drew to a close, I received an email from Daniel Raven-Ellison of London National Park City. 'I'm more excited', he wrote, 'about the tipping point where enough people are asking "what if" that eventually the question converts to becoming "why not?" What if all the children in our school had the opportunity to play on a regular basis? Why not?! We need more people asking "what if?" and then "why not?"'[35]

CHAPTER 8

What If Our Leaders Prioritised the Cultivation of Imagination?

The inability to imagine a world in which things are different is evidence only of a poor imagination, not of the impossibility of change.

—RUTGER BREGMAN, *Utopia for Realists*

Most of the institutions shaping the world today are incapable of imagining anything other than their everlasting existence. And so things carry on, no matter how toxic, how ridiculous, or how contrary to values that most people share. The US military, for example, is unable to imagine anything other than its own global dominance, forever. As the author Robert Koehler puts it, 'They're capable of imagining nothing else. . . . There's nothing in this controlling consciousness devoted to creating – or imagining – a world without nuclear weapons or a world free of war and poverty. That's just not part of the future "America" has any interest in envisioning. The next war is utterly unquestioned. "Us vs. them" is utterly unquestioned. There will always be enemies. What would we do without them?'[1]

This chapter is therefore dedicated to perhaps the most audacious what-if questions of all: What if our leaders cared about harnessing the collective imagination to solve our greatest challenges, signalled a real commitment to it and demonstrated it in their own policymaking and political manoeuvrings? What if they understood that our survival depends on being able to focus our full attention and imagination on the challenges confronting us and upon our ability to reimagine most aspects of how society works? What if they valued imagination in policymaking, education, public life, planning, development, democracy and economics? What if they nurtured conditions and real, boots-on-the-ground public policy that enabled the imagination of all to flourish – knowing that unleashing the public imagination is our best route to solving the world's many problems? I know how absurd this sounds, given our current state of affairs. I told you it was audacious.

But let's go there anyway. What if? And why not? First, how would our models of democracy need to change? Second, how would we ever take on the imagination-devouring dragon of endless growth and economic development and replace it with something more humane, more interesting, and better suited to meet the needs of the people and the planet? Third, what could this commitment look like as a broad policy – a Ministry of Imagination, say, or a National Imagination Strategy – and how might such a thing work? But of course, we have to look first at why these questions feel so impossible in our current state of affairs. Why are governments, and seemingly most of the people who work within them, so bereft of imagination and creativity in a time that so demands both? It's a complex question, I recognise.

One cold October day in 2018, I sat in the lobby of a hotel in Plymouth with Molly Scott Cato, an old friend and now Member of the European Parliament (MEP) for my region of the United Kingdom. She had just given a presentation on the need to cut plastic use, and afterwards we sat to talk. I was interested to hear her sense of how her recent change to a life in politics had impacted her personally. 'I can feel my imagination being really crushed in the four years I've done this job,' she told me. 'I've stopped dreaming. My mind is utterly overloaded all the time, and that is the nature of public life now. It'd be really interesting to ask MPs if they still dream. The knowing part of your brain is completely fed and preoccupied all the time, and you really don't have space for the imaginative part of your brain. The volume of mental stuff simply overwhelms the imagination.'

She reflected on how it must be for people in greater positions of power. 'What if you're having to make a decision about whether to bomb Libya or not?' she mused. 'Would it be helpful to imagine yourself as the mother of a child that might get killed as a result, or would that make it harder to make that decision? If you were too connected to your emotions and to your imagination, it might make it too hard to function.'

I headed home from our meeting thinking about the implications that people with massive amounts of power over the lives and well-being of others are unable to dream.

Many people who end up in top positions of power are the product of private boarding school education, which separates children from their parents at an early age. What sort of impact does that have on a person's imagination? The psychologist Joy Schaverien, author of *Boarding School Syndrome*, argues that 'early boarding can cause profound developmental damage.' She notes in particular that because the institutions them-selves provide 'little time for reverie . . . the life of the imagination may therefore suffer.'[2] I spoke to the journalist George Monbiot, himself a boarder from the age of eight, about how a system that produces 'a repressed, traumatised elite unable to connect emotionally with others is a danger to society'.[3]

'The effort', Monbiot told me, 'was very much to throw a tight loop around our imaginations, and confine them to a particular social and cultural arena.' The result was that many of his fellow students appeared 'to have had their imaginations surgically excised. . . . You come out of that system really not understanding how the other ninety-three percent of people live and work and struggle. This is why you have people who have been through that system arguing there's no such thing as poverty in this country.'[4]

While I was writing this chapter, the UK government, probably the least imaginative political administration in history, delivered its 2018 autumn budget. This was three weeks after the IPCC issued its chilling report which argued for 'rapid, far-reaching and unprecedented changes in all aspects of society'.[5] The UK government's response – from its best and brightest? An extra £1bn on defence, £520m for filling in potholes on roads, and not even a mention of climate change. We need leaders who have enough vision to imagine where these kinds of decisions are taking us, and enough vision to imagine a very different kind of future that we could yet create. And if they can't do either of those things, they need to get out of the way and make room for the imagination sprouting up elsewhere. We live in a time where, in the words of social theorist Roberto Unger, we are governed by people who 'confuse conformism with realism'.[6]

While I was writing this book, my country has been enmeshed in the appalling contortions of Brexit, its withdrawal from the European Union. Brexit has been a disaster. Not because of the decision or its implications – I am not setting out in this book to express an opinion on that. The disaster was the process. The Brexit referendum took a highly complex issue, which most people didn't really understand, and reduced it to a binary Yes or No. It was prey to massive amounts of misinformation and political interference, 'dark money' which influenced the vote, leaving a legacy of families and neighbours who don't speak to one another, and a younger generation feeling betrayed by the older one. Did it have to be like that?

Neither campaign, Remain nor Leave, engaged the imagination in making their case. All we got were dry arguments about how much money we'd lose or save, and big red buses with fictitious numbers on how much the United Kingdom would be able to reinvest in its National Health Service if it left the EU painted on the side. No one argued for the brilliant creative flourishing that leaving the EU could bring about, a cultural renaissance, the chance to create vibrant local economies and opportunity for reconnection. Conversely, very few people argued that we should stay in the EU because being connected to Europe brings untold cultural delights, means we are working together for a common goal of unity, solidarity and peace and a flourishing of the arts. No, it was all about how many millions of pounds we might save, or are unnecessarily spending, and provoking a fear of immigrants.

The resultant decision was neither a carefully considered nor a wise collective response, and the divisions it created will endure for generations. And it meant that no one could think about anything else for years – squashing imaginative what-if questions about what kind of future we might actually *want* to embrace. But how might we have done it differently? How might we have had a national exploration of such a big and important question in such a way that our imaginations were invited, enhanced and treasured?

The answers can be found in a suite of techniques known as 'deliberative democracy'. In essence, deliberative democracy refers to decision-making approaches that give people the opportunity to deliberate, to digest and to contemplate, in a safe context, particular issues. Ed Cox of the RSA (the Royal Society for the encouragement of Arts, Manufactures and Commerce), whose aim is 'to enrich society through ideas and action', suggests three principles that underpin it:

- Debate should be informed and informative, enabling people to explore issues from a range of perspectives based on sound argument rather than personality.
- Participants should be willing to talk and listen with civility and respect.
- Participants should represent a range of backgrounds and perspectives across the general population.[7]

It covers a spectrum of approaches and tools, but central to them all is the making of considered judgements, spaces where people of different perspectives come together to deliberate in an informed and well-facilitated way. One of the people who has been exploring these approaches in practice is the Belgian writer David van Reybrouck, whose book *Against Elections: The Case for Democracy* puts forward a different model for how societies could address big decisions such as Brexit in a better way. He calls it 'sortition', where citizens are chosen at random, as for jury duty, to represent their peers.

Van Reybrouck asked me to imagine how different the world would have been had David Cameron been an imaginative and innovative prime minister, and instead of calling the Brexit referendum, had brought together a random sample of people from across the country, first across different constituencies, and then in a national conference, who could invite to their meetings one weekend a month any experts or politicians they decided, supported by great facilitators. A referendum, as he put it, reveals people's individual preferences, whereas sortition gets to 'the collective priorities of people that have come together and focused on the material'. 'That is quite a different thing', he told me.[8]

How does being part of such a process impact the people involved, and nurture their imaginations? 'It's the sheer energy and happiness of people who feel taken seriously. Who are seeing that people are confident in them, who are trusting them. I don't think creativity and imagination can be released in a community that is not trusted by its leaders,' van Reybrouck explained to me. What if Brexit had felt like that? What if Brexit had been seen as the opportunity to introduce and familiarise the population with new deliberative democracy tools and approaches?

One of the most successful manifestations of deliberative democracy is citizens' assemblies. The idea dates back to ancient Greece, but its more modern manifestation begins in British Columbia, where the province's government created a citizens' assembly in 2004 to review the province's electoral system and to recommend changes to it, committing to a province-wide referendum based on its recommendations. One hundred and sixty people were chosen at random, with the constraint that the body must include a man and a woman from each of the province's seventy-nine electoral districts and two citizens representing aboriginal communities.

Beginning in 2004, the Citizens' Assembly on Electoral Reform met periodically on weekends for eleven months, during which participants learned about the electoral system, discussed it, and took part in fifty hearings across the province, where they listened to concerns and perspectives on the electoral process from citizens and a range of constituency groups. From this process, the Citizens' Assembly drafted a series of recommendation, captured in a report called *Making Every Vote Count*. The recommendations were put to a referendum, which failed to pass by just 2.31 percent. (The bar for passing had been put very high, requiring a 60 percent majority to pass.) Reflecting on the process, its chair, Jack Blaney, wrote: 'The members of the Citizens' Assembly . . . demonstrated how extraordinary ordinary citizens are when given an important task, and the resources and independence to do it right.'[9]

The most established example of citizens' assemblies is probably in Ireland. In 2008 the economy collapsed, revealing the extent to which politics and big finance worked to support each other's interests, and prompting calls for political reform. In 2011 a pilot project, We the Citizens, ran a citizens' assembly on political reform as an academic exercise, but it proved that the model could be trusted, and that Irish people could work together to deliberate on issues. This gave the Irish government the confidence in 2012 to launch the Convention on the Constitution, based on many of the approaches trialled by We the Citizens, to explore different aspects of the constitution, such as voting age, the electoral system, same-sex marriage and blasphemy. Ninety-nine people took part, of whom thirty-three were politicians and sixty-six were selected from across the country, representing the country's demographics. The process included ten weekend meetings over the course of fourteen months and created a safe, well-facilitated space for conversation. One of its key recommendations that emerged was a referendum on marriage reform to include gay marriage. The referendum was held in May 2015 and carried by 62 percent of the vote, with only a fraction of toxic divisiveness the Brexit discourse generated.

In 2016 the newly elected government set up the Irish Citizens' Assembly to explore more key issues, such as the Eighth Amendment (on whether Ireland should legalise abortion), fixed term parliaments and how Ireland could become a world leader in action on climate change.[10] This assembly met twelve times between October 2016 and April 2018. In May 2018, a referendum to repeal the legislation outlawing abortion went to the people, passing by 66.4 percent. This time, the ninety-nine participants didn't include any politicians, who excused themselves because, as Clodagh Harris, head of the Department of Government & Politics at University College Cork, who played a role in each of these versions of citizens' assemblies told me, 'In some ways, this was the politicians trying to remove themselves from a very sticky and potentially divisive issue.'[11]

I asked Harris how she felt citizens' assemblies can engage and enable the imagination. The first way, she told me, was that the inclusion of testimony. In a number of cases – most notably marriage equality and the

Eighth Amendment, repealing the law to outlaw abortion – the assemblies invited individuals and constituency groups to share their personal experiences. 'Participants had people's experience of crisis pregnancy both from a pro-life and a pro-choice perspective. It brought in the lived experience of being a gay person and unable to marry, and being a gay person and being worried about your parents, your two mums who are not able to marry and how can you look after them in old age, et cetera.'

She also suggested that the imagination benefitted from being given time and space, from the creation of space that is accessible, respectful, and where ideas can be questioned and challenged. In terms of her recommendations for such processes, she argues that people really ought to be paid for their time ('They're actually working, it's not a jolly') and that assemblies are given enough time to not feel rushed. 'I suppose,' she told me, 'at least if something is over two weekends and you have this period of time and space between the two weekends, people have a chance to reflect, revise, come back with more ideas.'

This shift towards democracy that creates spaces for greater deliberation, greater democracy and engagement and greater imagination need not only happen at the national scale. In Barcelona, a remarkable experiment is taking place. I recently visited the city and met Felix Beltran, a municipal activist there. The 2008 crash hit Spain especially hard. A couple of years later the Arab Spring inspired young people to express their unhappiness about the level of government corruption and the lack of real democracy. In 2011, infuriated by the economic austerity that followed the 2008 crash and inspired by the Arab Spring, people occupied city squares across Spain in what became known as the 15M movement – jump-started during a march on 15 May under a banner proclaiming WE ARE NOT GOODS IN THE HANDS OF POLITICIANS AND BANKERS – and also known as the Indignados, from Stéphane Hessel's book *Indignez-vous!* (Time for Outrage).

We learned that in Spain, if you default on your mortgage, the bank repossesses your house, sells it, keeps the money, and you remain personally liable for the full debt. Policies were crushing people, and for many, 15M was their first experience of deep democracy, of participation, of change. The political party Podemos burst onto the scene during this tumultuous time, winning seats in the national and European parliament. The 15M experience and the renewed sense of democracy prompted many people and organisations to try and build alternatives from within and through bottom-up policymaking. 'We took to the streets, the social networks, we took the squares – but change was blocked from above, by institutions, so we decided to win back the city,' Beltran told me. The 2015 city elections in Barcelona provided the opportunity.[12]

The progressive parties – ICV-EU, Podemos, Procés Constituent (a Catalan social movement), Equo (the environmental party) – came together and ran under what they called a 'confluence', a coming together on a shared platform: Barcelona en Comu (Barcelona Together) with Ada Colau, a former anti-evictions activist, on the ticket for mayor. Barcelona en Comu began by crowdsourcing a Code of Ethics which, among other things, stated that public representatives would earn only €2,200 a month, significantly less than the current salary. They also crowdsourced their programme of policies, and announced a fresh and transparent approach to funding. As Barcelona en Comu said at the time, 'We need to change the way politics is done, and not simply implement progressive policies.'

Their policy objectives include rehabilitation of housing and sanctions against empty buildings; limiting the number of tourist apartments and hotel vacancies through a Development Plan for Tourist Accommodation; introducing energy-efficiency criteria for new construction; promoting urban agriculture and car-free urban public spaces (superblocks); supporting care and care services, such as the first municipal dentist service; introducing a tourist tax; incorporating social and environmental criteria in public procurement; re-municipalisation of water supply alongside the establishment of Barcelona Energía, a 100 percent public electricity retailer, sourcing from renewable energy; setting a minimum of 30 percent of new apartments as social housing by law; promoting gender perspective and a feminist approach into all the initiatives carried out by the city council (what they call 'the feminisation of politics'); strengthening local trade; promoting social entrepreneurship and cooperatives; introducing citizen audits of municipal budgets and debt; establishing salary limits; and supporting local initiatives such as social centres, consumer cooperatives, community gardens, time banks and social currencies.

On 15 May 2015, Barcelona en Comu won a majority in the city's elections and Ada Colau became the mayor. Beltran described the process to me:

> The most important thing was to win back the city for the citizens. It was this winning mentality from the very beginning, the determination to be transparent and to run the institutions in a different way than had been done in Spain for years. We always had this system where the two traditional parties were the ruling power for forty years. People realised they were not doing progressive policies anymore. This crisis of representation was why this confluence had so much support from the street – all different classes.[13]

Similar movements are popping up around the world. The creation of democratic structures within which the imagination can flourish is a vital part of how we move forward, and Barcelona is at the forefront. The energy and work are spreading and taking root in many other cities under the title of 'Fearless Cities'.[14]

Every step we take towards a democracy that is more genuinely inclusive, more bottom-up, more empowering of local communities, is a step closer to imaginative thinking, action and cascading possibilities. As citizens' assemblies prove, those spaces need resources and good facilitation, but as Barcelona and Jackson and countless other places show, it is possible to develop governance models in which citizens have a real say in both developing a vision and participating in its rollout and implementation. As the filmmaker Adam Curtis told *The Economist*, 'People are frightened of instability. But the job of a good politician is to give them a story that says "yes this is risky, but it's also thrilling and it might just lead to something extraordinary."'[15]

Of course, as well as reimagining democracy, a renewal of the imagination needs also be reflected in the economies of the places where we live. An extractive economy, where the majority of retailers and businesses exist to suck wealth out of the local economy and redirect it elsewhere, is sucking imagination out along with it – a community's sense of what it feels is possible, its sense of being in control of its own future. If your local economy has become Amazon fulfilment centres and box stores, it is much harder to imagine the future with hope and optimism than if you live somewhere with a vibrant, diverse, creative local economy with high levels of local ownership and investment.

As communities, we need to start being more precise about what we value. For example, I often think about the distinction between imagination, creativity and innovation and how crucial that distinction is in terms of our capacity to move towards a sane and livable future. They all seem like good things, right? And they all seem like pretty much the same thing, right? So why is it that when I typed 'innovation' into a search engine, it generated 2,730 million hits and 'imagination' just 541 million? And why does Google return more than 90 million hits for 'innovation consultants', but a mere 7 million for 'imagination consultants'? Jeffrey Baumgartner, author of *The Way of the Innovation Master*, searched Monster.com for skills employers were seeking on one day in New York: 960 job postings were searching for candidates who were 'innovative', 1,000 were searching for 'creative' but just 9 wanted 'imaginative'.[16]

Creativity takes imagination and gives it some kind of form, turning it into something tangible, but it also comes with some baggage. As Oli Mould, a researcher at the Royal Holloway University of London, writes in his 2018 book *Against Creativity*, 'The dominant narrative of creativity is one of creating more of the same. Contemporary capitalism has commandeered creativity to ensure its own growth and maintain the centralization and monetization of what it generates.'[17] (As Ursula Le Guin once wrote, 'In the market place, the word *creativity* has come to mean the generation of ideas applicable to practical strategies to make larger profits. This reduction has gone on so long that the word *creative* can hardly be degraded further. I don't use it any more, yielding it to capitalists and academics to abuse as they like. But they can't have *imagination*.'[18]) From this degradation, it is an easy step to innovation: turning imagination and creativity into products that can be marketed, patented, trademarked.

Think about pizza for a moment. With pizza, you have something that fundamentally works. The basic model is sound. Everyone understands what it is. There are lots of opportunities to innovate with pizza, with new toppings, different kinds of dough, different kinds of crust. But it's still pizza. There is no need to *reimagine* pizza, because it works. It is fit for purpose. But there are a lot of things about the world right now that don't work. They are not fit for purpose. Our modern consumer economy is one of them. It is pushing the living world around us to the brink of extinction. Innovation won't cut it. It needs reimagining. And it's here – not only in adding new toppings but creating a different meal entirely – that the power of innovation can't even begin to hold a candle to imagination.

How do we do this? Well, for starters, our towns and cities have a powerful tool at their disposal for re-igniting the communal imagination, which is how they choose to influence the way money flows through that place. As Judy Wicks, founder of BALLE (Business Alliance for Local Living Economies), which supports a growing network of entrepreneurs and local economy activists across the United States, notes, globalisation 'has stripped us of imagination because it's all about replication, it's all about spreading your brand around the world. In order to do that, you have to reach the common denominator, you have to routinise, make things the same. It's the opposite of imagination'.[19] Local economies, she told me, are by nature more imaginative as they are rooted in a far deeper sense of what that place actually needs.

At the moment, in the place you live, money pours in, whether from government funding, grants, pensions, salaries and so on, but most of it then pours straight out again. Everywhere that money is leaking out (or every hole in the 'leaky bucket', as New Economics Foundation put it) is a potential livelihood, job, new enterprise, a new possibility.[20] Its potential to *stay* and to make things happen is intimately connected to the imagination of that place. We saw in the previous chapter how communities are using local economies to mobilise themselves and to reimagine and rebuild their economy in such a way that the future feels far richer with imagination and with hope. What might this look like if such an approach were initiated and led by the local government?

The City of Preston in Lancashire (population 140,000) offers some insight into how a shift in thinking and policymaking can unlock a city's imagination, with its 'guerrilla localism' and what people are now referring to as 'the Preston Model'.[21] Preston had been heading down the route of the kind of unimaginative development that can be found in cities the world over. One idea had been to redevelop the city's centre as the Tithebarn Shopping Centre, with a cinema multiplex and big stores. Then in 2011, large retailer John Lewis pulled out and the project collapsed. Cllr Matthew Brown was asked by the leader of the city council for initiatives that would boost the local economy, something he had long been interested in, seeking out examples from around the world. In 2013, he brought together the city's seven largest spenders of public money, including the police department, two universities, the city council, and the largest public housing provider. He commissioned the Manchester-based Centre for Local Economic Strategies (CLES) to examine where all the public money went that these 'anchor institutions' were spending.

CLES's findings knocked everybody sideways. They found that of the £750m spent every year, only 5 percent stayed in Preston, and only 39 percent stayed in Lancashire. In other words, £458m a year was leaking out of the county, and this was thanks to organisations that were supposed to be operating in Preston's best interests. The city council found that only 14 percent of its procurement spending was going back into Preston. (The national average is an already-pitiful 31 percent.)[22] With this information, suddenly there was an opportunity to talk about how to plug those leaks.

The community began exploring possible models that would harness the spending power of those seven 'anchor institutions' and rethink where the money flowed. The question was, as Cllr Brown relayed: 'What if we had a much more democratic economy and we had forms of economic activity, production and ownership that were a lot more rooted in the hands of the public and the community?' Brown was inspired by the cooperatives of Mondragon and the Evergreen Coops of Cleveland, Ohio, whose work of rethinking the role of anchor institutions and creating new coops to supply the local hospital's laundry, food and energy had

had a deep impact on him. 'Let's have a bit of imagination about how to get out of this mess,' he told me.[23]

By 2018 the City of Preston harnessed its imagination to get out of the mess so successfully that it was making the national headlines. A report by PricewaterhouseCoopers declared that Preston was the United Kingdom's 'most improved city'.[24] Seventy-five million pounds was now redirected to Preston-based suppliers, and £200m more was now staying in Preston. Because of the changes Brown and his colleagues have made, he told me, 'there's a lot more money around. You can see the confidence in the city because there's an extra twelve thousand employees in Preston'. Seventy-two thousand people now work in Preston. Three years ago, sixty thousand people worked there. But how did they do it?

For starters, the city government reimagined procurement. For example, rather than issuing one big tender for, say, the construction of a new public building, they began breaking the tender into many smaller ones so local firms could apply for them. There are plans to bring £5.5bn of the Lancashire Pension Fund, currently mostly overseas, back to Preston to invest in new buildings in the city centre. The city council opened a new covered market. New coops are emerging, including one that sources food from farmers within ten miles. The university embraced the idea of 'progressive procurement', now seeing itself as a 'civic anchor institution', a key social and economic actor within the community, capable of and responsible for nurturing the city's economy and cultural well-being. When the city's largest housing association needs to do maintenance on the estate, rather than outsourcing all the work to one company, it 'insources' – commissioning the many builders, electricians and other skilled tradespeople already living there. Preston is also working to create a community bank. 'I want to see a culture, both economically and politically, where people are encouraged to come forward with new ideas and they're listened to,' Cllr Brown remarked.

The story of Preston brings to mind an idea that could play a big role in fostering an 'economics of imagination'. A lot of ink has been spilled in recent years about Universal Basic Income. It's an excellent idea in many ways, and would help create conditions for both personal and collective imagination to thrive, in particular with a reduction of anxiety and stress.

But income is only one aspect of what enables us to feel secure. Universal Basic Assets (UBA) takes it further. As Marina Gorbis at the Institute for the Future defined it, UBA is 'a core, basic set of resources that every person is entitled to, from housing and healthcare to education and financial security'. She argues that the four countries that are at the top in global social mobility rankings are Denmark, Norway, Finland and Canada, each of which has 'a high level of access to public resources, like education, healthcare and transportation'.[25]

What if access to affordable housing were a Universal Basic Asset? What if we combined that with the guerrilla localism evolving in Preston, Jackson, Barcelona and elsewhere? What if housing could be built in a way that would maximise the economic opportunities already present in a community, enable money to stay there and make as much happen as possible? What if the housing were built by local companies, or by newly formed cooperatives, using locally processed materials, powered with community-owned renewable energy and held in community ownership so that it generated an ongoing income stream to make other things possible?

What if schools could procure food, energy, materials, services and building materials and labour to create the maximum economic benefit? The money the government invests to ensure that every child has access to a free, excellent and imaginative education would achieve so much more and enable so much more to happen, in such a diversity of ways. For example, in April 2019, I visited Mouans-Sartoux, a French town where all of the food served in all the schools, primary and secondary, is organic, and 70 percent of it is locally grown.[26] The municipality purchased a 7-hectare site on the edge of town to grow that 70 percent. The garden they created features polytunnels, orchards, and is buzzing with biodiversity. Sixty percent of school families now buy some organic produce, and 13 percent buy all organic. The boost to the local economy has also been significant.

As Cllr Brown put it, 'The game's up for the old system. We'd better start moving towards the new one bit by bit, beginning with the grass-roots and beginning locally. . . . We're at the early stage of something quite significant.'[27]

If you worked in government, and you were elected on a platform of bringing about unprecedented new thinking – truly imaginative thinking – where would you start? How would you build on ideas already in motion around the world? Imagine if your local or national government had a Ministry of Imagination. I appreciate that this might sound like something out of a Harry Potter book. But let's say it was a ministry whose role was to be the driver for the imagination within that administration. It would be a cross-cutting department, with a focus on how to bring imagination into all aspects and functions of government work. It would evaluate policy proposals from elsewhere in the government through a lens of whether they make the country more imaginative, or less. (So any policies likely to increase anxiety, stress and loneliness would not be permitted, for example.) It would train other departments to become more imaginative, more flexible, more playful. Its brief would be to reimagine everything.

When I thought of it, I figured that the idea of a Ministry of Imagination was pure conjecture, but it turns out there already is one, just by a different name: the Laboratorio para la Cuidad (Laboratory for the City) in Mexico City (population 8.9m). I had the opportunity to interview Gabriella Gómez-Mont, an artist and community curator with a long interest in thinking about the future, who founded what is, in effect, a Ministry of Imagination.[28] Gómez-Mont's background is in arts and culture, having worked as a journalist, documentary filmmaker, visual artist and experimental curator. The idea initially emerged in a workshop she attended at the Institute for the Future, a Palo Alto think tank. Her group came up with the idea of 'An Office for the Public Imagination': 'The idea of the impossible is where we start. We will imagine the impossible school. The impossible economy. The impossible family. The impossible treaty. The impossible planet. Our collective work is to make all of this impossible possible. To make the utopian practical. To build paths forward to reach the hoped-for world that we have together imagined.'

In 2013, she was asked by Miguel Angel Mancera, the newly elected mayor of Mexico City, to design, from scratch, a new kind of city department, one that would reinvent how government collaborates with citizens, and new models of participation and governance, and to ask: 'How do you democratise imagination and possibility?' Gómez-Mont drew together a team of eighteen people with an average age of twenty-nine, which also happens to be the average age of residents living in Mexico City. They came from a rich mixture of disciplines. Half the Laboratorio para la Cuidad team was made up of people you might expect in a government department: urban geographers, data analysts, political scientists, social scientists and engineers; the other half was made up of people from the arts, culture and humanities – such as artists, designers, filmmakers, architects, social innovation experts, activists and philosophers.

Once established, the team made a collective mental leap away from thinking of the city as a machine or a factory to seeing the city as a 'heterotopia', a multilayered patchwork of innovation occurring at all scales, from neighbourhood democracy initiatives to urban food production to entrepreneurial and community-based innovation of every stripe. 'We have an amazing history of communal practices,' Gómez-Mont told me. 'Everything from agriculture to economic coops to indigenous ways of doing governance and democracy. But we have not analysed them deeply enough, because in terms of imagination, unfortunately, we've been chasing dreams – a notion of progress of the first world – instead of looking our social composition in the eye and being able to build on that.' Once again, it's that idea that when we look squarely at the limitations our times impose, our imagination is far more engaged than when we attempt to cling to business as usual.

Rather than impose models from the top, the Laboratorio para la Cuidad seeks to understand the city and to base solutions on what's already happening. They do a lot of very deep research in order to understand this. Their 'Imagine Your City' survey tried to reach into the hopes and fears of those in the city. It asked:

Which three words come to mind when you think about
    Mexico City?
Which three things do you value the most?
How do you imagine the future of the city?

What does the government need to do to achieve your vision
of the city, and what do *you* need to do?

Thirty-one thousand answers came back, from a representative demo-
graphic cross section. Most of the respondents' visions of the future, it
turned out, were dystopian: 'We're all going to die . . .' in various unpleas-
ant ways, whether famine, water shortage or violent conflagration.

'So many times we think about democracy in terms of sustenance, if
you will,' Gómez-Mont told me, 'of access to water, access to food, access
to jobs. But what happens with access to possible futures?' Given the rich
creativity and experimentation happening across the city, her department started to think in terms of how differently the city administration,
and its citizens, might behave if they knew those stories. They might, for
example, reimagine participatory budgeting as a form of social research
and development.

Gómez-Mont's team are exploring how to create what she calls 'a
mega urban lab'. Although she says her department is 'definitely seen
as the weird department' by the rest of the administration, she also says
their work is having an impact and is respected. 'Imagination is not a
luxury,' she says (five words we should emblazon on T-shirts). 'We should
not only be thinking about building cities for the human body, but also
for the human imagination. . . . The more we distribute the capacity to
imagine different futures, the better off we will be.'

Mexico City is not the only place to recognise that putting imagination at the heart of a city's civic life is vital to its future. Bologna, Italy
(population 389,000) has long been a centre for progressive politics
and cooperatives. It sits at the heart of the Emilia-Romagna region,
where something akin to the approach to economic development being
modelled in Preston has long been the norm. Two out of every three
inhabitants are members of at least one cooperative, and 30 percent of
the region's GDP is generated by co-ops.[29] It is also the first region in
Italy to pass a law promoting the circular economy, the first to have a
proper strategy for a transition to a low-carbon economy, and it is home
to the first CSA scheme in the country. But when the economic crash hit
in 2008, it became clear that public participation and trust in institutions

had declined, and that the city's institutions had become overly bureau-cratic, to the point of stifling citizen-led action. As Bologna's Mayor Virginio Merola put it: 'It was all born from a bench, because a citizen asked for permission to repaint a bench. We realized that in order to give permission to repaint the bench, we had to go through five different sectors of the municipal machinery – five different authorizations. We began to understand that something was not working.'[30]

In 2014 the city council passed their new 'regulation on public collab-oration between citizens and the city for care and regeneration of urban commons' legislation. This set about creating a new infrastructure which made the council more responsive to citizens and invited and enabled them to take the initiative on shaping policy on new projects in their neighbourhoods, and on shaping the future of the city. It reimagined the city as comprising six districts, each with its own council and president, along with an Urban Innovation Foundation, to support community initiatives, and – my favourite – a Civic Imagination Office (CIO).

In 2016, 'civic imagination' was added to the 'culture, heritage, sport and tourism' remit of Deputy Mayor Matteo Lepore. As a report by Cities of Service notes, 'Lepore believed that the city government needed to reimagine policies and tools so that Bologna's citizens would feel a shared responsibility in taking care of public space and using resources sustainably.' The CIO oversees six 'laboratories', one in each of the city's districts, which act as permanent community hubs for collaboration and innovation. Their staff team brings together people from a wide range of backgrounds and, in collaboration with the Governance Unit at the City of Bologna and the sociology department at the University of Bologna, acts as a 'bridge' between the city and the citizens, to create 'pacts' and to oversee participatory budgeting. Pacts are projects that are proposed by the community that the CIO then help develop, assess the feasibility of, see how they fit with other developments planned, then partner and, sometimes, fund. By October 2018, 480 pacts had been implemented, from community gardens to tool libraries, from murals to repurposing empty buildings as community centres.[31]

A process of participatory budgeting determines a select few proj-ects that will receive city funding. In 2018, fourteen thousand people considered 174 project proposals of which 6 were funded, 1 in each district, sharing €1m of city funding. Unlike national elections, where only citizens can vote, thereby excluding the 15 percent of the population who are migrants, anyone over sixteen can take part. CIO also uses different workshops and Open Space Technology to create safe spaces and well-facilitated opportunities for people to imagine and develop new ideas and projects.

This works in Bologna, in part, because there has been a shift in the city council. The council staff trust the CIO, the Urban Innovation Foundation and the other bodies they have established, including an Active Citizenship Office, to connect to the communities, to provide the best support possible and to feed back what they find. As the CIO's director, Michele d'Alena, puts it, their approach means, 'We can listen to the soul of the neighbourhood, our office is on the ground.'[32] And those working for CIO take this very seriously. As Teresa Carlone, a community manager at the Urban Innovation Forum, put it, 'Everything they [the community] organise, we try to attend. . . . The majority of people in the district have my home number.'[33]

Why did they choose imagination as the concept to underpin their work? D'Alena told me how initially he was skeptical about using the word because he thought they needed a more 'practical' one. However, he has subsequently come to appreciate how effective focusing on imagination has been, having observed that 'imagine' was one of the most-used words in the many assemblies that they have run. 'The people want to imagine new ways to solve problems. "Imagine" is a very simple word. Everybody understands what it is. It is a clever way to speak about how to solve problems in a new way,' he told me.[34]

The city council also run an annual competitive programme for start-ups called 'Incredibol!' This supports new enterprises and uses the programme to allocate unused spaces in the city. For example, Dynamo is a bicycle rental and repair coop which also acts as a hub for, among other things, distributing local organic produce. Orchestra Senzaspine won Incredibol! in 2014 for its classical music programming for young people, and was then offered Mercato San Donato, an empty covered market, as their new home. The CIO and its network of District

Laboratories is a replicable model for any city government, and Bologna models what can happen when communities combine new approaches to democracy and grassroots decision-making with a localised approach to economic development.

In Mexico City and Bologna we've seen imagination reignited at the municipal level, but what about nationally? While the work under way in Mexico City and Bologna is visionary and bold, I'm doubtful that, say, the UK government would ever create a Ministry of Imagination, that it would be enough to face down our challenges, or that it would even be able to run in any manner resembling a functional one. Under our current administration, the idea seems ludicrous. Absent a seismic shift in politics, it is hard to imagine an administration where such an idea would even be taken seriously. And even if it were, the attempt to rebuild a national imagination would always be elbowed out of the way by an obsession with achieving economic growth, in the same way that governments who are, on paper, committed to sustainability and climate change mitigation override those values anytime new roads, airports or energy extraction are deemed 'good for the economy'.

Of course, you cannot legislate people into being imaginative. Nothing would shut down the imagination faster than politicians telling us to be more imaginative! But we do know that in order for the imagination to flourish, a person needs to feel safe, relaxed, connected to other people, be nourished with good food, surrounded by hopeful narratives of the future, invited into what-if spaces, exposed to art in all its forms, not feel under surveillance or time pressured, in as equal a society as possible, able to make meaningful contributions and exposed to nature as often as possible in their daily lives. Any National Imagination Strategy would need to start, therefore, by creating conditions that would nurture those things. It would establish a 'Right to Imagine'. There are things we can do to assist with this. People need safe spaces, well-facilitated meetings, opportunities to learn from others; this is no less true for civil servants, managers and staff in every organisation throughout the community than it is for individuals and community organisations. In the words of Ruth Ben-Tovim, we need to be 'bringing in the socially engaged creative practitioners who know how to work with communities.'[35]

The best model for a National Imagination Strategy I've yet come across is the Welsh government's Well-Being of Future Generations (Wales) Act 2015. In 1999, the Welsh Assembly government signalled a commitment to promote sustainable development. A decade later they published a report called *One Wales, One Planet*, which set out their vision for a sustainable Wales, only for a 2010 review by the National Audit Office and the World Wildlife Fund to determine that policy-making had made very little actual difference, focusing more on 'promoting' rather than 'delivering' sustainability. This debacle led to a big rethink that resulted in the 2015 Well-Being of Future Generations Act, including all public bodies from local government to the NHS, and from the National Museum to the National Park Authority. Its aim is to 'improv[e] the social, economic, environmental and cultural well-being of Wales' and each public body must carry out sustainable development, and 'must set and publish objectives and take all reasonable steps to meet them'.

Although one of the goals of the Well-Being of Future Generations Act is 'a prosperous Wales', it defines 'prosperous' as 'an innovative, productive and low carbon society which recognises the limits of the global environment and therefore uses resources efficiently and proportionately (including acting on climate change)'. Note there is no mention of economic growth. The aims of the economy are redefined to describe 'a nation in which, when doing anything to improve the economic, social, environmental and cultural well-being of Wales, takes account of whether doing such a thing may make a positive contribution to global well-being.'[36]

I spoke to Jane Davidson, former Welsh minister for environment, sustainability and housing, who is seen as the architect of the act. 'If you create legislation that is punitive,' she told me, 'it won't engage people's imaginations. Encouraging the imagination takes an enormous amount of bravery. It has to be a long-term commitment, and it has to have political support.'[37] The act, as she told me, 'gives permission to think differently'. Indeed that is its ambition. But how can it be enforced?

Firstly, it puts the onus on each public organisation to imagine its response, rather than explicitly setting out what each must do. That said, there are some things each body has to do: each must prepare a well-being statement, setting out what they're going to do; must report each year on their progress; and must respond to the future generations commissioner for Wales when asked. While Wales' pioneering One Planet Development legislation, which allows low-impact developments in the countryside provided they are zero carbon, have a low ecological footprint, use 100 percent renewable energy, increase biodiversity and (among other things) can generate 65 percent of their income from the site was already in place, the Well-Being of Future Generations Act gave it teeth. Now in any planning appeals relating to One Planet Development applications, the act can be used to tip the balance in their favour.[38]

That said, the degree to which the act has real teeth will come through case law. In June 2019, a proposed motorway relief road between Cardiff and Newport was overturned by Welsh First Minister Mark Drakeford on grounds of cost but also giving 'very significant weight' to environmental concerns. Future Generations Commissioner Sophie Howe, who had argued that the road 'did not reflect or support the ambitions' of the Wellbeing of Future Generations Act, welcomed the decision, stating her hope that 'this marks a shift in policy for Wales and the Welsh government'.[39] This is huge. From here, it is not a huge leap to imagine either a similar act, structured in the same way but focusing on imagination, or even adding the need to rebuild the national imagination to this particular act, thereby compelling every public body to set out what it will do to maximise the imaginative powers of everyone it works and interacts with. Framed in this way, a National Imagination Act would allow legal challenges to policymakers who, for example, try to purge the arts out of education, close down libraries, cut funding for the arts, or even impose austerity with all its knock-on implications for the imagination. Now, *that* would be a powerful bit of policymaking.

That's where I'd start, with a National Imagination Act, modelled on the Welsh one, framed in the context of a climate emergency, rapid social fragmentation and a biodiversity crisis. Rather than telling each public organisation how to be more imaginative, it would invite them, with help from skilled facilitators and inspiring examples, to create their own strategies. Such a legislative act would be a key step in the right direction and would appeal, I imagine, to people across the political spectrum. Its potential brings to mind the words of the philosopher Maxine Greene: 'It may be the recovery of imagination that lessens the social paralysis we see around us and restores the sense that something can be done in the name of what is decent and humane.'[40]

CHAPTER 9

What If All of This Came to Pass?

People talked. They communicated: the television and the radio were switched off, and any location became a place for dialogue and discourse. People changed. Ideas and inspirations with the potency to last a lifetime and to change it forevermore, were everywhere.

—JOHAN KUGELBERG (speaking of Paris in May 1968), 'A Jumble of Realia'

On the morning of 4 May 2006, people in London awoke to the news that a strange object had crashed into the street in Waterloo Place. Those who went to see what had happened were greeted by the sight of a twenty-feet-high 'rocket', a barrel-shaped object made from wood and banded with metal, its pointed end embedded into the tarmac, which had buckled up under the impact. It looked like something from a Jules Verne novel. There was steam issuing from it, a police cordon keeping people away, and no sense of what this object, which looked as though it had crash-landed from space during the night, was. The crowds grew, and the news spread.

The next morning, an enormous elephant, with a sultan and his retinue on its back, arrived at the rocket. A small mobile crane then arrived, removed the top of the rocket, and out came a huge child, a girl, eight metres tall, wearing flying goggles and blinking at the world she had arrived into. The girl then toured around London on an open-topped bus while the elephant walked around St James's, meeting the crowds and spraying them with water. The girl slept in front of Buckingham Palace in a huge deckchair, then had a shower and got dressed.

On Saturday, the elephant walked to Trafalgar Square, picked up the girl and carried her on his trunk to Grand Parade. 'The girl from the sultan's dreams' was so lifelike that people quickly forgot about the teams of footmen in red livery who were operating her. 'She's everyone's daughter,' one bystander said.[1] People were entranced. Children queued up to swing on her arm while she smiled at them. Sometimes she would lift up children and gaze into their eyes. On Sunday, the girl and the elephant walked back through huge crowds to where her rocket awaited. She climbed in, the rocket closed, and the elephant bid her farewell. Smoke and flames burst forth from the underside, and then the rocket opened once again. The girl had vanished.

The spectacle, it turned out, was the work of Royal de Luxe, a French street theatre company, and Artichoke, a UK public art and events team that defines 'event' in a whole new way. It was called *La visite du sultan des Indes sur son éléphant à voyager dans le temps* (A Visit from the Sultan of the Indies on His Time-Travelling Elephant). David Lammy MP, then the minister for culture, praised the project for 'reminding us that we can have street theatre. That we can smile. That we can believe in magic. That we can believe in wonder.'[2] Lyn Gardner, writing about the event in the *Guardian*, talked about how it brought 'joy and wonder to a million people . . . those who saw it will never forget it.'[3]

It was an event which, as Artichoke's director, Helen Marriage, described to me, was 'something so unlikely and unusual that people would remember it forever . . . this amazing thing happened and it was such an invitation, a universal invitation to people to just come and be delighted, that people forgot their inhibitions and regained that old sparkle in their eyes and in their voices as they all realised that together they could enjoy this amazing art work.' This was, it's worth noting, just nine months after the 7/7 bombings in London.[4]

The event was no small feat. It required closing off sections of the city to traffic, which itself required seven years of negotiations and preparations with organisations not renowned for their creativity or flexibility but, as Marriage put it, were terribly proud once it was actually happening. 'They still say it is the best thing they've ever done.

'We took everybody on a journey that said the arts, too, have their place in the life of a city', she continued, 'and that the city doesn't just have to be about shopping and traffic, that it's as important for people collectively to share these moments, moments like this, as it is for them to share or to experience moments in their own life. You know, when you fall in love or when their baby takes its first step. Moments are what you remember.'

Why do I start this final chapter with *The Sultan's Elephant*? Because awe is an undervalued emotion. The root of the word is in Old English and Norse and refers to the sense of fear and dread we feel in the face of a divine being. Until the mid-1700s, it was reserved for religious experiences. Then Irish philosopher Edmund Burke used the word to describe vast, powerful things we don't understand – it could just as easily be nature, looking at the stars or being moved by a piece of fiction or music. In 2015, Paul Piff and his colleagues at the University of California wrote that central to experiences of awe are 'perceptions of vastness that dramatically expand the observer's usual frame of reference in some dimension or domain'.[5]

When people experience awe – being immersed in the raw power of nature, gazing up at a feat of architecture such as Chartres Cathedral, witnessing a selfless act of heroism or bravery, seeing a musical, artistic or athletic virtuoso, being present for an era-defining political shift, standing in the crowd while a charismatic leader delivers a momentous address, or simply watching the light through autumn leaves – two key features define it: The first is a sense of vastness – whether vastness of space, time, beauty, understanding or connection – that makes us feel smaller and experience a dissolution of the self. The other is the need to adjust our understanding of the world, in order to accommodate the experience, or at least try to.

'Brief experiences of awe redefine the self in terms of the collective and orient our actions toward the interests of others,' writes Dacher Keltner, a professor of psychology at University of California. Research shows that experiencing awe can shift people from self-interest to collective interests, can bring about boosts in generosity, ethical behaviour, altruism and compassion, can improve our health and can stimulate wonder and curiosity.[6]

In one study, Paul Piff and his colleagues took two groups of students outdoors and invited each to spend one minute looking up. The first group stared up into a stand of two-hundred-foot Tasmanian eucalyptus trees on the campus of the University of California, Berkeley, the tallest stand of hardwood trees in North America. The other half stared up at a building. Both groups of students were then asked to fill out a questionnaire. While they were doing that, a researcher 'accidentally' dropped a bunch of pens on the floor. The students who stared up at the two-hundred-foot Tasmanian eucalyptus trees picked up more pens to help the researcher.[7]

Keltner argues that given the degree to which awe triggers people thinking more collectively, more compassionately and more pro-socially, we should 'build everyday awe', as much as possible. At the moment, researcher Amie Gordon estimates that on average we experience awe once every three days.[8] But like imagination, awe is struggling to find space in our lives today. Keltner writes that we live in

a time when, arguably, our culture is becoming more awe-deprived . . . so often our gaze is fixed on our smartphones rather than noticing the wonders and beauty of the natural world or witnessing acts of kindness, which also inspire awe . . . arts and music programs in schools are being dismantled; time spent outdoors and for unstructured exploration are being sacrificed for résumé-building activities. At the same time, our culture has become more individualistic, more narcissistic, more materialistic, and less connected to others.[9]

Paul Piff, speaking at a conference in 2016 called 'The Art and Science of Awe', said, 'As we work to reverse these long-term socio-economic and socio-political trends to foster more connections to others, stronger communities, more pro-sociality and more kindness, in the short term it would make more sense to foster more experiences of awe, for ourselves and for others. It might, at least, serve as a shortcut to the kinds of psychological shifts that we're hoping to bring about.'[10]

What would it look like if rather than protesting about the things that are wrong, dysfunctional and broken, we set out to give ourselves what futurist Stuart Candy calls 'visceral tastes' of the future, experiences of a positive, delightful future, that transform our sense of what's possible the way *The Sultan's Elephant* did? As the anthropologist and anarchist David Graeber writes, 'It is one thing to say 'Another World Is Possible.' It's another thing to experience it, however momentarily.'[11]

If we can mobilise ten thousand, twenty thousand, a hundred thousand people for a demonstration, what else could we do with even a fraction of that number? *The Sultan's Elephant* started with an overnight transformation, with Waterloo Place, a place people knew as one thing, suddenly, without warning, transformed into a source of intrigue, fascination, delight, suspense and story. We've all seen the documentaries showing the setup before a big garden show like Chelsea, where one day there is an empty space, and then after a team's concerted bout of working overnight under lights, suddenly the event space is a lush garden.

What if we could mobilise hundreds of people to transform a place into a physical manifestation of their idea of a future? If people woke up to find their local train station or local museum transformed into a renewable energy power station, an orchard, an edible food garden, a pop-up for local entrepreneurs, a play space, a welcome centre for refugees, a local art gallery, a brewery? It could be there for a day or two, and then, overnight, vanish again. Or perhaps people would love it so much that it would become permanent. Perhaps it would seek permission first. Perhaps it wouldn't.

Like the Tooting Twirl, or our cardboard box Transition Town Anywhere, once people have lived in it, experienced it, drunk coffee in it, met new people in it, they are forever changed, their expectations of that place are forever changed, their sense of what the future could be is forever changed. By day, it could feature actors acting out future scenarios, debates, public exploration of important questions, storytelling, performance and conversation. Newspapers could be distributed from that time in the future, telling the stories of what's happening. By night it could be lit like an enchanted urban forest, a cinema, a silent disco, a place to meet strangers, to talk.

Is this even possible? Can we really mobilise people to transform spaces in that way? Meet Jason Roberts. Roberts is from Dallas, Texas, and in 2010 he founded Better Block, a nonprofit that 'educates, equips, and empowers communities and their leaders to reshape and reactivate built environments to promote the growth of healthy and vibrant neighborhoods'.[12] Roberts's story starts when he and his partner visited European cities, seeing squares with public fountains, vibrant markets, tree-lined streets, cafes and conversation. He returned home and felt underwhelmed by the intersections of his car-dominated city, and the lack of vibrant public spaces he'd experienced in Europe. He identified an abandoned block in Dallas with boarded-up buildings, multi-lane traffic, and no safe space for pedestrians or cyclists. He discovered that the city's bylaws prevented everything the space needed to be vibrant and healthy: no crowds; no awnings; to be allowed to plant a few flowers would cost you $1,000.

Roberts wondered what would happen if he just broke every bylaw over the course a weekend – in the service, of course, of a better, healthier, more vibrant block. He summoned a group of friends and residents, and over a weekend they transformed the space.

> We brought in cafe seating. We brought in historic lights, and flowers, and we printed up all the rules that we were breaking, stuck them on the windows, and we invited the city staff and council members out and said 'come to our party' . . . it became so powerful for the community and for the city leadership to see this. They came back and said 'we don't know why these rules have been on the books for so long, we should change these things.'[13]

The group painted new cycle paths on the street. Some of the pop-up shops they created later became permanent.

Suspecting that the success of Better Block might have been a fluke, Jason undertook another, this time transforming an intersection with forty-two large trees in pots, pop-up shops and a pedestrian crossing. The second one worked just as well, and now Better Block is an international movement. Roberts calls this work 'guerrilla bottom-up place-making'. As we discovered in the Transition movement, people *will* come out and make things happen. 'People know something's wrong,' Roberts said. 'They don't necessarily know how to articulate, though, what the problem is.' Better Block helps, he argues, by working quickly and by having a deadline. He sees Better Block's work as 'a combination of an urban planning exercise meets a block party'.[14]

Roberts is a believer in deadlines. 'Want to know the best way to tidy a really messy flat?' he asked me. 'Call your friends and say you're going to throw a dinner party in four hours. It's amazing how clean your place gets and how efficient you get'. This sense of the focusing power of deadlines, and of setting a date when something will happen runs through his approach. In a talk he gave at TEDxOU he set out his three key pieces of simple but powerful advice for anyone wanting to create a Better Block: (1) Show up. (2) Give it a name. (3) Set a date and publish it (blackmail yourself). More recently, he launched 'Wikiblock', an open-source design toolkit for benches, chairs, planters, stages, beer garden fences and kiosks. People can download plans and take them to a maker space and build these better block elements, most of which assemble with no glue or nails.

Another quick makeover approach is 'PARK(ing) Day' which now happens around the world annually on the third Friday in September. John Bela, one of its founders, says, 'I like to think of Park(ing) Day installations as the gateway drug for urban transformation.'[15] It started in 2005 in downtown San Francisco, when a group of artists looking for affordable exhibition and performance space realised that car parking spaces were actually 'subsidised real estate'. They paid for a parking spot and transformed the space into a mini-park with grass, a potted tree and a bench, and then sat back to see what happened.

People came by, sat on the bench, ate their lunch, had conversations. 'A metred parking spot is an inexpensive short-term lease for a plot of precious urban real estate' Rebar, the San Francisco–based group who promote the idea, reflected.[16] They took the idea to social media and it took off in hundreds of cities around the world, 'a global experiment in remixing, reclaiming and reprogramming vehicular space for social exchange, recreation and artistic expression'.[17] Their PARK(ing) Day manual details various ways people have used their parking spots: a wedding ceremony, a free health clinic, a fingerpainting studio, a productive landscape, an ecology centre, a free head and neck massage, a public back porch, a public safety demonstration, a free worm composting demo, an urban farming display, a national park, a glass recycling centre, a free bicycle repair shop, a solar panel demonstration, an interactive sculpture, a memorial glen, a DIY lemonade stand, a political campaign, a croquet tournament, a public park, an outdoor classroom, a public dog park, an exercise bike, a notebook to elected officials, a chess tournament, an open poetry reading, a barbecue, a lawn bowling course, a marshland, a pirates' cove, a hula, an art gallery, a chicken coop, a dinner party, a public reading room, a public beach, a public picnic. What would you do with yours?

The French artist JR also lights the way for us in how to transform public spaces. 'I take photos, or sometimes photos that are not mine, and I blow them up on buildings, on facades, on rooftops, with paper black-and-white images,' JR told me.[18] In *Women Are Heroes*, he posted huge photos of local women on buildings, rooftops and trains, vast outdoor 'exhibitions' around the world.[19] In *Ellis*, JR movingly repopulated the now semi-derelict building that was once the United States' biggest immigration inspection center until its closure in 1954 with photos of immigrants upon their arrival there. He visited Israel and Palestine, taking photos of people doing the same job: bakers, lawyers, taxi drivers and so on, from both communities, posting them side by side.

As we saw at Art Angel, the work helps people learn to see again, to reconnect to the world around them. His work often pops up overnight, unannounced. I asked JR how he had seen his work shift the imagination of a place. He replied: 'In communities where I've worked over the years, I've seen how people have been proud and it's mainly a feeling of pride at being recognized. . . . For me that's one of the great ways to bring dignity back to people, by making them part of history. Making them feel part of history, not left aside.'

While much of his work is promoted through social media, JR is clear that social media is no substitute for genuine connection. 'That is a way to be more and more disconnected from each other', he told me. 'That's why any kind of project, and any kind of process that I try to build, is always incorporating the physical aspect . . . meeting people for real'. He involves people in choosing his subjects, producing the prints, pasting them up. It strikes me that JR's work is so resonant because it is about people learning to notice the places, people, stories, history and challenges around them. It wakes people, and creates connection.

As I write this, a fast-growing movement of non-violent civil disobedience, Extinction Rebellion, is emerging in the United Kingdom and spreading rapidly around the world, mobilising people for direct action on climate change and biodiversity loss. Campaigns addressing the climate emergency are percolating and emerging worldwide. There are a growing number of school strikes, kids walking out and demanding governments take climate change seriously. A new spirit of rebellion is rising. How would it be if each of those demonstrations, actions, strikes, always included some kind of manifestation of the future they want to see? Gardens, visual projections onto buildings, art installations, discussions, theatre, that show what they dream of, and want the world to be? Or perhaps overnight actions to transform a place? To bring into the present what the future could still be like, to add the provocation of awe to their ambitions.

What I have tried to do in this book is to make the case for a reprioritising of the imagination, the urgent shifting of priorities so that imagination, play and wonder are invited, encouraged and let loose, driven from all levels and in all sectors. It leads me to wonder what that would actually *feel* like. Are there examples from recent or distant history, when the public imagination has felt really alive? Not just for an elite clique of poets and artists, like the Romantics, or powerful leaders who commission imaginative and artistic people in service of their regimes (think Venice), but when for large swathes of ordinary people it has felt like a moment rich with art, beauty, possibility and change. What did it feel like to be there?

Most of the time, moments like this emerge in opposition to oppressive regimes, as autonomous spaces of resistance. Among the best known are the revolutions that took place around the world in 1968. In Prague, Berkeley, London, Mexico City, Belfast, Berlin and, perhaps most famously, Paris. In May 1968, French students and workers came within days of collapsing Charles de Gaulle's government, in a movement that had its roots deep in imagination. A lot of its thinking and presentation was inspired by the Situationists, a school of anarchism that valued play, imagination and 'the revolution of everyday life'.[20] They were masters of slogans, shared through graffiti and posters: 'I declare a permanent state of happiness.' 'Be realistic, demand the impossible.' 'Power to the imagination, imagination taking power.' 'Forget everything you've been taught. Start by dreaming.' 'Desiring reality is great! Realising your desires is even better!' And 'Form dream committees.'[21]

Students at the city's art schools, École des Beaux-Arts and École des Arts Décoratif, occupied the lithography studios, renaming them the Popular Workshop or *Atelier Populaire*. At the height of the uprising, students and activists were screenprinting more than 350 poster designs a day onto cheap newsprint using single-colour inks and then posting them on the walls of the city before they were taken down almost as quickly either by the police or by art collectors. (The original posters are now worth a small fortune.) Philippe Vermès, one of the Atelier's co-founders, later wrote, 'We worked day and night in shifts. People brought in food, hot coffee, and helped wherever they could. Anyone and everyone – students, factory workers, office employees, transporters, media people, mailmen, fishermen – could bring ideas and work on the actual screenprinting.'[22]

As Mark Kurlansky writes in *1968: The Year That Rocked the World*, 'It remains one of the most impressive outpourings of political graphic art ever produced.' It was a time of demonstrations, occupations, general assemblies, art, music, and the ever-present discussion of ideas.

But what did it *feel* like to be there?

One of the main things people recall is the conversations. People talked in a way almost unimaginable in our conversationally starved times. Kurlansky quotes Eleanor Bakhtadze, a student at the time, as saying: 'Paris was wonderful then. Everyone was talking.' Kurlansky adds: 'Ask anyone in Paris with fond memories of the spring of 1968, and that is what they will say. People talked. . . . Students on the street found themselves in conversation with teachers and professors for the first time. For the first time in this rigid, formal, nineteenth-century society, everyone was talking to everyone. "Talk to your neighbour" were words written on the walls.'[23]

The demonstrations spread, and the workers came out on a general strike in support. As oral historian Ronald Fraser put it, 'A calm but massive refusal was being expressed.' He quotes one activist as saying, 'It was fantastic. May was like that, like living on a constant high. Life was beautiful, the weather was lovely . . . everything we did immediately belonged to History. All the hierarchies had suddenly dissolved.' Another said 'in that month of talking you learnt more than in the whole of your five years studying. Learnt because you could talk to anyone and everyone. It really was another world – a dream world perhaps – but that's what I'll always remember: the need and the right for everyone to speak.'[24]

One English student who spent two weeks in Paris during those days later wrote that his first impression

> was of a gigantic lid being lifted, pent-up thoughts and aspirations suddenly exploding, on being released from the realm of dreams into the realm of the Real and Possible. In changing their environment people themselves were changed. Those who had never dared say anything before suddenly felt their thoughts to be the most important thing in the world and said so. The helpless and isolated suddenly discovered that collective power lay in their hands. People just went up and talked to one another without a trace of self-consciousness.[25]

You find similar stories more recently, though, too – places where the imagination has been given room to breathe: the Arab Spring, the Tiananmen Square uprising, Occupy ('another world is possible'), rave culture, UK roads protests. They all had a similar impact on those involved, where anything felt possible. The 15M movement occupied squares for six weeks in more than one hundred cities across Spain during the summer of 2011. Transition activist Juan del Rio shared his experience:

> Literally, 'cities' were built on the squares, and people from all ages and locations were meeting there in their thousands every day. With self-managed spaces, for reflection and discussion, for care, arts, celebration, inclusion and action. Cooperation, listening and support were always very present.
>
> Is it possible to create a collective permaculture garden, houses on the trees or meals for free for hundreds of people, while dreaming and discussing openly how to create a completely new system, in the main square of Barcelona surrounded by huge buildings that symbolise the power of capitalism? Yes, it was possible. We felt it was a historical moment, indeed it was, and it was because of the power of collective imagination.
>
> On a deeper cultural level it was for many the most transformative moment in their lives, both collectively and individually. For me it was one of the biggest transition experiences I've ever lived. I felt awake, energised and creative, despite the physical tiredness. It was an amazing opportunity to go from the ideas to the action, a moment to feel alive and connected to the planet and the people.[26]

It may feel unimaginable today, but there have also been times through history when societies shaped themselves around the imagination. It flourished just after the Russian Revolution. The Song period in China (960–1279) was a time of many public festivals, social clubs, woodblock printing (making literature widely available), theatre and art. They all flourished.[27] And Geneva, between 1792 and 1793, when the citizens used participatory democracy to draft a utopian constitution and in a bloodless revolution swept aside the old regime, followed by a month-long street party.[28] After the 2008 financial crash, Icelanders rewrote their constitution, and for a time, engaged in a complete reimagining, where anything and everything felt possible. Scottish friends tell me that the period of 2012–14, before the referendum on independence, was such a moment, filled with conversation, debate, ideas and possibility.

The Zapatistas, the rebellion of indigenous people that emerged from the Lacandon jungle in the Chiapas region of Mexico in 1994 and went public the day the North American Free Trade Agreement (NAFTA) came into effect, is a movement rooted in imagination. The Zapatistas see their goal as a revolution against neo-liberalism, but one rooted in participatory democracy, women's emancipation, education and art. Subcomandante Marcos, often seen as its figurehead, communicates many of his ideas through novels, poetry and other forms of writing, and once wrote, 'The only thing we proposed was to change the world. The rest we have improvised.'[29] They support and hold 'pockets of resistance' within which people can imagine a world beyond neo-liberalism. This sense that the imagination flourishes when freed of the burden of colonialism has been seen in many countries when they gain independence, and then experience a time where anything feels possible, and a new identity is debated and explored, what is sometimes called a 'postcolonial imagination'.[30]

It is also true, I think, that in hierarchical, unequal or colonised societies, history values and records the imagination and creative output that rests on the support of a wealthy patron, or supports the status quo, but the creative work of ordinary people is largely ignored. Andrew Simms of the Rapid Transition Alliance describes a project curated by the University of Exeter which gathered together a huge body of poetry from working-class people during the Lancashire 'Cotton Famine' of 1861–65, largely ignored at the time, but recently archived and published, acknowledging the imaginative lives of communities not generally acknowledged, let alone celebrated, for their imagination.[31]

The idea of creating a taste of the future in the present brings us back to Jackie Andrade's office at the University of Plymouth and how creating immersive experiences of the future might actually work, in ways similar to how functional imagery training works. Her colleague Jon May told me, 'Memories of the future really is what you're talking about. The idea that by briefly or temporarily putting yourself in the future and thinking about what it's like there, and then coming back to the present, that that influences the decisions you make about your behaviour between now and the future, and how you can cope and change things in order to bring that future state about.'

May felt that one aspect to its being successful would be to have a character in it, 'a wise old man who said, "Do you remember how we did this and we did that and we succeeded?" And then you come back to real life. You have got then the self-efficacy. It can be done. These were the things that were done. It was nice when we had done it.'[32]

Andrade and May talked about how important it would be to think of these immersions as multisensory. If we were actually able to hear louder birdsong. If we could smell delicious food being prepared. If we could hear more conversations in the streets than we've become used to today. She told me how with FIT, they start by asking people to imagine a specific time in the future, like their next birthday, if nothing had changed. They then ask them to imagine the same date if the changes they want to happen had taken place. Keeping the space open for a range of scenarios is a key part of why it works.

This idea of building a new relationship to the future is central to another approach, that of 'Future Design'. Future Design was conceived by Tatsuyoshi Saijo of the Research Institute for Humanity and Nature in Kyoto, Japan. The idea is simple, that in every act of decision-making that has implications for the future, some people participate who represent future generations, and who speak from their perspective. In some cases, they are distinguished by wearing a special robe.[33] Many studies have now shown that when future residents take part in decision-making, the groups tend to choose more sustainable options, and become more altruistic.[34]

What is most fascinating about this approach is the extent to which it affects the people who take on the role of future generations. As Saijo notes, they develop what he calls 'futureability': 'an increase in happiness as a result of deciding and acting to forgo current benefits as long as it enriches future generations.'[35] Research shows that people who take on the role find a lot of joy in acting as the future representative, and that it starts to occur naturally in their lives, in other groups and organisations that they are part of. Saijo's approach is being used by several different Japanese municipalities, and he is developing plans for a national Ministry of the Future, a new ministry within government who would scrutinise all government policies, and a Department of the Future in all local governments. While there is nothing new in the idea – the Iroquois, for example, included the voices of future generations in their decision-making for many hundreds of years – Saijo's approach offers fascinating insights into how taking that role of speaking for the future generations impacts and affects the people who take it on, both while in the sessions and beyond.

I wrote this book because I wanted to put the imagination back at the heart of how we think about the future, and about what kind of future we might create, the future that is still possible to create. Not a perfect, utopian future, but a future that recognises the limits imposed by circumstance as opportunities, and responds with imagination and care, creating a future where things turn out OK. One of my favourite interviews was with performing artist, author, activist and educator Dominique Christina, who told me how, in her opinion, all too often, when we are exploring how to address a problem, we become fixated on that problem: 'The problem is now in the centre of the room', she told me. 'Whatever is not working, or whatever is dysfunctional, is what's taking up all the space. . . . The brokenness [becomes] everything.'

She went on,

> there are enough amazing, miraculous, impossible, supernatu-
> ral people on this planet who love this planet and who operate
> from goodness and integrity and accountability. But we get so
> bogged down in staring straight into the abyss that we've lost
> our sight of heaven. . . . The way to respond to this stuff is to
> imagine what we want as opposed to constantly reacting to
> what we do not want. . . . The way in which we envision this
> world should be what's in the centre of the room, all the time,
> as opposed to the broken stuff always entering and centring
> in the room.[36]

I believe, as Gabriella Gómez-Mont put it, that 'imagination is not a luxury.' If Kyung Hee Kim is right, and our imagination has been declining since the mid-1990s, it at least partially explains what we are seeing in the world today. As Dr Peter Gray wrote in 2012: 'Well, surprise, surprise. For several decades we as a society have been suppressing children's creativity to ever greater extents, and now we find that their creativity is declining.'[37] It wasn't as though some people didn't see this coming.

We recognise that if a population isn't sufficiently nourished, we will see a decline in health and a rise in preventable illnesses. We recognise that if we fail to give a population a good education, it will fail to reach its potential. Yet the neglect of the imagination is generally overlooked, seen as a frivolous distraction from the overarching aim of building economic growth and technological progress. We saw in Reggio Emilia what the creation of a system of education designed specifically to prevent the resurgence of fascism would look like, yet we have designed an education system which it almost its opposite. We can see in Barcelona and other Spanish 'municipalist' cities what a model of democracy that invites the imagination could look like, yet in most other places, we persist in moving further and further away from such a thing. We saw at Art Angel what an approach to mental health that puts safety, hope and imagination at its heart would look like, yet most people's experience is just the opposite. Our imagination isn't accidentally dwindling; it is being co-opted, suffocated, corrupted and starved of the oxygen it needs.

We have relegated the imagination to the margins for too long, and now, as Robert Louis Stevenson put it, we 'sit down to a banquet of consequences'. Our failure to create the conditions, the spaces, the opportunities and the invitations for the imagination, and the implementation of political programmes such as austerity, directly smash to pieces much of what most of us need in order to live imaginative lives. We are living through a perfect storm of factors ruinous to the imagination. As we face vast crises that demand imaginative and urgent responses and a reimagining of everything, we are simply not up to it. This is really serious. Which makes it all the more important to reprioritise it as rapidly, and in as many ways and places, as we can.

It is my hope that this book might prompt a reconsidering of the strategies used by organisations and campaigns working in responses to the challenges we are facing, that they might work to make sure the expression of a positive vision of how the future could turn out, their dream of it, comes through loudly, imaginatively and passionately in all that they do. The physicist and writer Peter Russell once described this cultivation of a collective vision to me as acting like a strange attractor in chaos theory, something you throw in front of yourself which then draws you towards it, like a whirlpool.[38] While many of the technologies, economic models and know-how for creating a future in which we can all thrive already exist, what is missing is the *longing*. Imagination is so important because it helps us create longing, and if we can get that right, other things then follow.

I have taken you with me on a two-year exploration of the state of health of our collective imagination, the factors that might be behind this situation, and what we might do about it. I hope that, above all, I have managed to communicate what it feels like when the imagination is invited, cherished and cared for. Whether sitting listening to the dawn chorus, watching dots being added to a painting at Art Angel, or standing in Les Petits Producteurs in Liège, I recognised the same sense of possibility, the same spark.

I dream that these twenty years when the climate crisis, the collapse of the world's biodiversity, the unravelling of democracy and the multitude of other challenges converging on us with great urgency have been slowed down and even turned around, the years when the great rebuilding is well under way, will be the time of our lives. I dream that because imagination is at its heart, it will be a time of great music, great writing, great conversation, great art, great dancing. Our streets will fill with play and with the unexpected, with mime artists directing the traffic. Our lives will fill with everyday awe.

Our governments will learn from schools like Plymouth School of Creative Arts that great leaps forward come when people are invited to work with those in other areas of interest, to cross-pollinate ideas. Our town planners will realise that putting ateliers at the heart of High Streets and public places will transform the public's sense of what's possible. I dream that artists and activists will, together, create visceral pop-up experiences of the future, overnight transforming unloved but well-known places into immersive experiences (or 'memories of the future'), new jungles of possibility atop the paving stones of today which, once tasted, mean no one will be happy to go back to how it was before.

I dream that the imagination, once invoked, named, celebrated and let loose, becomes infectious. I dream of it as being a time when, as the poster from Paris in 1968 put it, 'beauty is in the street'. But much of what I dream of isn't really a dream at all, because it's already here, as I've tried to capture in these pages. Go out and find it, pay it a visit, make it happen where you live.

Thank you for reading. I opened this book with a quote by Susan Griffin, and I will close it with one. 'No one can stop us from imagining another kind of future, one which departs from the terrible cataclysm of violent conflict, of hateful divisions, poverty and suffering. Let us begin to imagine the worlds we would like to inhabit, the long lives we will share, and the many futures in our hands.'[39]

I leave you with one question, a question I hope by now has really got under your skin. What if the approach outlined here, and the great rekindling of the collective imagination, actually came to pass? What if? And why not?

Afterword

A couple of weeks before I finished writing this book, I was in Exeter to support my son and the many other young people gathering there – and across the country – for the United Kingdom's first School Strike 4 Climate. Inspired by Swedish teenage climate activist Greta Thunberg, and by similar strikes already under way in other countries, about eight hundred young people had gathered outside the offices of Devon County Council.

They were demanding that the government declare a climate emergency, that the National Curriculum be reformed to reflect the urgency of that climate emergency, that the government inform the public about the need to act on climate change and that the voting age be lowered to sixteen. All had taken the day off school, some with their school's support (my son's school had laid on a bus), and others in spite of threats of punishments.

There were banners, placards, chanting, songs, shouts of 'What do we want? Climate justice!' and 'Whose future? Our future!' It felt hopeful, hugely empowering and very noisy. After an hour or so, I noticed people around me looking across the park we were in and pointing. Coming over the horizon was another group, of about three hundred young people, singing their own songs, striding with purpose and focus, clasping their banners and flags. The reinforcements had arrived.

The young person addressing our group pointed them out, and the whole group turned to cheer them home. The group coming over the horizon grew and grew, and kept on coming. As they came together, both groups cheered to welcome the other. I asked one of the new arrivals who they were. She said, 'We're from the university, but as we walked we picked up more and more people.'

I then noticed that at the back of the group, which was still arriving, was a large banner with just two words, WHAT IF? It was the work of a group of students who, a few days earlier, had attended one of my workshops about this book. They had been fired by 'what if', and spent the evening trying to think of ways to bring that spirit to the day's activities.

The reaction to the school strike from the powers that be was predictable. Prime Minister Theresa May said, 'Disruption increases teachers' workloads and lesson time that teachers have carefully prepared for.' Minister Andrea Leadsom tweeted, 'It's called truancy, not a strike.' However, there was also a lot of support from people across the political spectrum, which was reflected later that morning when the group marched en masse to the centre of the city, past traffic with people waving and beeping their support.

The students with the WHAT IF? banner then set up inviting people to complete cards that started with the words WHAT IF? And they helped people print T-shirts with the words WHAT IF? I was struck that simply asking the question raised many of the subjects we've explored in this book. Responses included, 'What if we stopped staring at screens?', 'What if we were taken seriously?', 'What if people paid attention?', 'What if we all started singing the same song?', 'What if people listened to kids?', 'What if climate change were an entire subject?'

Reflecting on why she liked having WHAT IF? on her new T-shirt, one girl replied: 'It leaves an open question. If someone were to ask what it's for, I would bring up the topic of climate change and that it's February, and it's warm, and that I'm quite happy just wearing a T-shirt, and I'd ask, "What would your answer be? What if?"'[1]

Here was the next generation: informed, passionate, committed, articulate. And here was a movement that maybe, just maybe, would grow and grow, and from this day, its inception (in the United Kingdom at least), focus on 'what if' as well as what is. A movement that ingeniously created and held what-if spaces. That would tell stories about the future we dream of, founded on the idea of creating 'memories of the future'. That would sustain itself with a powerful sense of standing up against those negligent in their duty of care for the future, but also by the stories they share. It was a delicious taste of the possible.

ACKNOWLEDGMENTS

The creation of this book has been a real what-if process for me, a journey and an adventure. It has been such a privilege to have the time and space to immerse myself in this subject, and I must firstly acknowledge the amazingly kind support of the Lunt Foundation, especially Helene Rolin, Michael Lunt and Guibert del Marmol, in enabling me to do this. I will be forever grateful.

It would not have been possible without the support and comradeship of my family, everyone at Transition Network and Transition Town Totnes, both past and present. Thank you all for your patience and your encouragement. Thanks also to the University of Plymouth, whose fellowship really helped with the research.

When I say this has been a what-if adventure, I am especially pleased that of the almost one hundred people interviewed for this book, only about a quarter of them were known to me before I began this project. The rest I have uncovered as I've gone along, been told about by someone else or read about somewhere. While some interviews were done in person, the majority were done by Skype.

It feels important to me to note here that although I interviewed people in the United States, India, Brazil, Pakistan, Italy, Canada, Spain, Belgium, France, Colombia and Mexico, I didn't take a single flight in order to achieve this; they were all done virtually. I gave up flying in 2006 as a concrete step towards living a lower carbon life, and walking the walk in this way really matters to me. In the end, not every interview made it through the process of writing and editing, but I'd like to thank everyone who gave their time to speak to me, you all contributed something to this process and I am grateful: Ruth Ben-Tovim, Sven Birkerts, Rosalie Summerton and everyone at Art Angel, Dan Edelstyn, Hilary Powell, Michael Rosen, Lucy Neal, Scott Barry Kaufman, Holly Tiffin,

Jonathan Schooler, Inez Aponte, Philippe Van Parijs, Jo Chesterman, Richard Olivier, Mikkel Borg Bjergsø, Daniella Radice, Josh Golin, Donna Rose Addis, Jason Roberts, Lise Van Susteren, Martin Shaw, Toni Spencer, Ian Blackwell, Deborah Frances-White, Mark Sears, Rima Staines, Henry Giroux, Sarah Corbett, James Howard Kunstler, Hilary Jennings, Shaun Hill, Hannah Fox, Tony Whitehead, Ted Dewan, Doria Robinson, Neil Griffiths, Mohsin Hamid, Sarah Woods, Martin Kirk, Grace Turtle, Julian Dobson, Bruce K. Alexander, Karien Stroucken and Jennifer Coleman at the Institute of Imagination, Felix Beltran, Josiah Meldrum, Joy Schaverien, Dr Gordon Turnbull, David van Reybrouck, Michael Kiser, Jamie Hanson, Jeremy Finch and my fellow Spontaneity Shop improvisers, Matthieu Ricard, Marjorie Taylor, Manish Jain, Gabriella Gómez-Mont, Dr Larry Rosen, Vanessa Andreotti, Alex Schlegel, Maggie Jackson, Dan Schacter, Sally Weintrobe, Douglas Rushkoff, Gillian Judson, everyone at Catastrophe, Dr Adam Gazzaley, Hilary O'Shaughnessy, Evin O'Riordan, John McCarthy, JR, Dominique Christina, Daniel Raven-Ellison, Kieran Egan, Christian Jonet, Pascal Hennen, Eric Holthaus, Tom Hirons, Jonathan Cooper, Drew Dellinger, Kyung Hee Kim, Stuart Candy, Michel Bauwens, Chris Parsons and everyone at LandWorks, Robert Macfarlane, James Lawlor, Martin Ophoven, Carola Salvi, Michele d'Alena, John Thackara, Jay Griffiths, Quentin Blake, Ana Letícia Maciel, Luana Fonseca, David Sax, Stephen Duncombe, Anne-Marie Culhane, John Hickling, Alexandra Rowland, Tasha Bassingthwaighte, Ruth Sapsed, Karen MacLean, Nicolas Clerc, Cllr Matthew Brown, Andrew Brewerton, Bridget McKenzie, Dave Strudwick, Ste Weatherhead, Jackie Andrade, Jon May, Helen Marriage, James McKay, Clodagh Harris, Shana McDavis-Conway, Stella Duffy, Judy Wicks, Kali Akuno, Amy Seefeldt, Michael McCarthy, Johanna Morrell, Katy Murry, Ainslie Beattie, Jon Alexander, Molly Scott Cato, Ben Goldfarb, Tatsuyoshi Saijo. Thank you all. If you'd like to read any of those conversations in full, you'll find them at www.robhopkins.net.

I would also like to thank people who have particularly supported me along this journey: Chris Underhill, Tessa King, Amanda Cuthbert, Mark Lucas, Cyril Dion, Manda Brookman, Filipa Pimentel, Lara Lloyd, Joanna Smith, Mike Thomas, Indra Adnan, Pat Kane, Amber

Ponton, Sarah McAdam, Angie Greenham, Peter Lipman, Pete Yeo, Simon Blackbourn, all the Transition folks I've met along the way for their inspiration and hospitality.

Thanks also to Naresh Giangrande, Andrew Simms, Sophy Banks, Ben Brangwyn, Claire Milne, Matt Dunwell, Melanie Laurent, Deborah Benham, Julien Dossier, Ophélie, Johnny and Fanny Thwaites, Dave Pollard, Cheryl Dahle, Mat Henney, Manda Scott, Frances Northrop, everyone at New Lion Brewery, Juliette Timsit, Xavier Combe, Pete Yeo, Fabienne Briant, Sylvie Mingant, Tom Doust at the Institute of Imagination, Dominique Le Ster, Ruth Potts, and Olivier De Schutter.

I am grateful to everyone at Chelsea Green, to Margo Baldwin for seeing the potential in this idea, to Brianne Goodspeed, my brilliant editor, and to Elizabeth Babcock, Rose Baldwin, Sandi Eaton, Matt Haslum, Eliza Haun, Melissa Jacobson, Darrell Koerner, Sarah Kovach, Sean Maher, Christina Butt, Jeffrey Slayton, Jenna Stewart, Pati Stone, Natalie Wallace, and Michael Weaver for their work on this book.

Finally, I would also like to acknowledge with respect and gratitude those who have fired my own imagination during my life: Dr Christine Blasey Ford, Sterling Morrison, Rebecca Solnit, Grayson Perry, Kim Gordon, Vincent van Gogh, Tove Jansson, Chuck D, Matt Haynes, Clare Wadd, Fiona McIntyre, Bill Mollison, Mariame Kaba, David Holmgren, Sylvia Plath, Michael Shuman, Barbara Kingsolver, Albert Bates, Sasami, Mark E. Smith, Naomi Klein, Nils Frahm, Ursula K. Le Guin, Sir Ken Robinson, Mary Warnock, Quentin Blake, Jonathan Richman, Ruth Mock, Nicholas Carr, Ada Colau, the Frack Free Four, Marie-Eve Leclerc, Banksy, Darren McGarvey, Joanna Macy, Richard Wilkinson and Kate Pickett, Marley Marl, Robert Smith, Sherry Turkle, Can, Nina Simone, Matthew B. Crawford, Kate Tempest, Campaign for a Commercial-Free Childhood, Venice, Roxanne Shante, the Last Poets, Aretha Franklin, George Monbiot, Anna Campbell, Theaster Gates, Angela Carter, John Crowley, the Situationists, the Impressionist room at the Musée d'Orsay in Paris, Ryan Griffin at astrangelyisolatedplace.com, the blogs of hurryslowly.co, Tom Vague, Greta Thunberg and all the school strikers, Paul Haig, Emil Ferris, Extinction Rebellion, Geir Jenssen, James Bernard, Nick Drake, Martin Newell, Laurie Steen, Adam Curtis and Sarah Gillespie.

NOTES

Introduction: What If Things Turned Out OK?

1. The phrase is borrowed from a 2013 Real Bread Campaign report titled *Rising Up: Baking Real Bread Improves People's Lives*, https://www.sustainweb.org/publications/rising_up/.
2. Such an operation already exists in London, just off Brick Lane. It's called Rise Bakery ('baking lives better'). Find them online at http://www.risebakery.london/.
3. You can visit a brewery like this on Sheffield station – the Sheffield Tap.
4. However, many of the examples I use are taken from real initiatives currently under way in communities around the UK and Europe: (1) A sustainable thirteen-unit apartment complex built with straw-bale walls exists in Cressy, Switzerland, for instance. Whereas the average Swiss citizen uses 160 litres of water per day, at Cressy, thanks to composting toilets, they use just 48 litres per day. Much of their energy is generated on-site and is renewable. (2) A number of local authorities are now passing regulations to require that all the new plantings be edible plants, and are choosing to establish productive edible trees in public places. (3) Several Edible Bus Stops have been planted across London already (http://theediblebusstop.org). (4) The innovative education system I describe is based on the current Finnish model.
5. IPCC (Intergovernmental Panel on Climate Change), 'Summary for Policymakers of IPCC Special Report on Global Warming of 1.5°C Approved by Governments', news release, 8 October 2018.
6. Kevin Anderson and John Broderick, *Natural Gas and Climate Change* (Manchester, UK: Tyndall Manchester, CEMUS, Teesside University, 17 October 2017), 12, https://www.research.manchester.ac.uk/portal/files/60994617/Natural_Gas_and _Climate_Change_Anderson_Broderick_FOR_DISTRIBUTION.pdf.
7. IPCC, 'Summary for Policymakers'.
8. Adam Gazzaley and Larry D. Rosen, *The Distracted Mind: Ancient Brains in a High-Tech World* (Cambridge, MA: MIT Press, 2016), 100.
9. Susan Griffin, 'To Love the Marigold', in *The Impossible Will Take a Little Longer*, ed. Paul Rogat Loeb (New York: Basic Books, 2014), 170.
10. Andrew Simms and Peter Newell, *How Did We Do That? The Possibility of Rapid Transition* (London: STEPS Centre/New Weather Institute, 2017), https://steps -centre.org/wp-content/uploads/2017/04/How_Did_We_Do_That.pdf.
11. Andrew Simms, *Nine Meals from Anarchy: Oil Dependence, Climate Change and the Transition to Resilience* (London: New Economics Foundation, 2008).

12. This story is told in 'The Lessons from Kinsale – Part One', *Transition Culture* (blog), 12 December 2005, https://www.transitionculture.org/2005/12/12/the -lessons-from-kinsale-part-one/.

13. Transition Town Totnes, *Totnes & District Local Economic Blueprint*, 2015, http:// www.reconomy.org/wp-content/uploads/2015/10/TD-Local-Economic-Blueprint -final_low_res.pdf.

14. Find out more about the Totnes Local Entrepreneur Forum and its history at https://reconomycentre.org/home/lef/local-entrepreneur-forum-2015-wrap-up/.

15. Check us out: http://www.newlionbrewery.co.uk. Better still, pop in and say hi. Say I sent you. . . .

16. There are three key pieces of research on Transition Streets and its impacts: GfK NOP Social Research, *LCCC Baseline Research Mini Report – Totnes*, 2012, https:// www.transitionstreets.org.uk/wp-content/uploads/2012/07/LCCCBaselineResearch MiniReport%E2%80%93Totnes.pdf; Fiona Ward, Adrian Porter and Mary Popham, *Transition Streets: Final Project Report*, September 2011, https://www .transitionstreets.org.uk/wp-content/uploads/2012/07/TransitionStreets-finalreport -27Sep2011.pdf; Helen Beetham, *Social Impacts of Transition Together (SITT): Investigating the Social Impacts, Benefits and Sustainability of the Transition Together/ Transition Streets Initiative in Totnes*, 2011, https://www.transitionstreets.org.uk /wp-content/uploads/2012/07/SocialimpactsofTransitionStreets-finalreport.pdf.

17. David Fleming, *Lean Logic: A Dictionary for the Future and How to Survive It* (White River Junction, VT: Chelsea Green Publishing, 2016), 209.

18. Maxine Greene, 'Imagination and Becoming (Bronx Charter School of the Arts)', 2007, https://maxinegreene.org/uploads/library/imagination_bbcs.pdf.

19. Paolo Lugari, '*Un nuevo renacimiento en el trópico*', Fundación Centro Experimental Las Gaviotas, 2009, http://www.centrolasgaviotas.org/docs/conferencia.pdf.

20. Amitav Ghosh, *The Great Derangement: Climate Change and the Unthinkable* (London: University of Chicago Press, 2016), 9.

21. George Monbiot, 'How Do We Get Out of This Mess?', *Guardian*, 9 September 2017, https://www.theguardian.com/books/2017/sep/09/george-monbiot-how-de -we-get-out-of-this-mess.

22. David Wallace-Wells, 'The Uninhabitable Earth', *New York*, 10 July 2017, http:// nymag.com/intelligencer/2017/07/climate-change-earth-too-hot-for-humans.html.

23. Kyung Hee Kim, 'The Creativity Crisis: The Decrease in Creative Thinking Scores on the Torrance Tests of Creative Thinking', *Creativity Research Journal* 23, no. 4 (2011): 285–95.

24. Kyung Hee Kim, interview with author, *Imagination Taking Power* (blog), 20 September 2018, https://www.robhopkins.net/2018/09/20/kyung-hee-kim-on-the-creativity-crisis/.

25. Alvaro Pascual-Leone et al., 'Modulations of Muscle Responses Evoked by Transcranial Magnetic Stimulation During the Acquisition of New Fine Motor Skills', *Journal of Neurophysiology* 74, no.3 (1995): 1037–45.

26. Guang Yue and Kelly Cole, 'Strength Increases from the Motor Program: Comparison of Training with Maximal Voluntary and Imagined Muscle Contractions', *Journal of Neurophysiology* 67, no. 5 (1992): 1114–23.

27. Jackie Andrade et al., 'Functional Imagery Training to Reduce Snacking: Testing a Novel Motivational Intervention Based on Elaborated Intrusion Theory', *Appetite* 100 (2016): 256–62.

28. Jackie Andrade and Jon May, interview with author, *Imagination Taking Power* (blog), 18 December 2018, https://www.robhopkins.net/2018/12/18/jackie -andrade-and-jon-may-on-imagination-lemons-and-functional-imagery-training/.

29. Jennifer Coleman, in discussion with the author, 18 June 2017.

30. Scott Barry Kaufman, in discussion with the author, 1 May 2017.

31. Fleming, *Lean Logic*.

32. IPCC, 'Summary for Policymakers'.

33. Will Steffen et al., 'Trajectories of the Earth System in the Anthropocene', *Proceedings of the National Academy of Sciences (USA)* 115, no. 33 (August 2018): 8252–59.

34. Michael Winship, 'Naomi Klein: "There Are No Non-Radical Options Left Before Us"', *Salon*, 4 February 2016, https://www.salon.com/2016/02/04/naomi_klein _there_are_no_non_radical_options_left_before_us_partner/.

35. One of the key insights of Yuval Noah Harari's *Sapiens: A Brief History of Humankind* (London: Penguin Random House, 2011).

Chapter 1: What If We Took Play Seriously?

1. Playing Out's website is http://playingout.net/.

2. You can hear the podcast I recorded in the street, featuring all interviews with parents and children in this chapter, at the *Imagination Taking Power* (blog), https://www. robhopkins.net/2017/05/18/traffic-just-needs-to-be-put-in-its-place -and-then-this-happen/.

3. Jo Chesterton, in discussion with the author, 9 May 2017.

4. Jo Chesterton, in discussion with the author.

5. Enrique Peñalosa and Susan Ives, 'The Politics of Happiness', *Yes!*, 20 May 2004, https://www.yesmagazine.org/issues/finding-courage/the-politics-of-happiness.

6. Evelyn Sharp, *The London Child* (London: J. Lane, 1927), 87.

7. *Playday 2007: Our Streets Too!* 'Street Play Opinion Poll Summary', http://www .playday.org.uk/resources/research/2007-research/.

8. Richard Louv, 'A Timely Truth', *National Trust*, 2011, 34–37.

9. Mayer Hillman et al., *One False Move: A Study of Children's Independent Mobility* (London: Policy Studies Institute, 1990).

10. Documented in Hugh Cunningham, *The Invention of Childhood* (London: BBC Books, 2006); and I especially love this black-and-white film from 1972, which tells the story of how a group of children fought for the right to play in the streets of their neighbourhood of De Pijp, https://youtu.be/YY6PQAI4TZE.

11. Captured in Hanna Rosin's article 'The Overprotected Kid', *Atlantic*, April 2014.

12. Howard Chudacoff, *Children at Play: An American History* (New York: New York University Press, 2007).

13. Tim Gill, *No Fear: Growing Up in a Risk Averse Society* (Calouste Gulbenkian Foundation, 2007), 42.

14. Melinda Wenner, 'The Serious Need for Play', *Scientific American*, February 2009, https://www.scientificamerican.com/article/the-serious-need-for-play/.

15. Stuart Brown, 'Play as an Organizing Principle: Clinical Evidence and Personal Observations', in *Animal Play: Evolutionary, Comparative, and Ecological Perspectives*, ed. Marc Beko and John A. Beyer (Cambridge: Cambridge University Press, 1998), 243–45.

16. Jaak Panksepp, 'Play, ADHD and the Construction of the Social Brain: Should the First Class Each Day Be Recess?', *American Journal of Play* 1, no. 1 (2008): 72.

17. Stephen Moss, *Natural Childhood*, National Trust, 2012, https://www.nationaltrust .org.uk/documents/read-our-natural-childhood-report.pdf.

18. Michael Yogman et al., 'The Power of Play: A Pediatric Role in Enhancing Development in Young Children', *Pediatrics* 142, no. 3 (September 2018): 1–16.

19. Richie Poulton et al., 'Evidence for a Non-associative Model of the Acquisition of a Fear of Heights', *Behaviour Research and Therapy* 36 (May 1998): 537–44.

20. Moss, *Natural Childhood*.

21. You can watch this series at https://www.channel4.com/programmes/old-peoples -home-for-4-year-olds.

22. You can hear the podcast I made at the Street Games Festival, including interviews with organisers, parents and children, at https://www.robhopkins.net/2017/04/25 /podcast-an-afternoon-playing-in-the-street/.

23. Alex Spiegel, 'Old-Fashioned Play Builds Serious Skills', *Morning Edition*, aired 21 February 2008 on NPR, http://www.npr.org/templates/ story/story.php?storyId =19212514.

24. Jay Griffiths, interview with author, *Imagination Taking Power* (blog), 16 March 2019, https://www.robhopkins.net/2019/03/26/jay-griffiths-a-child-can-transform -a-twig-and-a-pile-of-leaves-into-absolutely-anything/.

25. Mattel, Hello Barbie Doll, Mattel & Fisher Price Customer Service, 2015, https:// service.mattel.com/us/productPopup.aspx?prodno=DNR56&siteid=27.

26. Jason Boog, 'Hello Barbie's War on Imagination', *Salon*, 19 December 2015, https://www.salon.com/2015/12/19/hello_barbies_war_on_imagination_the _childhood_destroying_gift_you_dont_want_to_give_your_kid/.

27. Shoshana Zuboff, *The Age of Surveillance Capitalism: The Fight for A Human Future at the New Frontier of Power* (London: Profile Books, 2019), 266–67.

28. Josh Golin, interview with author, *Imagination Taking Power* (blog), 20 March 2017, https://www.robhopkins.net/2017/03/20/josh-golin-on-toys-marketing-and -when-barbie-goes-bad/.

29. Philip Olterman, 'German Parents Told to Destroy Doll That Can Spy on Children', *Guardian*, 17 February 2017, https://www.theguardian.com/world/2017/feb/17/german-parents-told-to-destroy-my-friend-cayla-doll-spy-on-children.

30. Zuboff, *The Age of Surveillance Capitalism*, 267.

31. Carly Dauch et al., 'The Influence of the Number of Toys in the Environment on Toddlers' Play', *Infant Behaviour* 50 (2018): 78–87.

32. Sarah Jewell, 'The Nursery That Took All the Children's Toys Away', *Independent*, 11 November 1999, https://www.independent.co.uk/news/education/education-news/the-nursery-that-took-all-the-childrens-toys-away-1125048.html.

33. Leah Stella Stephens, 'Imagination. Creativity. Curiosity: What Happens When We Neglect the Jewels of Our Minds?' *Medium*, 27 March, 2016, https://www.imaginationmatters.org/index.php/2017/10/20/imagination-creativity-curiosity/

34. Tom Salinsky and Deborah Frances-White, *The Improv Handbook: The Ultimate Guide to Improvising in Comedy, Theatre and Beyond* (London: Bloomsbury, 2016), 52.

35. You can hear the podcast I made of all the improv class interviews in this chapter as part of *Imagination Taking Power* (blog), 'I Suck, and I Love to Fail: A Weekend of Learning to Improvise', https://www.robhopkins.net/2017/09/26/i-suck-and-i-love-to-fail-a-weekend-of-learning-to-improvise/.

36. This story is told in the film *Bogotá Change*, directed by Andreas Dalsgaard: https://www.youtube.com/watch?v=4lOkLNIT3gI&t=873s.

37. I am grateful to Grace Turtle for telling me this story. Grace Turtle, interview with author, *Imagination Taking Power* (blog), 4 September 2018, https://www.robhopkins.net/2018/09/04/grace-turtle-everywhere-i-look-there-is-this-mass-realisation-that-we-need-to-re-engage-our-imagination/.

38. Antanas Mockus, 'The Art of Changing a City', *New York Times*, 16 July 2015, https://www.nytimes.com/2015/07/17/opinion/the-art-of-changing-a-city.html.

39. Grace Turtle, 'Searching for Neverland: A Theatre of Impossible Futures', *Medium*, 19 June 2018, https://medium.com/@Graceleoturtle/searching-for-neverland-a-theatre-of-impossible-futures-851acf8cea5b.

40. Grace Turtle, interview with author, *Imagination Taking Power* (blog), 4 September 2018, https://www.robhopkins.net/2018/09/04/grace-turtle-everywhere-i-look-there-is-this-mass-realisation-that-we-need-to-re-engage-our-imagination/.

41. The story of how this activity was conceived, planned and carried out is told in a blog post by Ruth Ben-Tovim: 'The Evolution and Practice of the "Transition Town Anywhere" Activity', 19 November 2012, https://www.transitionculture.org/2012/11/19/the-evolution-and-practice-of-the-transition-town-anywhere-activity/.

42. Ben-Tovim, 'The Evolution and Practice of the "Transition Town Anywhere" Activity'.

43. Ruth Ben-Tovim, email message to author, 31 October 2018.

44. Isabela Maria Gomez de Menezes, in discussion with the author, 19 January 2019.

45. Filipa Pimentel, in discussion with the author, 1 February 2019.

46. Franco 'Biffo' Berardi, *Futurability: The Age of Impotence and the Horizon of Possibility* (London: Verso Publications, 2017).

47. Alvin Rosenfeld and Nicole Wise, *The Over-Scheduled Child: Avoiding the Hyper-Parenting Trap*, (New York: St. Martin's Griffin, 2000) quoted in Walter Kirn with Wendy Cole, 'What Ever Happened to Play?', *Time*, 22 April 2001, https://content.time.com/time/nation/article/0,8599,107264,00.html.

48. Peter and Iona Opie, 'The Private World of Children's Games', *Observer*, 6 August 1961, 31.

Chapter 2: What If We Considered Imagination Vital to Our Health?

1. Will Hutton, 'The Bad News Is We're Dying Early in Britain – And It's All Down to "Shit-Life Syndrome"', *Guardian*, 19 August 2018, https://www.theguardian.com/commentisfree/2018/aug/19/bad-news-is-were-dying-earlier-in-britain-down-to-shit-life-syndrome.

2. Gazzaley and Rosen, *The Distracted Mind*, 170.

3. Denis Campbell, 'Three in Four Britons Felt Overwhelmed by Stress, Survey Reveals', 14 May 2018, *Guardian*, https://www.theguardian.com/society/2018/may/14/three-in-four-britons-felt-overwhelmed-by-stress-survey-reveals.

4. The Prince's Trust/Ebay, *Youth Index 2019* (London: Prince's Trust, 2018), https://www.princes-trust.org.uk/about-the-trust/news-views/ebay-youth-index-2019.

5. Jean M. Twenge, 'Are Smartphones Causing More Teen Suicides?' *Guardian*, 24 May 2018, https://www.theguardian.com/society/2018/may/24/smartphone-teen-suicide-mental-health-depression.

6. Baroness Kidron et al., *Disrupted Childhood: The Cost of Persuasive Design*, 5Rights, June 2018, https://5rightsfoundation.com/static/5Rights-Disrupted-Childhood.pdf.

7. Cited in Peter Gray, *The Decline of Play*, TEDxNavesink, 13 June 2014, https://www.youtube.com/watch?v=Bg-GEzM7iTk.

8. Alexandra Alter, 'Uneasy About the Future, Readers Turn to Dystopian Classics', *New York Times*, 27 January 2017, https://www.nytimes.com/2017/01/27/business/media/dystopian-classics-1984-animal-farm-the-handmaids-tale.html; Christopher Schmidt, 'Why Are Dystopian Films on the Rise Again?', *JSTOR Daily*, 19 November 2014, https://daily.jstor.org/why-are-dystopian-films-on-the-rise-again/.

9. Sarah H. Konrath et al., 'Changes in Dispositional Empathy in American College Students Over Time: A Meta-Analysis', *Personality and Social Psychology Review* 15, no. 2 (2011): 180–98.

10. Timothy D. Wilson et al., 'Just Think: The Challenges of the Disengaged Mind', *Science* 345, no. 6192 (2014): 75–77.

11. Art Angel's website is www.artangeldundee.org.uk.

12. Rosalie Summerton, email message to author, 4 October 2018.

13. Derek Ramsay, in discussion with the author, 3 October 2018.

Notes

14. Hester Parr, *Art Angel: A Research Report*, Department of Geography, University of Dundee, September 2005, 22, https://www.researchgate.net/publication /267389289_Art_Angel_A_Research_Report.

15. Interview with Art Angel artist, 3 October 2018.

16. Donna Rose Addis et al., 'Age-Related Changes in the Episodic Simulation of Future Events', *Psychological Science* 19, no. 1 (2008): 33–41; Randy L. Buckner, 'The Role of the Hippocampus in Prediction and Imagination', *Annual Review of Psychology* 61 (2009): 27–48; Donna Rose Addis et al., 'Hippocampal Contributions to the Episodic Simulation of Specific and General Future Events', *Hippocampus* 21, no. 10 (2011): 1045–52; Donna Rose Addis, 'Are Episodic Memories Special? On the Sameness of Remembered and Imagined Event Stimulation', *Journal of the Royal Society of New Zealand* 48, no. 2/3 (2018): 64–68; Donna Rose Addis and Daniel L. Schacter, 'The Hippocampus and Imagining the Future: Where Do We Stand?', *Frontiers of Human Neuroscience* 5, no. 173 (2012): 1–20, https://dash.harvard.edu/bitstream/handle/1/10636300/76560509.pdf.

17. Donna Rose Addis, interview with author, *Imagination Taking Power* (blog), 23 February 2018, https://www.robhopkins.net/2018/02/23/donna-rose-addis -on-the-hippocampus-the-future-and-brain-networks/.

18. Jessica R. Andrews-Hanna, 'The Brain's Default Network and Its Adaptive Role in Internal Mentation', *Neuroscientist* 18, no. 3 (2011): 251–70.

19. Theodore D. Wachs et al., 'Issues in the Timing of Integrated Early Interventions: Contributions from Nutrition, Neuroscience, and Psychological Research', *Annals of the New York Academy of Sciences* 1308 (2014): 89–106; Robert F. Anda et al., 'The Enduring Effects of Abuse and Related Adverse Experiences in Childhood: A Convergence of Evidence from Neurobiology and Epidemiology', *European Archives of Psychiatry and Clinical Neuroscience* 256, no. 3 (April 2006): 174–86.

20. Bessel van der Kolk, *The Body Keeps the Score: Mind, Brain, and Body in the Transformation of Trauma* (London: Penguin Books, 2014).

21. Gordon Turnbull, *Trauma: From Lockerbie to 7/7: How Trauma Affects Our Minds and How We Fight Back* (London: Corgi, 2012); Gordon Turnbull, interview with author, *Imagination Taking Power* (blog), 27 November 2018, https://www .robhopkins.net/2017/11/27/professor-gordon-turnbull-on-how-trauma -impacts-the-imagination/.

22. Daniel Schacter, interview with author, *Imagination Taking Power* (blog), 16 March 2018, https://www.robhopkins.net/2018/03/16/dan-schacter-on-the-memory -and-the-imagination/.

23. Interview with Art Angel artist.

24. Sarah Corbett, *How to Be a Craftivist: The Art of Gentle Protest* (London: Unbound, 2017); Sarah Corbett, interview with author, *Imagination Taking Power* (blog), 22 June 2017, https://www.robhopkins.net/2017/06/22/sarah-corbett-on-craftivism -and-the-imagination.

25. Rosalie Summerton, interview with author, *Imagination Taking Power* (blog), 15 October 2018, https://www.robhopkins.net/2018/10/15/rosalie-summerton-on -how-art-angel-heals-the-imagination/.

26. Johann Hari, *Lost Connections: Uncovering the Real Causes of Depression – And the Unexpected Solutions* (London: Bloomsbury, 2018), 161.

27. Ruth Cain, 'How Neoliberalism Is Damaging Your Mental Health', *Conversation*, 30 January 2018, https://theconversation.com/how-neoliberalism-is-damaging -your-mental-health-90565.

28. Neil Straus, 'Why We're Living in the Age of Fear', *Rolling Stone*, 6 October 2016, https://www.rollingstone.com/politics/politics-features/why-were-living-in-the -age-of-fear-190818/.

29. Roberto Stefan Foa and Yascha Mounk, 'The Democratic Disconnect', *Journal of Democracy* 27, no. 3 (July 2016).

30. Patrick Maguire and Anoosh Chakelian, 'Facts and Figures: The Deepest Cuts: Austerity Measured', *New Statesman*, 12–18 October 2018, 26.

31. Angela Monaghan and Jessica Elgot, '"Brexit Boom" Gives Britain Record 134 Billionaires, Fuelling Inequality Fears', *Guardian*, 7 May 2017, https://www .theguardian.com/business/2017/may/07/brexit-boom-creates-record-number -of-uk-billionaires-sunday-times-rich-list.

32. Richard Wilkinson and Kate Pickett, *The Inner Level: How More Equal Societies Reduce Stress, Restore Sanity and Improve Everyone's Well-Being* (London: Allen Lane, 2018), 55–56.

33. Royal College of Psychiatrists, *No Health Without Public Mental Health the Case for Action. Position Statement ps4/2010* (London: Royal College of Psychiatrists, 2010), https://www.rcpsych.ac.uk/PDF/Position%20Statement%204% 20website.pdf.

34. Summerton, interview.

35. Jamie Hanson et al., 'Association Between Income and the Hippocampus', *PLOS One* 6, no. 5 (May 2011): 1–8.

36. Joy Schaverien, interview with author, *Imagination Taking Power* (blog), 29 November 2017, https://www.robhopkins.net/2017/11/29/joy-schaverien-trauma -on-a-collective-scale-or-on-an-individual-scale-can-freeze-the-imagination/.

37. Turnbull, interview.

38. Matthew Walker, *Why We Sleep: The New Science of Sleep and Dreams* (London: Penguin, 2017).

39. Rubin Naiman, 'Falling for Sleep', *Aeon*, 11 July 2016, https://aeon.co/essays/ the-cure-for-insomnia-is-to-fall-in-love-with-sleep-again.

40. Giuseppe Curcio et al., 'Clinical Review: Sleep Loss, Learning Capacity and Academic Performance', *Sleep Medicine Reviews* 10 (2006): 323–37.

41. Rubin Naiman, *Wired and Tired*, 13 March 2018, HurrySlowly.co blog, https:// hurryslowly.co/021-rubin-naiman/.

42. Po Bronson, 'Snooze or Lose', *New York Magazine*, 7 October 2007, http://nymag .com/news/features/38951/.

43. Walker, *Why We Sleep*.

44. Catherine Monk et al., 'Research Review: Maternal Prenatal Distress and Poor Nutrition – Mutually Influencing Risk Factors Affecting Infant Neurocognitive Development', *Journal of Child Psychology and Psychiatry* 54, no. 2 (2013): 115–30.

45. Irakli Loladze, 'Hidden Shift of the Ionome of Plants Exposed to Elevated CO_2 Depletes Minerals at the Base of Human Nutrition', *eLife* 3 (May 2014), https:// elifesciences.org/articles/02245.

46. William Jagust et al., 'Central Obesity and the Aging Brain', *Arch Neurol* 62, no. 10 (2005): 1545–48.

47. Mei-Kei Leung et al., 'Increased Gray Matter Volume in the Right Angular and Posterior Parahippocampal Gyri in Loving-Kindness Meditators', *Social Cognitive and Affective Neuroscience* 8, no. 1 (2013): 34–39; Eileen Luders et al., 'Global and Regional Alterations of Hippocampal Anatomy in Long-Term Meditation Practitioners', *Human Brain Mapping* 34, no. 12 (2013): 3369–75; Kirk I. Erickson et al., 'Exercise Training Increases Size of Hippocampus and Improves Memory', *PNAS* 108, no. 7 (2011): 3017–22; Lisanne F ten Brinke et al., 'Aerobic Exercise Increases Hippocampal Volume in Older Women with Probable Mild Cognitive Impairment: A 6-Month Randomised Controlled Trial', *British Journal of Sports Medicine* 49, no. 4 (2015): 248–54.

48. Robert Macfarlane, interview with author, *Imagination Taking Power* (blog), 4 June 2018, https://www.robhopkins.net/2018/06/04/the-metaphors-we-use-deliver -us-hope-or-they-foreclose-possibility/.

49. Powerfully documented in Vicky Cooper and David Whyte, eds., *The Violence of Austerity* (London: Pluto Press, 2017).

50. Aditya Chakrabortty, 'In an Era of Brutal Cuts, One Ordinary Place Has the Imagination to Fight Back', *Guardian*, 6 March 2019, https://www.theguardian .com/commentisfree/2019/mar/06/brutal-cuts-fight-back-preston -dragons-den.

51. Henry Giroux, 'Trump's War on Dangerous Memory and Critical Thought', *TruthDig*, 16 March 2017, https://www.truthdig.com/articles/trumps-war-on -dangerous-memory-and-critical-thought/.

52. Henry Giroux, interview with author, *Imagination Taking Power* (blog), 19 April 2017, https://www.robhopkins.net/2017/04/19/henry-giroux-on-the-attack-on -the-public-imagination/.

53. Susan Engel, 'Open Pandora's Box: Curiosity in the Classroom', *The Sarah Lawrence Child Development Institute Occasional Papers*, http://www.slc.edu/cdi /Occasional_Paper_Engel.php.

54. Data from a survey conducted by YouGov, with a sample size of 621 children and 2,238 adults, for Institute of Imagination, London (unpublished).

55. PR Newswire, 'New Study of Professional Creatives Reveals a Decline in Creativity', 25 September 2013, http://www.prnewswire.co.uk/news-releases/new -study-of-professional-creatives-reveals-decline-in-creativity-225134292.html.

56. Richard Sennett: 'Entrevista: Lo gratuito conlleva siempre una forma de dominación', *El País Semanal*, 18 August 2018, https://elpais.com/elpais/2018/08/09/eps /1533824675_957329.html.

57. Thomas Piketty, *Capital in the Twenty-First Century* (Harvard: Harvard University Press, 2014).

58. Rod Tweedy, 'A Mad World: Capitalism and the Rise of Mental Illness', *Red Pepper*, 9 August 2017, https://www.redpepper.org.uk/a-mad-world-capitalism -and-the-rise-of-mental-illness/.

59. Joseph Allen et al., 'Associations of Cognitive Function Scores with Carbon Dioxide, Ventilation, and Volatile Organic Compound Exposures in Office Workers: A Controlled Exposure Study of Green and Conventional Office Environments', *Environmental Health Perspectives* 124, no. 1 (2016): 805–12.

60. Paul Hawken, *Drawdown: The Most Comprehensive Plan Ever Proposed to Reverse Global Warming* (London: Penguin Books, 2018).

61. Jem Bendell, 'Deep Adaptation: A Map for Navigating Climate Tragedy', *IFLAS Occasional Paper 2,* 27 July 2018, http://www.lifeworth.com /deepadaptation.pdf.

62. Frances C. Moore et al., 'Rapidly Declining Remarkability of Temperature Anomalies May Obscure Public Perception of Climate Change', *Proceedings of the National Academy of Sciences of the United States of America*, published ahead of print 25 February 2019, https://doi.org/10.1073/pnas.1816541116.

63. Nick Obradovich and Frances C. Moore, 'The Data Is In. Frogs Don't Boil. But We Might', *Washington Post*, 25 February 2019, https://www.washingtonpost.com /weather/2019/02/25/data-are-frogs-dont-boil-we-might/.

64. Susan Clayton et al., *Mental Health and Our Changing Climate: Impacts, Implications and Guidance* (Washington, DC: American Psychological Association and ecoAmerica, March 2017), https://www.apa.org/news/press/releases/2017/03 /mental-health-climate.pdf.

65. James Bridle, 'Air Pollution Rots Our Brains. Is That Why We Don't Do Anything About It?', *Guardian*, 24 September 2018, https://www.theguardian .com/commentisfree/2018/sep/24/air-pollution-cognitive -improvement-environment.

66. Rebecca Solnit, *Men Explain Things to Me* (London: Granta, 2014), 105.

67. Summerton, interview.

68. Institute for the Future, 'An Office for Public Imagination: Group Text/Exercise at IFTF Reconstitutional Convention', n.d.

69. Eric Liu and Scott Noppe-Brandon, *Imagination First: Unlocking the Power of Possibility* (San Francisco: Jossey-Bass, 2009), 21.

70. Lucy Neal, interview with author, *Imagination Taking Power* (blog), 18 March 2019, https://www.robhopkins.net/2019/03/18/lucy-neal-imagination-is-the-most-important-thing-in-the-whole-wide-world/.

Chapter 3. What If We Followed Nature's Lead?

1. Henry Porter, 'To Be Alone in the Dawn Chorus Reminds Us How Precious Life Is', *Guardian*, 4 May 2013, https://www.theguardian.com/commentisfree/2013/may/04/dawn-chorus-thing-of-beauty.

2. What's a 'wildlife disco'? Have a look at http://www.soundartradio.org.uk/services/projects/wildlife-disco/.

3. Rob Hopkins, '"You Only Get So Many Mays in Your Life": Why Our Imagination Needs the Dawn Chorus', *Imagination Taking Power* (blog), 10 May 2017, https://www.robhopkins.net/2017/05/10/204/.

4. Hank Johnston, 'A Camping Trip with Roosevelt and Muir', *Yosemite* 56, no. 3 (1994): 2–4.

5. Sierra Club, *Theodore Roosevelt 1858–1919*, Sierra Club, The John Muir Exhibit, https://vault.sierraclub.org/john_muir_exhibit/people/roosevelt.aspx.

6. Johnston, 'A Camping Trip'.

7. Sierra Club, *Theodore Roosevelt*.

8. Theodore Roosevelt, *An Autobiography* (Frankfurt: Outlook Verlag GmbH, 2018; original 1913), 253.

9. Monique Grooten and Rosamund Almond, *Living Planet Report 2018: Aiming Higher* (Gland, Switzerland: World Wildlife Fund, 2018).

10. Michael McCarthy, *The Moth Snowstorm: Nature and Joy* (London: John Murray, 2015), 14; Damien Carrington, 'Warning of "Ecological Armageddon" After Dramatic Plunge in Insect Numbers', *Guardian*, 18 October 2017, https://www.theguardian.com/environment/2017/oct/18/warning-of-ecological-armageddon-after-dramatic-plunge-in-insect-numbers.

11. John Vidal, 'Protect Nature for World Economic Security, Warns UN Biodiversity Chief', *Guardian*, 16 August 2010, https://www.theguardian.com/environment/2010/aug/16/nature-economic-security.

12. McCarthy, *The Moth Snowstorm*, 87.

13. Michael McCarthy, interview with author, *Imagination Taking Power* (blog), 20 February 2019, https://www.robhopkins.net/2019/02/20/michael-mccarthy/.

14. Looking up 'List of Extinct Species' on Wikipedia will give you a very sobering few hours. . . .

15. American Museum of Natural History, *Passenger Pigeons*, https://www.amnh.org/exhibitions/permanent-exhibitions/birds-and-reptiles-and-amphibians-halls/hall-of-new-york-city-birds/passenger-pigeons.

16. Mentioned to me by Drew Dellinger in my conversation with him; Drew Dellinger, interview with author, *Imagination Taking Power* (blog), 11 July 2018,

https://www.robhopkins.net/2018/07/11/drew-dellinger-if-we-had-more
-imagination-we-could-have-less-capitalism/.

17. Madeline Bunting, 'Disarming the Weapons of Mass Distraction', 15 March 2018, *New York Review of Books*, https://www.nybooks.com/daily/2018/03/15/disarming
-the-weapons-of-mass-distraction/.

18. You'll find many others in Robert Macfarlane, *Landmarks* (London: Penguin Books, 2016).

19. Macfarlane, interview.

20. Mark Wilson, 'Infographic: In 80 Years We Lost 93% of Variety in Our Food Seeds', *Fast Company*, 5 November 2012, https://www.fastcompany.com/1669753
/infographic-in-80-years-we-lost-93-of-variety-in-our-food-seeds.

21. Hope Shand, 'Biological Meltdown: The Loss of Agricultural Diversity', *Reimagine*, n.d., https://www.reimaginerpe.org/node/921.

22. Manish Jain, interview with author, *Imagination Taking Power* (blog), 31 January 2018, https://www.robhopkins.net/2018/01/31/manish-jain-our-work-is-to
-recover-wisdom-and-imagination/.

23. Agustín Fuentes, *The Creative Spark: How Imagination Made Humans Exceptional* (New York: Dutton, 2017), 274.

24. Douglas Mann, 'Monarch Butterflies Have Declined 90%: Conservationists Seek Extra Protection', *Newsweek*, 27 August 2014, https://www.newsweek.com/monarch
-butterflies-have-declined-90-conservationists-seek-extra-protection-267094.

25. Susan Clayton et al., *Mental Health and Our Changing Climate*.

26. Lise van Susteren, interview with author, *Imagination Taking Power* (blog), 24 April 2018, https://www.robhopkins.net/2018/04/24/847/.

27. Mark Cocker, *Our Place: Can We Save Britain's Wildlife Before It Is Too Late?* (London: Jonathan Cape, 2018), 195.

28. Peter Aspinall et al., 'The Urban Brain: Analysing Outdoor Physical Activity With Mobile EEG', *British Journal of Sports Medicine* 49, no. 4 (February 2015): 272–76.

29. Ruth Ann Atchley et al., 'Creativity in the Wild: Improving Creative Reasoning through Immersion in Natural Settings', *PLOS ONE* 7, no. 12 (2012): e51474.

30. Daniel Levitin, *The Organised Mind: Thinking Straight in the Age of Information Overload* (London: Dutton, 2015).

31. Carolyn Gregoire, 'The New Science of the Creative Brain on Nature', *Outside*, 18 March 2016, https://www.outsideonline.com/2062221/new-science-creative
-brain-nature.

32. Howard Frumkin et al., 'Nature Contact and Human Health: A Research Agenda', *Environmental Health Perspectives* 125, no. 7 (July 2017): 1–18.

33. Gregory N. Bratman et al., 'The Benefits of Nature Experience: Improved Affect and Cognition', *Landscape and Urban Planning* 138 (June 2015): 41–50.

34. BBC News, '"Nature" Being Prescribed by GPs in Shetland', 5 October 2018, https://www.bbc.co.uk/news/uk-scotland-north-east-orkney-shetland-45758016.

35. RSPB Scotland/NHS Scotland, *Nature Prescriptions Calendar*, n.d., https://www
    .healthyshetland.com/site/assets/files/1178/730-1309-17-18 _nature_prescriptions
    _calendar_4sep.pdf.

36. Marc G. Berman et al., 'The Cognitive Benefits of Interacting with Nature',
    Psychological Science 19, no. 12 (2008): 1207–12.

37. Denise Winterman, 'The Surprising Uses for Birdsong', BBC News, 8 May 2013,
    https://www.bbc.com/news/magazine-22298779.

38. Neil E. Klepeis et al., 'The National Human Activity Pattern Survey (NHAPS): A
    Resource for Assessing Exposure to Environmental Pollutants', *Journal of Exposure
    Analysis and Environmental Epidemiology* 11 (24 July 2001): 231–52; Damien
    Carrington, 'Three-quarters of UK Children Spend Less Time Outdoors Than
    Prison Inmates – Survey', *Guardian*, 25 March 2016, https://www.theguardian.
    com/environment/2016/mar/25/three-quarters-of-uk-children-spend-less-time
    -outdoors-than-prison-inmates-survey.

39. Francesca Boyd et al., 'Who Doesn't Visit Natural Environments for Recreation
    and Why: A Population Representative Analysis of Spatial, Individual and
    Temporal Factors Among Adults in England', *Landscape Use and Urban Planning*
    175 (2018): 102–13.

40. Rob Hopkins, 'Dreaming of Eternity: Three Days in the Ruhr Valley', *Imagination
    Taking Power* (blog), 20 September 2017, https://www.robhopkins.net/2017/09/20/394/.

41. LandWorks, https://www.landworks.org.uk/landworks-prisoner-training/.

42. LandWorks, 'The Facts', www.landworks.org.uk/landworks-prisoner-training
    /prison-education-facts/.

43. Chris Parsons, interview with author, *Imagination Taking Power* (blog), 11 June
    2018, https://www.robhopkins.net/2018/06/11/chris-parsons-on-landworks
    -imagination-and-moving-beyond-prison/.

44. London National Park City, 'Map of London', http://www.nationalparkcity.london/map.

45. Daniel Raven-Ellison, interview with author, *Imagination Taking Power* (blog), 9
    April 2018, https://www.robhopkins.net/2018/04/09/daniel-raven-ellison-on-what
    -if-london-were-a-national-park-city/.

46. London National Park City, 'What Is the London National Park City?', n.d.,
    http://www.nationalparkcity.london/about/about-find-out-more/what-is-the
    -london-national-park-city.

47. More on the concept of 'food deserts' at http://www.foodispower.org/food-deserts/.

48. Doria Robinson, interview with author, TransitionNetwork.org (blog), 7 January
    2014, https://transitionnetwork.org/news-and-blog/doria-robinson-on-scaling-up
    -community-resilience-in-the-shadow-of-chevron/.

49. Urban Tilth, 'About Us', https://www.urbantilth.org/about-us/.

50. Doria Robinson, interview with author, *Imagination Taking Power* (blog), 27
    November 2018, https://www.robhopkins.net/2018/11/27/doria-robinson-on-how
    -urban-agriculture-can-heal-a-communitys-imagination/.

Chapter 4: What If We Fought Back to Reclaim Our Attention?

1. According to Martin Bailey's book *The Sunflowers are Mine: The Story of Van Gogh's Masterpiece*, (London: White Lion Publishing, 2019), it is believed the sunflowers were either a gift from Patience Escalier, or were cut by Van Gogh himself in the garden of a bathhouse he had been drawing two weeks earlier.
2. Sherry Turkle, *Reclaiming Conversation: The Power of Talk in a Digital Age*, (New York: Penguin Books, 2016).
3. Steven Naifeh and Gregory White Smith, *Van Gogh: The Life*, (London: Profile Books, 2012), 618.
4. Hugh McGuire, 'Why Can't We Read Books Any More? Or, Can Books Save Us from What Digital Does to Our Brains', *Medium*, 22 April 2015, https://medium.com/@hughmcguire/why-can-t-we-read-anymore-503c38c131fe.
5. Nielsen, *The Nielsen Total Audience Report Q1 2018*, The Nielsen Company (US), https://www.nielsen.com/content/dam/corporate/us/en/reports-downloads/2018-reports/q1-2018-total-audience-report.pdf.
6. Chris Berdick, 'Dealing with Digital Distraction: Solutions Run the Gamut – from Tech Breaks to Tech Take-Overs', *The Hechinger Report*, 22 January 2018, https://hechingerreport.org/dealing-digital-distraction/.
7. Bianca Bosker, 'The Binge Breaker: Tristan Harris Believes Silicon Valley Is Addicting Us to Our Phones. He's Determined to Make It Stop', *Atlantic*, November 2016, https://www.theatlantic.com/magazine/archive/2016/11/the-binge-breaker/501122/; Tristan Harris, 'How a Handful of Tech Companies Control Billions of Minds Every Day', TED.com, April 2017, https://www.ted.com/talks/tristan_harris_the_manipulative_tricks_tech_companies_use_to_capture_your_attention#t-49051.
8. Matthew B. Crawford, *The World Beyond Your Head: On Becoming an Individual of an Age of Distraction* (New York: Farrar, Straus and Giroux, 2015), 9; Monica Rozenfled, 'Technology Is Addictive by Design', *Institute*, 6 June 2018, http://theinstitute.ieee.org/ieee-roundup/blogs/blog/technology-is-addictive-by-design; James Williams, *Stand Out of Our Light: Freedom and Resistance in the Attention Economy* (Cambridge: Cambridge University Press, 2018).
9. Jon D. Elhaiab et al., 'Fear of Missing Out, Need for Touch, Anxiety and Depression Are Related to Problematic Smartphone Use', *Computers in Human Behaviour* 63 (October 2016): 509–16.
10. Common Sense Media, *Technology Addiction: Concern, Controversy and Finding a Balance: Executive Summary*, May 2016, 2.
11. Elhaiab et al., 'Fear of Missing Out'.
12. Tony Dokoupil, 'Is the Internet Making Us Crazy? What the New Research Says', *Newsweek*, 9 July 2012, https://www.newsweek.com/internet-making-us-crazy-what-new-research-says-65593.

13. Sarah Marsh, 'NHS to Launch First Internet Addiction Clinic', *Guardian*, 22 June 2018, https://www.theguardian.com/society/2018/jun/22/nhs-internet-addiction-clinic-london-gaming-mental-health.

14. Dr Ryan Kemp, email message to author, 22 November 2018.

15. Julia Carrie Wong, 'Former Facebook Executive: Social Media Is Ripping Society Apart', *Guardian*, 12 December 2017, https://www.theguardian.com/technology/2017/dec/11/facebook-former-executive-ripping-society-apart.

16. Sven Birkerts, *Changing the Subject: Art and Attention in the Internet Age* (Minneapolis: GrayWolf Press, 2015), 243.

17. Scott Barry Kaufman, 'The Real Neuroscience of Creativity', *Scientific American*, 19 August 2013, https://blogs.scientificamerican.com/beautiful-minds/the-real-neuroscience-of-creativity/.

18. Junaid Mubeen, 'Why "Sleep on It" Is Our Most Useful Advice for Learning', *Medium*, 4 March 2018, https://medium.com/s/story/why-sleep-on-it-is-the-most-useful-advice-for-learning-and-also-the-most-neglected-86b20249f06d.

19. Jonathan Schooler, interview with author, *Imagination Taking Power* (blog), 6 April 2017, https://www.robhopkins.net/2017/04/06/jonathan-schooler-on-why-daydreaming-is-a-good-thing/.

20. Benjamin Baird et al., 'Inspired by Distraction: Mind Wandering Facilitates Creative Incubation', *Psychological Science* 23, no. 10 (2012): 1117–22.

21. Schooler, interview.

22. Turkle, *Reclaiming Conversation*, 62.

23. Leonard Mlodinow, *Elastic: Flexible Thinking in a Constantly Changing World* (London: Allen Lane, 2018), 125.

24. Larry Rosen, interview with author, *Imagination Taking Power* (blog), 23 January 2018, https://www.robhopkins.net/2018/01/23/dr-larry-rosen-on-activism-and-imagination-in-the-age-of-the-distracted-mind/.

25. Larry Rosen, interview with author; Gazzaley and Rosen, *The Distracted Mind*.

26. Bruce K. Alexander, interview with author, *Imagination Taking Power* (blog), 27 June 2018, at https://www.robhopkins.net/2017/06/27/bruce-k-alexander-on-addiction-and-the-imagination/.

27. Maggie Jackson, *Distracted: The Erosion of Attention and the Coming Dark Age* (Amherst, NY: Prometheus Books, 2008), 13.

28. Maggie Jackson, interview with author, *Imagination Taking Power* (blog), 15 May 2018, https://www.robhopkins.net/2018/05/15/maggie-jackson/.

29. Douglas Rushkoff, interview with author, *Imagination Taking Power* (blog), 12 March 2018, https://www.robhopkins.net/2018/03/12/douglas-rushkoff-weve-disabled-the-cognitive-and-collaborative-skills-needed-to-address-climate-change/.

30. Rushkoff discusses this in a film called *Present Shock* made by Dark Rye, which you can find at https://vimeo.com/91720717.

31. Williams, *Stand Out of Our Light*.

32. Tim Wu, *The Attention Merchants: The Epic Struggle to Get Inside Our Heads* (London: Atlantic Books, 2016), 350.

33. Jonathan Beller, 'Paying Attention', *Cabinet*, Winter 2006–7, http://www.cabinet-magazine.org/issues/24/beller.php.

34. Tincan Project, *Slow Sunday: Spend Time Well*, a great guide you'll find at http://www.tincan.net.au/spend-time-well/.

35. As set out in Cal Newport, *Digital Minimalism: On Living Better with Less Technology* (London: Penguin Business, 2019).

36. Turkle, *Reclaiming Conversation*.

37. Craig Mod, 'How I Got My Attention Back', *Wired*, 13 January 2017, https://www.wired.com/2017/01/how-i-got-my-attention-back/.

38. David Sax, interview with author, *Imagination Taking Power* (blog), 30 April 2018, https://www.robhopkins.net/2018/04/30/david-sax-how-analog-can-feed-imagination/.

39. Arwa Mahdawi, 'Simon Cowell Giving Up His Phone Is the Ultimate Show of Affluence', *Guardian*, 5 June 2018, https://www.theguardian.com/commentisfree/2018/jun/05/simon-cowell-giving-up-his-phone-is-the-ultimate-show-of-affluence.

40. Camp Grounded, http://www.campgrounded.org.

41. Dr Ryan Kemp, email message to author, 22 November 2018.

42. Sarah Marsh, 'NHS to Launch First Internet Addiction Clinic', *Guardian*, 22 June 2018, https://www.theguardian.com/society/2018/jun/22/nhs-internet-addiction-clinic-london-gaming-mental-health.

43. Daniel Levitin, *The Organized Mind: Thinking Straight in the Age of Information Overload* (New York: Dutton, 2014).

44. Gazzaley and Rosen, *The Distracted Mind*.

45. Laura Marulanda and Thomas William Jackson, 'Effects of E-Mail Addiction and Interruptions on Employees', *Journal of Systems and Information Technology* 14, no. 1 (2012): 82–94.

46. William Power, *Hamlet's Blackberry: A Practical Philosophy for Building a Good Life in the Digital Age* (Melbourne, Scribe, 2010), 60.

47. Sandi Mann and Rebekah Cadman, 'Does Being Bored Make Us More Creative?', *Creativity Research Journal* (2014): 26.

48. Colin Ellard, 'The Generic City: Boring Landscapes Impede on Our Biological Need for Intrigue. So Why Are So Many Buildings So Hideous?' *Slate*, 27 November 2015, http://www.slate.com/articles/health_and_science/science/2015/11/psychology_of_boring_architecture_the_damaging_impact_of_big_ugly_buildings.html?via=gdpr-consent.

49. Turkle, *Reclaiming Conversation*, 66.

50. Mann and Cadman, 'Does Being Bored Make Us More Creative?', 2.

51. Matthieu Ricard, interview with author, *Imagination Taking Power* (blog), 5 February 2018, https://www.robhopkins.net/2018/02/05/matthieu-ricard-i-think-the-buddha-might-have-got-rid-of-twitter-with-his-palace/.

52. Martin Shaw, interview with author, TransitionCulture.org (blog), 17 September 2012, https://www.transitionculture.org/2012/09/17/an-interview-with-dr-martin-shaw-a -lot-of-opportunity-is-going-to-arrive-in-the-next-20-years-disguised-as-loss/.

53. Tom Hirons and Rima Staines, interview with author, *Imagination Taking Power* (blog), 21 June 2018, https://www.robhopkins.net/2018/06/21/tom-hirons -and-rima-staines-on-hedgespoken-a-vehicle-for-the-imagination/.

54. Christopher Ingraham, 'The Long, Steady Decline Of Literary Reading', *Washington Post*, 7 September 2016, https://www.washingtonpost.com/news/wonk /wp/2016/09/07/the-long-steady-decline-of-literary-reading/.

55. P. Matthijs Bal and Martijn Veltkamp, 'How Does Fiction Reading Influence Empathy? An Experimental Investigation on the Role of Emotional Transportation', *PLOS One* 8, no. 1 (2013): 1–12.

56. Charles Chu, 'In the Time You Spend on Social Media Each Year, You Could Read 200 Books', *Quartz*, 29 January 2017, https://qz.com/895101/in-the-time -you-spend-on-social-media-each-year-you-could-read-200-books/.

57. Turkle, *Reclaiming Conversation*, 9, 13.

58. Jean M. Twenge, *iGen: Why Today's Super-Connected Kids Are Growing Up Less Rebellious, More Tolerant, Less Happy – And Completely Unprepared for Adulthood* (New York: Atria Books, 2017), 80; NHS, 'Loneliness Increases Risk of Premature Death', 13 March 2015, https://www.nhs.uk/news/mental-health/loneliness -increases-risk-of-premature-death/.

59. University of Sheffield report for the BBC, *Changing UK: The Way We Live Now*, 2008, http://www.statistics.gov.uk/pdfdir/stalone0409.pdf.

60. Quoted in Luke Kemp, 'Are We on the Road to Civilizational Collapse?', BBC, 19 February 2019, http://www.bbc.com/future/story/20190218-are-we-on-the-road -to-civilisation-collapse.

61. Turkle, *Reclaiming Conversation*, 25.

62. James Bridle, *New Dark Age: Technology and the End of the Future* (London: Verso, 2018).

63. Zuboff, *The Age of Surveillance Capitalism*, 11.

64. Rushkoff, interview.

65. Turkle, *Reclaiming Conversation*.

Chapter 5: What If School Nurtured Young Imaginations?

1. Marjorie Taylor, *Imaginary Companions and the Children Who Create Them* (New York: Oxford University Press, 1999).

2. Marjorie Taylor, interview with author, *Imagination Taking Power* (blog), 23 October 2018, https://www.robhopkins.net/2018/10/23/marjorie-taylor-on-imaginary -friends-i-have-not-seen-a-decline/.

3. BBC News, 'No Playground for "Super School"', 6 May 2007, http://news.bbc.co .uk/1/hi/england/cambridgeshire/6629655.stm.

4. Valerie Strauss, 'In Texas, a Revolt Brews against Standardized Testing', *Washington Post*, 23 March 2012, https://www.washingtonpost.com/blogs/answer-sheet /post/in-texas-a-revolt-brews-against-standardized-testing/2012/03/15 /gIQAI5N0VS_blog.html.

5. Tim Lott, 'Ditch the Grammar and Teach Children Storytelling Instead', *Guardian*, 19 May 2017, https://www.theguardian.com/lifeandstyle/2017/may/19/ditch -the-grammar-and-teach-children-storytelling-instead.

6. Liu and Noppe-Brandon, *Imagination First*, 188.

7. Bob and Roberta Smith to Michael Gove, 25 July 2011, http://bobandrobertasmith .co.uk/letter-to-michael-gove/.

8. Will Gompertz, *Think Like an Artist . . . and Lead a More Creative, Productive Life* (London: Penguin Books, 2015), 188.

9. Ian Youngs, 'Art Party Conference Puts the Art into Party Politics', BBC News, 24 November 2013, https://www.bbc.com/news/entertainment-arts-25050676.

10. Chris Sharratt, 'Art in Schools Faces Extinction: How Can We Fix the Crisis?', *Frieze*, 8 October 2018, https://frieze.com/article/art-schools-faces-extinction-how -can-we-fix-crisis.

11. Dominic Sandbrook, *The Great British Dream Factory: The Strange History of Our National Imagination* (London: Allen Lane, 2015), 426.

12. Cultural Learning Alliance, 'Further Decline in Arts GCSE and A Level Entries,' 23 August 2018, https://culturallearningalliance.org.uk/further-decline-in-arts -gcse-and-a-level-entries/.

13. Cultural Learning Alliance, 'Further Decline in Arts'.

14. Quoted in Rick Rogers, *Get It: The Power of Cultural Learning*, Culture and Learning Consortium, 2009, https://www.cloreduffield.org.uk/userfiles/documents /publications/Get_it_the_power_of_cultural_learning.pdf.

15. The foregoing stats are from Cultural Learning Alliance, *Imagine Nation: The Value of Cultural Learning*, 2017, https://culturallearningalliance.org.uk /wp-content/uploads/2017/08/ImagineNation_The_Case_for_Cultural _Learning.pdf.

16. Rose Wylie, 'Culture Is a Birthright: Eight Leading UK Artists on the Perils of Excluding Arts in Schools', *Frieze*, 12 June 2018, https://frieze.com /article/culture-birthright-eight-leading-uk-artists-perils-excluding -arts-schools.

17. See Clayground Collective, *Thinking Hands? Report: Symposium to Explore the Role of Hand Skills Development in Seeing, Thinking and Learning*, 2014, http://www .claygroundcollective.org/wp-content/uploads/2016/02/Thinking-Hands -Symposium-Report-Final.pdf.

18. Sean Coughlan, 'Surgery Students "Losing Dexterity to Stitch Patients"', BBC News, 30 October 2018, https://www.bbc.com/news/education-46019429.

19. Kim, interview.

20. Peter Gray, *Free to Learn: Why Unleashing the Instinct to Play Will Make Our Children Happier, More Self-Reliant, and Better Students for Life* (New York: Basic Books, 2013); Gray, *The Decline of Play*.

21. Andrea Ridgeway et al., 'Effects of Recess on the Classroom Behaviour of Children with and without Attention-Deficit Hyperactivity Disorder', *School Psychology Quarterly* 18, no. 3 (2013): 253–68.

22. Rachael Pells, 'Four-Year-Olds Suffering Panic Attacks, Eating Disorders, Anxiety and Depression, Report Says', *Independent*, 14 April 2017, https://www.independent.co.uk/news/education/education-news/uk-schools-mental-health-surge-support-issues-children-pupils-nasuwt-barnardos-a7682751.html.

23. Interview by email with teacher, 19 February 2017.

24. Interview by email with student teacher, 12 November 2018.

25. Ken Robinson and Lou Aronica, *Creative Schools: The Grassroots Revolution That's Transforming Education* (New York: Penguin Book, 2016), 7.

26. Andrew Brewerton, interview with author, *Imagination Taking Power* (blog), 4 February 2019, https://www.robhopkins.net/2019/02/04/we-decided-to-create-a-school-talking-imagination-with-andrew-brewerton/.

27. Seefeldt, interview with author, *Imagination Taking Power* (blog), 18 November 2018, https://www.robhopkins.net/2018/11/18/amy-seefeldt-on-creating-a-centre-for-imagination/.

28. Adam Lusher, 'Ten-Year-Olds Denied SATs Marks Because of Semi-Colons That Fail to Meet Official Shape and Size Standards', *Independent*, 11 July 2017, https://www.independent.co.uk/news/education/education-news/sats-tests-primary-school-testing-key-stage-2-shambles-draconian-marking-mark-scheme-wrong-shaped-a7835551.html.

29. Gillian Judson, 'Two Key Points for Understanding Imagination in Education', *Getting Smart*, 24 September 2016, https://www.gettingsmart.com/2016/09/imagination-misunderstood/.

30. Gillian Judson, interview with author, *Imagination Taking Power* (blog), 26 February 2018, https://www.robhopkins.net/2018/02/26/gillian-judson-on-imaginative-education-and-the-joys-of-being-a-perfinker/.

31. Ruth Sapsed, interview with author, *Imagination Taking Power* (blog), 5 December 2018, https://www.robhopkins.net/2018/12/05/ruth-sapsed-on-cambridge-curiosity-and- imagination/.

32. Neil Griffiths, in discussion with the author, 29 July 2018.

33. Quoted in Mandy Maddock, *Enemies of Boredom: An Evaluation Report of the Hundred Languages of Children Exhibition and Programme of Events, Cambridge, Summer 2004* (Cambridge: Cambridge Curiosity and Imagination / Refocus Cambridge, 2005).

34. As set out in Valarie Mercilliott Hewett, 'Examining the Reggio Emilia Approach to Early Childhood Education', *Early Childhood Education Journal* 29, no. 2 (Winter 2001).

35. Loris Malaguzzi, 'Your Image of the Child: Where Teaching Begins', *Child Care Information Exchange* 3 (1994), 52–61.
36. Jay Griffiths, *Kith: The Riddle of the Childscape* (London: Penguin Books, 2014).
37. You can find the school's website at http://www.ecole-domaine-du-possible.fr/.
38. Jean Rakovitch, in discussion with the author, 18 December 2018.
39. Karen MacLean, interview by author, *Imagination Taking Power* (blog), 10 December 2018, https://www.robhopkins.net/2018/12/10/karen-maclean/.
40. MacLean, interview.
41. Seefeldt, interview.
42. Seefeldt, interview.
43. Amy Leigh Seefeldt, 'Centring the Ecological Imagination: A Catalyst for Change' (master's thesis, Schumacher College, 2016), https://issuu.com/amyseefeldt/docs/161130_amys_dissertation.
44. Seefeldt, interview.
45. Seefeldt, interview.
46. If you are interested in finding out more about this, and can read Portuguese, then see http://idg.receita.fazenda.gov.br/acesso-rapido/direitos-e-deveres/educacao-fiscal/folhetos-orientativos/arquivos-e-imagens/guia-sobre-beneficios-fiscais-nas-doacoes-para-os-fundos-e-programas-ucs-naf.pdf.
47. Cambridge Curiosity and Imagination, http://cambridgecandi.org.uk/about/about.
48. Cambridge Curiosity and Imagination, 'Fantastical Cambridge', n.d., http://cambridgecandi.org.uk/projects/footprints/fantastical-cambridgeshire.
49. Sapsed, interview.
50. Dave Strudwick, interview by author, *Imagination Taking Power* (blog), 21 February 2019, https://www.robhopkins.net/2019/02/21/dave-strudwick-on-how-a-school-of-creative-arts-can-foster-the-imagination/.
51. Dave Strudwick, in discussion with author, 19 December 2018.
52. Manish Jain, interview with author, *Imagination Taking Power* (blog), 31 January 2018, https://www.robhopkins.net/2018/01/31/manish-jain-our-work-is-to-recover-wisdom-and-imagination/.
53. Australian Associated Press, 'Scott Morrison tells students striking over climate change to be "less activist"', *Guardian*, 26 November 2018, https://www.theguardian.com/environment/2018/nov/26/scott-morrison-tells-students-striking-over-climate-change-to-be-less-activist.
54. Brewerton, interview.

Chapter 6: What If We Became Better Storytellers?

1. Stephen Duncombe, interview with author, *Imagination Taking Power* (blog), 26 September 2018, https://www.robhopkins.net/2018/09/26/stephen-duncombe-on-imagination-spectacle-and-desire/.
2. Zygmunt Bauman, *Retrotopia* (Cambridge: Policy Press, 2017).

3. Annie Murphy Paul, 'Your Brain on Fiction', *New York Times*, 17 March 2012, https://www.nytimes.com/2012/03/18/opinion/sunday/the-neuroscience-of-your -brain-on-fiction.html.

4. Annette Simmons, *The Story Factor: Inspiration, Influence and Persuasion through the Art of Storytelling* (New York: Basic Books, 2006), 54.

5. Fabienne Briant, email message to author, 3 April 2019.

6. Donella Meadows, *Envisioning a Sustainable World* (presented at the Third Biennial Meeting of the International Society for Ecological Economics, San Jose, Costa Rica, 24–28 October, 1994), http://donellameadows.org/archives/envisioning-a -sustainable-world/.

7. Umair Haque, 'I'm Burned Out on Collapse – And I Bet You Are Too: The Hidden Psychological Toll of Living through a Time of Fracture', *Medium*, 8 December 2018, https://eand.co/im-burned-out-on-collapse-and-i-bet-you-are-too-70114c184c02.

8. Meadows, *Envisioning a Sustainable World.*

9. Denise Baden, 'Environmental Storytelling Can Help Spread Big Ideas for Saving the Planet', *Aerogramme Writers' Studio*, 8 January 2019, https://www.aerogramme studio.com/2019/01/08/environmental-storytelling-can-help-spread-big-ideas-for -saving-the-planet/.

10. James McKay, interview with author, *Imagination Taking Power* (blog), 7 January 2019, https://www.robhopkins.net/2019/01/07/james-mckay-the-man-who -draws-the-future/.

11. James McKay and Benjamin Dickson, eds., *A Dream of a Low Carbon Future* (Leeds: Engineering and Physical Sciences Research Council, University of Leeds, 2016).

12. The speech he gave is available at https://www.quentinblake.com/news/quentin -blake-hay-festival-2013.

13. Ghislaine Kenyon, *Quentin Blake: In the Theatre of the Imagination* (London: Bloomsbury, 2016), 212.

14. Hey Design, *Design Inspiration: Quentin Blake Illustrations*, 22 October 2016, https://medium.com/@heydesign/design-inspiration-quentin-blake-illustrations -68d24adf9234.

15. McKay, interview.

16. Martin Shaw, interview with author, *Imagination Taking Power* (blog), 4 May 2017, https://www.robhopkins.net/2017/05/04/martin-shaw-on-imagination-i-would -describe-it-as-ripe-for-invasion/.

17. Alexandra Rowland, interview with author, *Imagination Taking Power* (blog), 14 January 2019, https://www.robhopkins.net/2019/01/14/alexandra-rowland -on-hopepunk-grimdark-story-and-imagination/.

18. Alexandra Rowland, 'One Atom of Justice, One Molecule of Mercy, and the Empire of Unsheathed Knives', *Festive Ninja: Optimistic Indie Roleplaying* (blog), 2018, https://festive.ninja/one-atom-of-justice-one-molecule-of-mercy-and-the -empire-of-unsheathed-knives-alexandra-rowland/.

19. Rowland, interview.
20. Mohsin Hamid, *Exit West* (London: Hamish Hamilton, 2017), 215–216.
21. Mohsin Hamid, 'Mohsin Hamid on the Dangers of Nostalgia: We Need to Imagine a Brighter Future', *Guardian*, 25 February 2017, https://www.theguardian .com/books/2017/feb/25/mohsin-hamid-danger-nostalgia-brighter-future.
22. Mohsin Hamid, interview with author, *Imagination Taking Power* (blog), 15 May 2017, https://www.robhopkins.net/2017/05/15/mohsin-hamid-imagination-allows -us-to-imagine-futures-not-bound-by-the-tyranny-of-the-past-and-the-present/.
23. Shana McDavis-Conway, interview with author, *Imagination Taking Power* (blog), 13 February 2019, https://www.robhopkins.net/2019/02/13/1208/.
24. You can see Deborah Frances-White doing this exercise at a conference at https:// youtu.be/gWuEH-qg0Nw.
25. Steve McAllister, '10 Stories of Transition in the US: Transition Fidalgo & Friends' Vision 2030', *Transition US* (blog), 2018, http://www.transitionus.org/stories/10 -stories-transition-us-transition-fidalgo-friends%E2%80%99-vision-2030.
26. McAllister, '10 Stories of Transition'.
27. Evelyn Adams, email message to author, 11 January 2019.
28. Transition Fidalgo and Friends, *Vision 2030: Our Vibrant, Sustainable Community*, 2014, iii, http://www.transitionfidalgo.org/wp-content/uploads/2015/04/Vision_2030.pdf.
29. Milton Friedman, *Capitalism and Freedom* (Chicago: University of Chicago Press, 2002), xiv.
30. McKay, interview.

Chapter 7: What If We Started Asking Better Questions?

1. Rob Hopkins, 'Podcast: The Tooting Twirl: "Let Nobody Say After Today That It's Not Possible"'. *Imagination Taking Power* (blog), 17 July 2017, https://www .robhopkins.net/2017/07/17/podcast-the-tooting-twirl-let-nobody-say-after -today-that-its-not-possible/.
2. Rob Hopkins, 'Podcast: The Tooting Twirl'.
3. Liu and Noppe-Brandon, *Imagination First*, 33.
4. Rob Hopkins, 'Podcast: The Tooting Twirl'.
5. Ruth Ben-Tovim, in discussion with the author, 16 January 2019.
6. Ben-Tovim, discussion.
7. Lucy Neal, interview with author, *Imagination Taking Power* (blog), 18 March 2019, https://www.robhopkins.net/2019/03/18/lucy-neal-imagination-is-the-most -important-thing-in-the-whole-wide-world/.
8. Mockus, 'The Art of Changing a City'.
9. Martin Shaw, in discussion with the author, 8 February 2017.
10. Quoted in Nagesh Belludi, 'Turning a Minus into a Plus . . . Constraints Are Catalysts for Innovation', *Right Attitudes*, http://www.rightattitudes.com/2017/11 /29/creativity-thrives-when-constrained/.

11. IPCC, 'Summary for Policymakers'.

12. Catrinel Haught-Tromp, 'The Green Eggs and Ham Hypothesis: How Constraints Facilitate Creativity', *Psychology of Aesthetics, Creativity, and the Arts* 11, no. 1 (2017): 11.

13. I did some great interviews about craft brewing that I ended up not including in this book. But if you're interested, go to http://www.robhopkins.net and look up interviews with Shaun Hill, Evin O'Riordan, Mikkel Borg Bjergsø and Michael Kiser.

14. Anderson and Broderick, *Natural Gas and Climate Change*.

15. Ruth Ben-Tovim, discussion.

16. Raven-Ellison, interview.

17. Hannah Fox, in discussion with the author, 24 October 2018.

18. Hannah Fox, interview by author, *Imagination Taking Power* (blog), 4 September 2017, https://www.robhopkins.net/2017/09/04/hannah-fox-on-how-a -communitys-imagination-reshaped-a-museum/.

19. C. White et.al., *Proving the Cultural Value of the Arts for Health Methods & Analysis Report for the Happy Museum: Cultural Value & Making*, University of Derby, 2014, http://happymuseumproject.org/wp-content/uploads/2016/03/Proving-Cultural -Value-of-the-Arts-for-Health.pdf.

20. Hannah Fox, discussion.

21. Search the Make Works database at https://make.works/derby/.

22. Andrea Hadley-Johnson, in discussion with the author, 20 July 2017.

23. Josiah Meldrum, interview by author, *Imagination Taking Power* (blog), 4 December 2017, https://www.robhopkins.net/2017/12/04/545/.

24. Meldrum, interview.

25. The Bank Job project, with videos and updates, can be found at https:// bankjob.pictures/.

26. The Rolling Jubilee campaign, https://rollingjubilee.org.

27. You can watch that segment of *Last Week Tonight* at https://youtu.be/hxUAntt1z2c.

28. Hilary Powell and Dan Edelstyn, interview by author, *Imagination Taking Power* (blog), 12 April 2018, https://www.robhopkins.net/2018/04/12/hilary-powell-and -dan-edelstyn-on-the-bank-job/.

29. David Sax, *The Revenge of Analog: Real Things and Why They Matter* (New York: PublicAffairs, 2016), 239.

30. Part of the Transition model, as set out in Rob Hopkins, *The Transition Companion: Making Your Community More Resilient in Uncertain Times* (Dartington: Green Books, 2011).

31. All my interviews in Liège can be found here: 'A Dazzlingly Delicious Taste of the Future in Liége', *Imagination Taking Power* (blog), 26 March 2018, https://www .robhopkins.net/2018/03/26/a-delicious-taste-of-the-future-in-liege/.

32. McDavis-Conway, interview.

33. Kali Akuno, interview by author, *Imagination Taking Power* (blog), 13 November 2018, https://www.robhopkins.net/2018/11/13/kali-akuno-on-imagination-and -the-ways-we-can-and-must-resist/.

34. John Dudna, 'Towards the Horizon of Abolition: A Conversation with Mariame Kaba', *The Next System Project*, 9 November 2017, https://thenextsystem.org/learn /stories/towards-horizon-abolition-conversation-mariame-kaba.

35. Daniel Raven-Ellison, email message to author, 24 January 2019.

Chapter 8: What If Our Leaders Prioritised the Cultivation of Imagination?

1. Robert Koehler, 'The American Way of War: Evolution Stops Here', *ZNet*, 3 June 2018, https://zcomm.org/znetarticle/the-american-way-of-war-evolution -stops-here/.

2. Joy Schaverien, 'Boarding School Syndrome: Broken Attachments, a Hidden Trauma', *British Journal of Psychotherapy* 27, no. 2 (2011): 138, 142.

3. George Monbiot, 'The British Boarding School Remains a Bastion of Cruelty', *Guardian*, 16 January 2012, https://www.theguardian.com/commentisfree/2012 /jan/16/boarding-school-bastion-cruelty.

4. George Monbiot, interview by author, *Imagination Taking Power* (blog), 24 July 2017, https://www.robhopkins.net/2017/07/24/george-monbiot/.

5. IPCC, 'Summary for Policymakers'.

6. Roberto Unger, 'Social Theorist Roberto Unger Talks with Jo Fidgen about Why He Thinks His Fellow Left-of-Centre Progressives Lack Imagination,' aired 24 November 2013 on BBC Radio 4, https://www.bbc.co.uk/programmes/b03hvn6n.

7. Ed Cox, 'Our Call for Action on Deliberative Democracy', *RSA*, 4 July 2018, https://www.thersa.org/discover/publications-and-articles/rsa-blogs/2018/07/our -call-for-action-on-deliberative-democracy.

8. David van Reybrouck, interview by author, *Imagination Taking Power* (blog), 1 November 2017, https://www.robhopkins.net/2017/11/01/ticking-a-box-is-no -longer-an-option-david-van-reybrouck-on-elections-imagination-and-brexit/.

9. Quoted in Graham Smith, *Democratic Innovations: Designing Institutions for Citizen Participation* (Cambridge: Cambridge University Press, 2011), 74.

10. An Tionól Saoránach (The Citizens' Assembly), *The Citizens' Assembly Fact Sheet*, June 2018, https://www.citizensassembly.ie/en/About-the-Citizens-Assembly /CA-Fact-Sheet-June-2018.pdf.

11. Clodagh Harris, in discussion with author, 8 December 2018.

12. Felix Beltran, interview by author, *Imagination Taking Power* (blog), 7 December 2017, https://www.robhopkins.net/2017/12/07/felix-beltran-on-how-barcelona -en-comu-are-reimagining-democracy/.

13. Beltran, interview.

14. For more on Fearless Cities, see http://fearlesscities.com/en.

15. N.B., 'The Antidote to Civilisational Collapse: An Interview with the Documentary Filmmaker Adam Curtis', *Economist*, 6 December 2018, https://www.economist.com/open-future/2018/12/06/the-antidote-to-civilisational-collapse.

16. Jeffrey Baumgartner, *Imagination: The Number One Tool for Innovation and Creativity*, n.d., http://www.innovationmanagement.se/imtool-articles/imagination-the-number-one-tool-for-innovation-and-creativity/.

17. Oli Mould, *Against Creativity* (London: Verso, 2018).

18. Ursula K. Le Guin, 'The Operating Instructions', in *The Wave in the Mind: Talks and Essays on the Writer, the Reader and the Imagination* (Boulder: Shambhala, 2004), 207.

19. Judy Wicks, interview by author, *Imagination Taking Power* (blog), 6 November 2018, https://www.robhopkins.net/2018/11/06/judy-wicks-on-imagination-entrepreneurship-and-local-economies/.

20. Bernie Ward and Julie Lewis, *Plugging the Leaks: Making the Most of Every Pound That Enters Your Local Economy*, New Economics Foundation, Esmée Fairbairn Foundation and the Neighbourhood Renewal Unit, September 2002, https://neweconomics.org/uploads/files/9215d0d00f79789377_cxm6bu0ue.pdf.

21. The term 'guerrilla localism' was coined by Aditya Chakrabortty, 'In 2011 Preston Hit Rock Bottom. Then It Took Back Control', *Guardian*, 31 January 2018, https://www.theguardian.com/commentisfree/2018/jan/31/preston-hit-rock-bottom-took-back-control; Clifford Singer, 'The Preston Model', *The Next System Project*, 9 September 2016, https://thenextsystem.org/the-preston-model.

22. Singer, 'The Preston Model'.

23. Matthew Brown, interview by author, *Imagination Taking Power* (blog), 23 January 2018, https://www.robhopkins.net/2019/01/23/cllr-matthew-brown-on-how-the-preston-model-unlocks-the-imagination/.

24. Richard Partington, 'Preston Named as Most Improved City in UK', *Guardian*, 1 November 2018, https://www.theguardian.com/politics/2018/nov/01/preston-named-as-most-most-improved-city-in-uk.

25. Marina Gorbis, 'There Could Be a Real Solution to Our Broken Economy. It's Called "Universal Basic Assets"', *Medium*, 4 April 2017, https://medium.com/institute-for-the-future/universal-basic-assets-abb08ca2f0fc.

26. As part of a larger journey I blogged about at https://www.robhopkins.net/2019/04/20/1303/.

27. Rob Hopkins, 'The Inspiring tale of Re-Imagining Preston's Economy', 16 June 2015, Transition Network, https://transitionnetwork.org/news-and-blog/the-inspiring-tale-of-the-re-imagining-of-prestons-economy/.

28. Gabriella Gómez-Mont, interview by author, *Imagination Taking Power* (blog), 3 October 2018, https://www.robhopkins.net/2018/10/03/gabriella-gomez-mont-imagination-is-not-a-luxury/.

29. John Duda, 'The Italian Region Where Co-ops Produce a Third of Its GDP', *Yes!*, 5 July 2016, https://www.yesmagazine.org/new-economy/the-italian-place-where -co-ops-drive-the-economy-and-most-people-are-members-20160705.

30. Cities of Service, *Engaged Cities Award Case Study: Co-Creating Urban Commons An Engaged Cities Award Case Study Created by Cities of Service in Partnership with 2018 Award Winner Bologna, Italy,* January 2019, https://citiesofservice .org/wp-content/uploads/2019/01/Bologna_Cities_of_Service _Case_Study.pdf.

31. Cities of Service, *Engaged Cities Award Case Study*; Bloomberg Cities, 'How Bologna is Working with Residents to Re-imagine Public Spaces', *Medium*, 14 December 2018, https://medium.com/@BloombergCities/how-bologna-is -working-with-residents-to-re-imagine-public-spaces-52112472ed49; Michele d'Alena et al., 'Civic Imagination Office as a Platform to Design a Collaborative City, Service Design Proof of Concept', *Politecnico di Milano*, 18–20 June 2018, http://www.servdes.org/wp/wp-content/uploads/2018/07/53.pdf.

32. Cities of Service, 'The Power of Imagination: Engaged Cities Award Summit 2018', video posted to YouTube 8 August 2018, https://www.youtube.com/ watch?v=lj9-vFeqVTU.

33. Cities of Service, *Engaged Cities Award Case Study.*

34. Michele d'Alena, interview by author, *Imagination Taking Power* (blog), 4 March 2019, https://www.robhopkins.net/2019/03/04/michele-dalena-on-bologna -the-city-with-a-civic-imagination-office/.

35. Ruth Ben-Tovim, discussion.

36. Llwodraeth Cymru / Welsh Government, *Well-being of Future Generations (Wales) Act 2015: The Essentials, 2nd edition,* May 2015, https://gov.wales/docs/dsjlg /publications/150623-guide-to-the-fg-act-en.pdf.

37. Jane Davidson, in discussion with the author, 15 January 2019.

38. Llwodraeth Cymru / Welsh Government, *One Planet Development Technical Advice Note 6 Planning for Sustainable Rural Communities,* October 2012, https://gov.wales /docs/desh/publications/121114oneplanetguideen.pdf.

39. BBC News, 'M4 Relief Road: Newport Motorway Plans Scrapped', 4 June 2019, https://www.bbc.co.uk/news/uk-wales-48512697.

40. Maxine Greene, *Releasing the Imagination: Essays on Education, the Arts and Social Change* (San Francisco: Jossey-Bass, 1995), 35.

Chapter 9: What If All of This Came to Pass?

1. Royal de Luxe, *The Sultan's Elephant* (film), produced by Artichoke, London, 2006, https://youtu.be/Bc0PoWfPzmI.

2. Royal de Luxe, *The Sultan's Elephant.*

3. Lynn Gardner, 'And for Our Next Trick . . .', *Guardian*, 27 August 2008, https:// www.theguardian.com/stage/2008/aug/27/theatre.

4. Helen Marriage, interview by author, *Imagination Taking Power* (blog), 24 January 2019, https://www.robhopkins.net/2019/01/25/helen-marriage-on-the-sultans-elephant-and-large-acts-of-public-imagination/.

5. Paul Piff et al., 'Awe, the Small Self, and Pro-Social Behaviour', *Journal of Personality and Social Psychology* 108, no. 6 (2015): 884.

6. Dacher Keltner, 'Why Do We Feel Awe?', *Greater Good Magazine*, 10 May 2016, https://greatergood.berkeley.edu/article/item/why_do_we_feel_awe.

7. Piff et al., 'Awe'.

8. Cited in Keltner, 'Why Do We Feel Awe?'

9. Keltner, 'Why Do We Feel Awe?'

10. Paul Piff, *Can Awe Combat Narcissism?* (presented at The Art and Science of Awe conference, Greater Good Science Centre, University of California, Berkeley, June 2016), https://www.youtube.com/watch?v=w7Q7wTt4IbA.

11. David Graeber, 'The New Anarchists', *New Left Review* 13 (January/February 2002), 72.

12. Better Block, http://betterblock.org/about/.

13. Jason Roberts, 'How to Build a Better Block', TEDxOU, 21 February 2007, https://www.youtube.com/watch?v=ntwqVDzdqAU.

14. Jason Roberts, interview by author, *Imagination Taking Power* (blog), 8 May 2017, https://www.robhopkins.net/2017/05/08/jason-roberts-when-you-say-about-imagination-i-think-about-visionaries/.

15. Benjamin Schneider, 'How Park(ing) Day Went Global,' *CityLab*, 15 September 2017, https://www.citylab.com/life/2017/09/from-parking-to-parklet/539952/.

16. Rebar Group Inc., *The Park(ing) Day Manual: A Primer on User-Generated Urbanism and Temporary Tactics for Improving the Public Realm*, n.d., 1, https://parkingday.org/src/Parking_Day_Manual_Consecutive.pdf.

17. Schneider, How Park(ing) Day Went Global'.

18. JR, interview by author, *Imagination Taking Power* (blog), 3 July 2017, https://www.robhopkins.net/2017/07/03/talking-imagination-and-participation-with-jr/.

19. Marco Berrebi and JR, *Women Are Heroes: A Global Project by JR* (New York: Abrams, 2009).

20. Ken Knabb, ed., *Situationist International Anthology*, revised and expanded edition (Berkeley: Bureau of Public Secrets, 2006).

21. These and many other Situationist slogans from May 1968 can be found in Knabb, ed., *Situationist International*.

22. Philippe Vermès, 'The Late Sixties', in *Beauty Is in the Street: A Visual Record of the May '68 Paris Uprising*, ed. Johan Kugelberg and Philippe Vermès (London: Four Corners Books, 2011), 10.

23. Mark Kurlansky, *1968: The Year That Rocked the World* (London: Jonathan Cape, 2004), 229, 227.

24. Ronald Fraser, *1968: A Student Generation in Revolt* (London: Chatto & Windus, 1988), 191, 190, 195.

25. Quoted in Rosemary Pink, 'The Boy Scout Guide to Situationism', *Vague*, Vague Publishing, 1985.

26. Juan del Rio, email message to author, 28 January 2018.

27. OER Services, *Culture under the Song Dynasty*, n.d., https://courses.lumenlearning .com/suny-hccc-worldcivilization/chapter/culture-under-the-song-dynasty/.

28. Guillaume Chenevière, *Rousseau, une histoire genevoise* (Geneva: Editions Labor et Fides, 2012).

29. Quoted in Leonidas Oikonomakis, 'Why We Still Love the Zapatistas: The Construction of a New World Is Much More Than an Academic Exercise', *Roar*, n.d., https://roarmag.org/magazine/why-we-still-love-the-zapatistas/.

30. See, for example, Nigel C. Gibson, *Fanon: The Postcolonial Imagination* (Cambridge: Polity Press, 2003).

31. See http://cottonfaminepoetry.exeter.ac.uk/.

32. Andrade and May, interview.

33. Keishiro Hara et al., *Reconciling Intergenerational Conflicts with Imaginary Future Generations – Evidence from a Participatory Deliberation Practice in a Municipality in Japan*, Kochi University of Technology Social Design Engineering Series, 24 October 2017.

34. Yoshio Kamijo et al., 'Negotiating with the Future: Incorporating Imaginary Future Generations into Negotiations', *Sustainability Science* 12, no. 3 (2016): 409–20.

35. Tatsuyoshi Saijo, *Future Design: Bequeathing Sustainable Natural Environments and Sustainable Societies to Future Generations, Working Paper – Social Design Engineering Series*, Kochi University of Technology, 20 July 2018.

36. Dominique Christina, interview by author, *Imagination Taking Power* (blog), 1 November 2018, https://www.robhopkins.net/2018/11/01/dominique-christina-on -using-the-raw-material-of-possible-to-say-all-of-the-urgent-things/.

37. Peter Gray, 'As Children's Freedom Has Declined, so Has Their Creativity', *The Creativity Post*, 29 September 2012, http://www.creativitypost.com/education/as _childrens_freedom_has_declined_so_has_their_creativity.

38. Peter Russell, interview by author, *Transition Culture* (blog), 5 February 2011, https://www.transitionculture.org/2007/02/05/exclusive-to-transition-culture -peter-russell-on-life-after-oil-change-and-consciousness/.

39. Griffin, 'To Love the Marigold'.

Afterword

1. Rob Shorter, unpublished audio recording.

INDEX

Index

Index

Index

Index

ABOUT THE AUTHOR

Miriam Klingl / Werde

ROB HOPKINS is a co-founder of Transition Town Totnes and Transition Network, and the author of *The Power of Just Doing Stuff*, *The Transition Handbook*, and *The Transition Companion*. In 2012 he was voted one of the *Independent*'s top 100 environmentalists and was on Nesta and the *Observer*'s list of Britain's 50 New Radicals. Hopkins has also appeared on BBC Radio 4's *Four Thought* and *A Good Read*, in the French film phenomenon *Demain* and its sequel *Apres Demain*, and has spoken at TEDGlobal and three TEDx events. An Ashoka Fellow, Hopkins also holds a doctorate degree from the University of Plymouth and has received two honorary doctorates from the University of the West of England and the University of Namur. He is a keen gardener, a founder of New Lion Brewery in Totnes, and a director of Totnes Community Development Society, the group behind Atmos Totnes, an ambitious community-led development project. He blogs at www.transitionnetwork.org and www.robhopkins.net, and you can find him on Twitter at @robintransition.

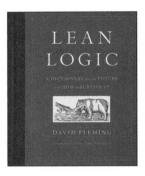

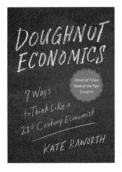